China and Globalization 2.0

China is now at the forefront of globalization, particularly with the One Belt, One Road policy. What does a Chinese globalization look like, though? This series will explore the distinct legacies and evolutions of China's worldview, even as China exports its development model to countries around the world.

Bai Gao • Zhihong Zhen
Editors

The China-Europe Railway Express

State Building and Market Building

社会科学文献出版社
SOCIAL SCIENCES ACADEMIC PRESS (CHINA)

palgrave
macmillan

Editors
Bai Gao
Department of Sociology
Duke University
Durham, NC, USA

Zhihong Zhen
School of Sociology and Political Science
Shanghai University
Shanghai, China

Translated by Yu Nan

ISSN 2523-7209 ISSN 2523-7217 (electronic)
China and Globalization 2.0
ISBN 978-981-19-2881-9 ISBN 978-981-19-2882-6 (eBook)
https://doi.org/10.1007/978-981-19-2882-6

Jointly published with Social Sciences Academic Press

The printed edition is not for sale in China Mainland. Customers from China Mainland please order the print book from Social Sciences Academic Press.

Translation from the Chinese language edition: "《中欧班列：国家建设与市场建设》" by Bai Gao and Zhihong Zhen, © Social Sciences Academic Press 2017. Published by Social Sciences Academic Press. All Rights Reserved.

This Palgrave Macmillan imprint is published by the registered company Springer Nature Singapore Pte Ltd.
The registered company address is: 152 Beach Road, #21-01/04 Gateway East, Singapore 189721, Singapore

Acknowledgments

This research project was one of the key projects of the Center on China's High-Speed Rail Development Strategy at Southwest Jiaotong University from 2016 to 2017. We would like to express our gratitude to Southwest Jiaotong University for providing us with research funding and an international cooperation platform.

During the field research process, we received generous support and selfless assistance from many individuals. Without their help, this research would have been difficult to complete. First and foremost, we would like to extend our gratitude to Dr. Wu Yabin, a distinguished researcher at the Center on China's High-Speed Rail Development Strategy at Southwest Jiaotong University and the Executive Dean of the Global Value Chain Research Institute at the University of International Business and Economics. Dr. Wu facilitated our connections with research units throughout the project. Without his assistance, this project would have taken on a different form. We would also like to express our special thanks to Professor Zhen Zhihong, the Deputy Director of the China High-Speed Rail Development Strategic Research Center, for his critical organizational role and valuable experience in guiding the research team during field investigations. His expertise was instrumental in helping the team uncover and capture valuable empirical materials.

Secondly, we are deeply grateful to the governments, relevant departments, and experts from the five cities that we visited. Despite their busy schedules, they agreed to interviews and warmly received our research team. We refrain from listing names, but their innovative spirit in operating China-Europe freight trains greatly inspired our team.

I would like to extend special thanks to all the authors for their dedication and professionalism throughout the extensive editing process, which involved four to six rounds of revisions.

The viewpoints presented in this book, as well as any potential errors, are the sole responsibility of the authors and are not related to those who aided.

August 11, 2017 Bai Gao

Contents

Notes on Contributors

Huihui Feng PhD in Human Geography, is a Research Fellow at National Research Center on Strategic Development of High-Speed Railway, Southwest Jiaotong University. Her main research areas include tourism transportation and regional planning.

Bai Gao is a professor at Duke University. His main research areas include economic sociology, comparative-historical sociology, international political economy, and comparative political economy.

Shuxing Han Master's student at the School of Sociology, Shanghai University.

Dongkun Li is an Associate Professor and Master's Supervisor at the School of Public Administration, Southwest Jiaotong University.

Xinyue Luo Master's student at the School of Public Administration, Southwest Jiaotong University.

Ying Ma Distinguished Research Fellow at the Center on China's High-Speed Rail Development Strategy Research of Southwest Jiaotong University, Assistant Research Fellow at the International Economics and Trade Research Institute of Shanghai University of International Business and Economics.

Lihua Wang Ph.D. in History, Lecturer at the Center on China High-Speed Rail Development Strategy Research, Southwest Jiaotong University. His research focuses on urban history and frontier history.

Bin Wang Ph.D. in Sociology, is a Lecturer at China High-Speed Rail Development Strategy Research Center, Southwest Jiaotong University.

Haoyu Wang Lecturer at the China High-Speed Rail Development Strategy Research Center of Southwest Jiaotong University, specializing in the field of ethnical sociology.

Jianmei Xiao Lecturer at the China High-Speed Rail Development Strategy Research Center of Southwest Jiaotong University, with a research focus on religious studies.

Zhihong Zhen is a professor at Shanghai University. His main research areas include economic sociology, international political economy, population studies, and aging.

Dajie Zuo Distinguished Research Fellow at the Center on China's High-Speed Rail Development Strategy at Southwest Jiaotong University and an associate professor at the School of Transportation and Logistics of Southwest Jiaotong University. His primary research focus is on transportation organization and optimization.

List of Figures

List of Tables

CHAPTER 1

Introduction: State Building and Market Building—An Economic and Sociological Analysis of China-Europe Railway Express

Bai Gao

1.1 China-Europe Railway Express: Unprecedented Market Building

In 2013, the Chinese government launched the "Belt and Road" Initiative (BRI). The BRI spans over 60 nations with a combined population of over 3.2 billion, or roughly 45% of the world's population, and a combined GDP of $12 trillion, or 16% of the world economy. The total volume of trade reaches $7,185.55 billion, representing 21.7% of global trade. The total trading volume between China and BRI countries stood at $953.59 billion in 2016, making up 25.7% of China's total international trade. The significance of these countries' exports to China continues to grow, with the proportion rising from 23.9% in 2011 to 27.8% in 2016. China has

B. Gao (✉)
Department of Sociology, Duke University, Durham, NC, USA
e-mail: bai.gao@duke.edu

B. Gao, Z. Zhen (eds.), *The China-Europe Railway Express*, China and Globalization 2.0,
https://doi.org/10.1007/978-981-19-2882-6_1

also become the largest import market for major trading partners along the route.[1]

The BRI is an unprecedented market development project. The "Belt" is short for the "Silk Road Economic Belt," which encourages economic integration throughout Eurasia by building transportation infrastructure along the ancient Silk Road, thereby building the largest economic belt in the world in the twenty-first century. The purpose of the Silk Road Economic Belt is to integrate the economies of Eurasia. It is expected to bring about major growth in trade between Asian and European countries, significant reduction in various trade barriers, and additional bilateral, multilateral, and even comprehensive free trade agreements covering Eurasia; a significant increase in cross-border flows of capital, products, services, and technology; a global production system that will include many Central Asian, South Asian, Middle Eastern, and Central and Eastern European countries hitherto excluded from the international division of labor, providing them with previously unheard-of development opportunities; The entire area of Eurasia will be covered by a highly integrated logistics system made up of various modes of transportation such as highways, railroads, air, and sea; future e-commerce will present considerable development potential for small and medium-sized companies in various countries, with the completion of transportation infrastructure and the integration of numerous supporting systems.

The China-Europe Railway Express (CR Express) is a key driver of the Silk Road Economic Belt market construction project. The logistics industry that developed around CR Express is critical to the Eurasian market. The CR Express has grown rapidly since its inception seven years ago. Data from China State Railway Group Co., Ltd. (China Railway) shows that the CR Express has operated 5046 trains since its inception in 2011 until May 13, 2017. Of those, 1702 trains were operated in 2016 alone, while 593 trains were operated in the first quarter of 2017, an increase of 175% year over year; there were 198 return trains, up 187% from the previous year. The CR Express currently links 28 cities in 11 European nations and 27 cities in China,[2] spanning 21 provinces and municipalities. By

[1] Jianing Cao , "Interpreting Big Data: 'Belt and Road' Initiative Becomes a New Engine for International Trade," Belt and Road Portal, April 10, 2017. https://www.yidaiyilu.gov.cn/xwzx/gnxw/10787.htm.

[2] "Seven Countries' Railway Departments Sign Agreement to Deepen China-Europe Railway Express Cooperation," ThePaper.cn, April 23, 2017. http://www.sohu.com/a/13586635_260616.

2020, CR Express had hoped to have 5000 annual train trips between China and Europe.

The development of the CR Express differs significantly from city to city. For instance, Chongqing stands out in terms of international collaboration as it was the first city to operate the Chongqing-Xinjiang-Europe railway, abbreviated as "Yuxin'ou" railway. In addition to establishing the sole international joint venture logistics platform among the cities served by China-Europe trains, it has also accomplished the extraordinary feat of enabling goods to be cleared at the point of origin and transported directly to Europe without having to pass through customs inspections in numerous countries along the way. The logistics platform construction in Chengdu started with three private companies and was later taken over by a state-owned enterprise (SOE) in April 2016. The number of rail services in Chengdu increased quickly after the switch from private to public ownership, catching up to Chongqing in 2016. What sets Yiwu apart from other cities on the China-Europe Railway Express is that since the start it has been run by a private company called Yiwu Tianmeng Industrial Investment Co Ltd., which manages the logistics platform for the Yiwu-Xinjiang-Europe railway, or "Yixin'ou." Tianmeng has not only extended the "Yixin'ou" from Spain to the UK and Belarus but also to Iran, Afghanistan, and Iraq. In contrast to the other cities examined in this book, Zhengzhou lacks a strong manufacturing sector as its primary support. In Zhengzhou, the development of China-Europe Railway Express focuses on creating a dedicated logistics and trade channels. Furthermore, Zhengzhou's logistics system extends beyond railways, as it is integrated with equally robust air and land transportation systems. While Wuhan is geographically advantageous, its approach to developing China-Europe Railway Express differs from that of others. Wuhan implements a strategy that stresses quality and seeks to raise the value of each container unit, unlike other cities that rely on government subsidies to obtain higher volume. Wuhan also emphasizes the openness of its logistics platform and promotes competition among businesses of various kinds on the platform, in contrast to other cities that concentrate on vertical integration to recuperate the costs of logistics platform building.

The development of CR Express presents two challenges to the economics perspective. First, from a financial standpoint, the operating costs are considerable. These trains have relied heavily on substantial subsidies from local governments since their inceptions. Some contend that CR Express make little economic sense since it is used by local governments as vanity projects to score political points. Without government subsidies, it could not be sustained. Second, even from the viewpoint of new structural economics, which is more willing to recognize the role of the government in economics than other schools, China-Europe Railway Express do not fall under the category of industries that the government should support. According to new structural economics, the only time government economic intervention can be successful is when it is founded on comparative advantage. The China-Europe Railway Express, representing railway transportation, do not possess any apparent comparative advantage. Rail services are significantly slower than air service and have no economic advantage over maritime shipping.

Despite these, however, why have CR Express progressed so quickly? Why are there such stark differences between cities in the development of China-Europe Railway Express? Existing social science literature can offer us useful insights.

1.2 State Building and Market Building

The perspective of economic sociology on the process of market construction as a part of the state-building process provides a valuable analytical framework for understanding the development of the CR Express. Simultaneously, the practical development of the CR Express enriches economic sociology's understanding of the relationship between the state and the market by providing significant empirical evidence.

In the existing economic sociology literature, there are two opposing views on the relationship between the state and the market. According to one viewpoint, represented by Max Weber, the market in rational capitalism, as exemplified by Western Europe, is built on specific legal and political structures. A legal framework that upholds property rights and contractual obligations is necessary for this capitalist market to operate efficiently and to ensure that profits are generated via legitimate business operations rather than parasitic extraction. Institutional economics has also backed up this claim, particularly through Douglass North's historical investigation. According to this view, the market and the government are different entities that can be analyzed objectively and can impact each another. The state plays a few critical roles in market development. Market development is dependent on the definition of property rights, the establishment of industrial governance structures, the development of market exchange rules, and market monitoring.[3]

Another perspective, represented by Karl Polanyi, offers a different angle on this relationship. He argues that market building and state building are mutually dependent and intertwined processes. He points out that, unlike other commodities produced for free exchange in the market, land, labor, and money are "fictitious commodities" that cannot be independently generated from market activities. However, labor is simply the activity of human beings, land is nature divided into parcels, and the money that circulates in national economies almost always relies on the "full faith and credit" of one or another government. In a market economy, the necessary activity of regulating the supply of these fictitious commodities falls to the state and encompasses different initiatives. Therefore, it is impossible to talk about market building without also talking about state building.[4] Market functions have developed as a result of state building. The establishment and development of markets depend on the establishment of state functions.

Although economic sociology emphasizes the importance of state building in the process of market building, it distinguishes between two scenarios when analyzing the role of the state: the state as an active agent influencing market building and the state as a structural condition influencing market building. In the first scenario, the state, composed of numerous actors, actively and intentionally pursues various public policies for different reasons. These policies can have expected or unforeseen, positive or negative impacts on market building and development. In the second scenario, the state passively influences market building and development. In this case, the state merely serves as a political platform for diverse actors to pursue their own interests, and the extent of their influence on the policymaking process depends on their relationship with the state. The state is also viewed as an organizational structure, in which the division of duties and the allocation of authority among its departments have a big impact on the public policies that determine how markets are

[3] Neil Fligstein, *The Architecture of Markets: An Economic Sociology of Twenty-First-Century Capitalist Societies* (Princeton: Princeton University Press)

[4] Fred Block and Peter Evans, "The State and the Economy," in Neil J. Smelser and Richard Swedberg, eds. *The Handbook of Economic Sociology*, Second Edition (Princeton: Princeton University Press, 2005), pp. 505–506.

built. The government is also seen as an essential factor in deciding where economic activity occurs.[5]

1.3 The State as an Active Agent: Industrial Policy Perspectives

The literature on the industrial policy adopted by the developmental state offers a direct analytical framework for comprehending the forces that have fueled the rapid expansion of the China-Europe Railway Express when it comes to the role of the state as an active agent in the process of market building.

First, while operating within the parameters of private property rights and market economies, the primary goal of developmentalism is to achieve industrialization and sustained growth in per capita GDP, allowing for state intervention in the market from a long-term perspective. This is highlighted in the classical developmentalist literature, with a focus on Japan and South Korea. The subject of study in the developmentalist literature is both political and economic systems instead of the economic system alone. Setting such a research scope is significant as developmentalism takes the existence of the nation-state as a basic assumption. Classical economic liberalism, in contrast, argues for the independence of economic operations from politics and nationalism. On the contrary, developmentalism, at its core, is a theory and practice of industrialization approached from the perspective of the nation-state, where the interaction between politics and economy plays a crucial role. In fact, according to developmentalism, industrialization cannot occur without the interplay between politics and economy.[6]

Second, the goal of state industrial policies is to promote the growth of sectors that can generate maximum benefits and high added values in a nation's international trade. Comparative political economy literature on developmentalism emerged in the early 1980s with analyses of the Japanese economic miracle. Chalmers Johnson, in his book *MITI and the Japanese*

[5] Leon N. Lindberg and John L. Campbell, "The State and the Organization of Economic Activity," in John L. Campbell, J. Rogers Hollingsworth, and Leon N. Lindberg, eds. *Governance of the American Economy* (New York: Cambridge University Press, 1991), pp. 357–358.

[6] Yasuke Murakami, "An Anticlassical Political-Economic Analysis: A Vision for the Next Century" (Stanford: Stanford University Press, 1996), pp. 145–146.

Miracle: The Growth of Industrial Policy, 1925–1975, argues that while capitalist nations all operate within market economies, the states have different patterns of involvement in economic affairs. Johnson highlights the sharp contrast between a regulatory state and a developmental state. A regulatory state, such as the United States, focuses largely on establishing and enforcing the rules of game for the market, leaving the rise and fall of particular industries to market forces. In contrast, a developmental state, represented by Japan, is concerned with determining the industrial structure that will benefit its economy the most from international trade. Developmental states believe that the higher the added value of an industry in international trade, the greater its strategic value within a nation's economy. The state should utilize various policy tools at their disposal to promote the development of strategic industries.

Contrary to neoclassical economics' individualistic methodology, industrial policy analysis stresses a nation-state or a specific region's overall economic interests rather than individual business. "Western economics has consistently downplayed the role of the state and has not regarded collective actors involved in economic activities as entities equivalent to individual actors."[7] However, as a representative of the Japanese Ministry of International Trade and Industry remarked, "Industrial policy must be formulated at the level of sovereign nations, considering the available resources. Factors such as national security and the improvement of international competitiveness in industrial policy cannot be effectively addressed without acknowledging the coexistence of sovereign nations."[8] In other words, industrial policy focuses on broader, macro-level public interests rather than the profitability of individual business.

Third, one of the primary reasons why developing countries implement industrial policies to encourage the growth of strategic sectors is that the market in a latecomer nation cannot provide opportunities for such industrial development. Latecomer countries' economic progress is beset by a slew of internal contradictions. Low productivity implies that the nation should entice savings with high interest rates but, at the same time, its need to encourage investment also demands low interest rates. It needs a low exchange rate to promote exports but, at the same time, it also needs

[7] Bai Gao, Economic Ideology and Japanese Industrial Policy (Shanghai People's Publishing House, 2008 [1997]), p. 32.

[8] Bai Gao, Economic Ideology and Japanese Industrial Policy (Shanghai People's Publishing House, 2008 [1997]), pp. 32–33.

a high exchange rate to relieve the burden of debt payments and imports. It must adopt protectionist policies to prevent its infant industries from international competition but, at the same time, it also needs to promote free trade to empower its own exports and import. Because of these unbalanced conditions, the states in latecomer nations frequently interfere in the market to accommodate the competing interests of diverse parties. Even within the same market, importers and exporters, and borrowers and savers, often face disparate market pricing due to state intervention. In other words, the state in a latecomer nation not only sees few prices that truly represent the market, but it frequently purposefully inflicts pricing distortions in an effort to attract investments.[9] This deliberate pricing distortion in state industrial policy, intended at encouraging businesses to engage in fledgling industries and produce profits, has an economic justification. Unlike Western neoclassical economics, which analyzes capitalist market economies in a purely abstract manner, developmental economics focuses on understanding unique historical processes of production, distribution, exchange, and consumption during the industrialization process.[10] Yasuke Murakami has noted that a general trend seen in the process of economic development is that sectors heavily influenced by nature, such as agriculture, tend to experience diminishing marginal returns or rising marginal costs, whereas sectors where human intervention plays a more significant role frequently exhibit increasing marginal returns or decreasing marginal costs. Thus, if rising output levels in an infant industry result in falling marginal costs and rising marginal returns, the businesses in that industry will ultimately become competitive on a global scale.[11]

Fourth, in the classical East Asian developmentalism represented by Japan and South Korea, the developmental state's industrial policy does not entail picking a single "champion" out of a variety of companies and concentrating resources to it. Instead, it promotes oligopolistic competition, enabling a few stronger businesses within a sector to compete and increase their level of global competitiveness. To help local businesses increase their competitiveness against global competitors, the developmental state opposes excessive competition and contends that resources

[9] Alice H. Amsden, "Asia's Next Giant: South Korea and Late Industrialization" (New York: Oxford University Press, 1989), p. 13.

[10] Yasuke Murakami, "An Anticlassical Political Economic Analysis: A Vision for the Next Century" (Stanford: Stanford University Press, 1996).

[11] Yasuke Murakami, "An Anticlassical Political Economic Analysis: A Vision for the Next Century" (Stanford: Stanford University Press, 1996), pp. 146–148.

should be comparatively concentrated due to the limited availability of national resources. Overly competitive industries dilute their scarce resources, which prevents them from reaching economies of scale.[12] "Industrial policy seeks to capitalize on falling marginal costs. Its objective is to preserve healthy competition in sectors with declining marginal costs. Without such a policy, these industries will not be able to unleash their growth potential."[13]

1.4 Chinese Characteristics of Industrial Policies

The implementation of industrial policies in China differs significantly from that of Japan and South Korea, the representatives of classical developmentalism. The major difference lies in the strong presence of local governments and SOEs in China.[14]

In discussions about industrial policies in Japan and South Korea, the central government is frequently highlighted. However, this approach does not work in China. Chinese local governments play a crucial role in formulating and implementing industrial policies. They are able to selectively interpret and apply the industrial policies of the central government in accordance with their own preferences, and they occasionally develop local industrial policies that go against those of the central government. Chinese local governments use subsidies for industries they want to grow as a key instrument for implementing industrial policy. The fierce competition among local governments has played a significant role in driving the development of the railway logistics market symbolized by the China-Europe Railway Express. Trade between China and Europe has long been heavily reliant on maritime transport, but, by 2016, China-Europe Railway Express had grown to over 1700 trains, each carrying 41 standard containers. It is unthinkable without local government competition.

[12] Bai Gao, Economic Ideology and Japanese Industrial Policy (Shanghai People's Publishing House, 2008 [1997]), p. 41.

[13] Yasuke Murakami, "An Anticlassical Political Economic Analysis: A Vision for the Next Century" (Stanford: Stanford University Press, 1996), p. 183.

[14] Regarding the GDP competition among local governments, refer to Zhou Li'an's "A Study on the Model of Promotion Tournament for Chinese Local Officials" in the *Economic Research Journal*, July 2007, pp. 36–50. Regarding the role of state-owned enterprises in industrial policy, refer to Liu Xiaolu's "Classification Reform and Policy Adjustment of State-Owned Enterprises from the Perspective of Industrial Policy" on China.com.cn, March 24, 2017. http://www.china.com.cn/opinion/think/2017-03/24/content_40495116.htm.

Moreover, another major difference between China and Japan or South Korea is the significant role played by SOEs in implementing and carrying out China's industrial policies. In theory, the Chinese government has much more sway over SOEs than it does over private or foreign companies because the government appoints the senior executives of SOEs. In reality, it is typical to see SOEs monopolizing particular industries within a given sector and being in charge of implementing and executing industrial strategies via administrative orders. SOEs are typically the primary actors in carrying out both central and local government industrial policies. Since the reforms and opening-up, SOEs have been required to operate per market principles; however, they continue to play a crucial role in implementing government industrial policies when the central and local governments want businesses to enter particular industries where the market is not yet fully developed. The existence and considerable role of SOEs in the Chinese economy have had a profound impact on how the Railway Express between China and Europe operate.

1.5 The State as a Structural Factor

The state, viewed as a structural factor in the process of market building, plays a crucial role in explaining the differences among cities in operating China-Europe Railway Express. In our analysis of the development of CRE, three structural influences of the state are particularly important.

Firstly, the state functions as an organizational structure that allocates various powers and divides responsibilities internally. This division of labor among bureaucracies affects the interplay among different policy departments within the government, as they may pursue their own interests when formulating and implementing industrial policies. These interactions involve not only different branches of government but also societal forces. They frequently give rise to specific government–business relationships, and the nature of these relationships has a significant impact on how the government formulates policies, what kind of policies it formulates, and how it implements those policies [Leon N. Lindberg and John L. Campbell, "The State and the Organization of Economic Activity," in John L. Campbell, J. Rogers Hollingsworth, and Leon N. Lindberg, eds. Governance of the American Economy (New York: Cambridge University Press, 1991), pp. 358–359]. The development of the China-Europe Railway Express platform is profoundly influenced by the state capacity for intervention, regulation, and coordination as well as by the power dynamics among diverse social actors that place major restrictions on government actions. It can generally be expected that local governments will lean toward a smaller number of companies as the main actors for implementing and executing their policies if the key decision-makers have strong policy preferences and policymaking and implementation departments are relatively centralized. Reliance on a single SOE is also more likely in these circumstances. On the other hand, there is a higher chance that a relatively diverse and inclusive industrial platform will emerge if the top decision-makers of the local government lack specific policy preferences, and the authority for policymaking is decentralized among various functional divisions, resulting in dispersed policymaking and implementation power. In fact, there are various potential outcomes between these two scenarios.

Furthermore, the state, more visible in China, functions as a critical structural condition that defines resource allocation [Leon N. Lindberg and John L. Campbell, "The State and the Organization of Economic Activity," in John L. Campbell, J. Rogers Hollingsworth, and Leon N. Lindberg, eds. Governance of the American Economy (New York: Cambridge University Press, 1991), pp. 358–359]. Specific industrial policies always have explicit measures for resource allocation. They can range from direct fiscal spending to providing favorable conditions in terms of credit, land, and taxation. These industrial policies significantly influence how resources are allocated for businesses. Businesses that actively participate in industries supported by the government are more likely to have better access to resources. This pattern of resource distribution also suggests a drop in government funding for other areas of the economy. Changes in resource allocation brought on by industrial policy frequently represent significant variables that might affect how well a business operates.

Lastly, another example of how the state, as a structural condition, impacts the direction of market building is that both the policy paradigm of the central government and the policy legacies of local governments, affect how local governments develop their CEFT programs. Policy paradigms "consist of both implementation plan, in the form of policies, and the means-ends designations, in the form of the principles of governmental action" [Frank Dobbin, Forging Industrial Culture (Princeton: Princeton University Press, 1994), p. 19]. In the discussion of industrial policies, the policy paradigm represents a dominant perspective, policy principles, or authoritative views. Therefore, it serves as a framework for government officials, industry professionals, and the general public to understand relevant economic phenomena, and it usually forms the basis for various economic actors to anticipate the direction of industrial development [Bai Gao, Economic Ideology and Japanese Industrial Policy (Shanghai People's Publishing House, 2008 [1997]), p. 17]. In China's political system, where the central government appoints local officials, the central government's policy paradigm is more important for local governments. It doesn't just give local government officials a "method of looking at issues" to understand economic phenomena; it also tries to take away the chance that they may have divergent viewpoints on the same policy area from an independent stance.

1.6 Plans for the Book

The preceding discussion offers helpful perspectives for our empirical analysis.

This study selects five major cities operating the CR Express—Chongqing, Yiwu, Chengdu, Zhengzhou, and Wuhan—as the empirical cases. These cities were chosen because they have operated China-Europe trains with remarkable success and each of them is a representative in its own right. Chongqing is a pioneer in operating China-Europe trains; Chengdu is a latecomer to the top; Zhengzhou is a typical city without major local manufacturing industrial clusters but has achieved relatively successful development of the trains; Yiwu is the sole city that primarily develops logistics platforms with a private company; Wuhan has a distinctive growth model marked by inclusivity and balance. In every case study, we conducted extensive literature research and interviewed many people in pertinent enterprises and government agencies.

The impact of the state as a structural factor on market building is reflected in two sets of linkages in the political economy of the CR Express, and they are central to comprehending the current state of freight train operations. The first set of relationships involves the central and local governments. This includes the relationship between the central government and local governments, as well as the complexities that arise between China Railway, formerly the Ministry of Railways, but now a national SOE, and local governments in implementing the development of China-Europe Railway Express. We have devoted a chapter to especially discussing China Railway's position in the development of CR Express from its viewpoint. The second set of relationships consists of SOEs and private enterprises. The degree of inclusivity of logistics platforms in various locations that serve China-Europe Railway Express reveals the tensions in this relationship.

The logistics industry represented by the China-Europe Railway Express does in fact act as a pillar industry that propels the BRI's construction, encourages the westward opening up, and makes it easier for Eurasia's economic integration. The goal of the state efforts to promote the land-based logistics industry represented by railways is to foster the growth of global trade between China and the countries along various routes.

Therefore, we cannot assess state industrial policies by using the standard metrics for evaluating the market activities of businesses. The industrial policies of developmental states described in the literature on classical developmentalism are in blatant conflict with the market principle or the profit principle. These principles are more visible in liberal market economies such as the United Kingdom and the United States, where companies are viewed as vehicles for shareholders to make profits.

And last, when adopting industrial policies, developmental states frequently prefer oligopolistic competition over choosing national "champions." They rely on a few leading companies to compete in domestic market, through which they enhance their international competitiveness.

CHAPTER 2

China Railway and the China-Europe Railway Express: Practices and Prospects

Dajie Zuo

Since the initiation of the China-Europe Railway Express (CR Express) in 2011, with important milestones such as the Belt and Road Initiative (BRI) proposed in 2013 and the release of the China-Europe Railway Express Development Plan in 2016, CR Express' development can be roughly divided into three phases: the exploration period (2011–2013), the vigorous development period (2013–2016), and the standardization and enhancement period (after 2016). During the exploration phase, China State Railway Group Co., Ltd. (referred to as China Railway) primarily faced challenges such as optimizing the organization of train transport processes and improving customs clearance and inspection and quarantine efficiency. In the prosperity phase, China Railway's operation of the CR Express was primarily constrained by the insufficient return cargo sources, leading to a decline in key technical and economic

D. Zuo (✉)
Center on China's High-Speed Rail Development Strategy at Southwest Jiaotong University, Chengdu, China

School of Transportation and Logistics of Southwest Jiaotong University, Chengdu, China
e-mail: bai.gao@duke.edu

B. Gao, Z. Zhen (eds.), *The China-Europe Railway Express*, China and Globalization 2.0,
https://doi.org/10.1007/978-981-19-2882-6_2

indicators for the trains. In the standardization and enhancement phase, balancing the interests of localities and China Railway and maximizing the brand value of the CR Express became new challenges for China Railway. Therefore, a systematic review of the institutional changes and evolutionary mechanisms of China Railway's operation of the CR Express holds significant importance for further standardizing and enhancing the quality and level of the China-Europe freight train services.

2.1 China Railway and the CR Express

2.1.1 The Role and Position of China Railway in China's Comprehensive Transportation System

2.1.1.1 Introduction to China State Railway Group Co., Ltd.

2.1.1.1.1 Subsidiaries of China Railway

(1) Railway Bureaus (Companies) (18 in total): Harbin Railway Bureau, Shenyang Railway Bureau, Beijing Railway Bureau, Taiyuan Railway Bureau, Hohhot Railway Bureau, Zhengzhou Railway Bureau, Wuhan Railway Bureau, Xi'an Railway Bureau, Jinan Railway Bureau, Shanghai Railway Bureau, Nanchang Railway Bureau, Guangzhou Railway (Group) Corporation, Nanning Railway Bureau, Chengdu Railway Bureau, Kunming Railway Bureau, Lanzhou Railway Bureau, Urumqi Railway Bureau, and Qinghai-Tibet Railway Company.
(2) Specialized Transport Companies (3 in total): China Railway Container Transport Co., Ltd. (referred to as CRCT), China Railway Special Cargo Transport Logistics Co., Ltd., and China Railway Express Co., Ltd.

2.1.1.1.2 CRCT

(1) Business Scope of CRCT

CRCT primarily engages in domestic and international container rail transport, container multimodal transport, international railway intermodal transport; logistics services including warehousing, loading/

unloading, packaging, and distribution; containers, specialized container vehicles, specialized container facilities, railway tarpaulins, and related operation and leasing businesses. Additionally, CRCT conducts international and domestic freight agency services and related economic, technical, information consulting, and service businesses.

(2) Operating Locations

The company has established 18 large container center stations equipped with advanced international technology and logistics functions in Beijing, Shanghai, Guangzhou, Shenzhen, Tianjin, Harbin, Shenyang, Qingdao, Chengdu, Chongqing, Xi'an, Zhengzhou, Wuhan, Dalian, Ningbo, Kunming, Urumqi, and Lanzhou. It currently operates two subsidiary companies, China Railway International Freight Agency Co., Ltd. (CRIF) and China Railway Specialized Container Transport Co., Ltd., and has six container handling stations in Beijing East, Yangpu, Chengdu East, Chongqing East, Dalang, and Kunming East. In addition, container business is conducted at 609 other stations.

(3) Product and Service

(a) Rail Transport

Container rail transport services are characterized by safety, punctuality, convenience, and speed. The company operates container trains between major cities in China, providing high-quality services to customers. Notably, the double-deck container trains running between Beijing and Shanghai have filled a gap in Asian railway transportation. The company can also customize rail transport routes to meet specific customer requirements, offering personalized container train transport services.

(b) Logistics Services

Leveraging the advantages of railway container transport, the company's specialized logistics division is establishing modern logistics bases with advanced information processing, warehousing, and distribution capabilities. These facilities integrate railway, road, and port services to provide high-quality logistics services to a wide range of customers.

(c) End-to-End Transport

For customers with scattered cargo transportation needs, the company has introduced a new product called "Container Full-Service Express Transport," which combines warehousing, transport, loading and unloading, consolidation, delivery, and information services. This comprehensive logistics service offers door-to-door pickup and delivery, single-ticket service, and one-time billing for less-than-truckload cargo.

(d) Container Leasing

As the owner of containers, the company provides container leasing services to users. Through leasing agreements with lessees, the company offers qualified containers for use within specified terms. Container leasing can take various forms, including one-way leasing, long-term leasing, spot leasing, and regional leasing, following international practices.

2.1.1.2 The Backbone Role of China Railway in the Comprehensive Transportation Network

2.1.1.2.1 China's Vast Territory and Its Industrial Distribution Determine the Backbone Role of Railways

China has a vast territory, spanning approximately 5400 kilometers from east to west and 5200 kilometers from north to south. This vast expanse has led to an uneven distribution of resources and industries across the country. The western, northwestern, and southwestern regions are rich in natural resources, while the eastern region is the hub of industrial and economic activity. As a result of this geographical distribution, there is a significant flow of bulk and long-distance cargo, particularly in energy and raw materials, from the western to the eastern regions and from the northern to the southern regions of China. Land-based transportation typically covers distances ranging from 800 to 1000 kilometers, and sometimes even exceeds 2000 kilometers. The transportation distance to coastal ports generally falls within the range of 500 to 700 kilometers.

2.1.1.2.2 National Economic Development and Social Progress Determine the Backbone Role of Railways

Railways serve as an effective means to narrow regional disparities and promote sustainable social development. Accelerating railway construction in underdeveloped regions can significantly improve their external transportation conditions, shorten distances to central cities and national markets, reduce transportation costs for local products, enhance market competitiveness, and create more equitable development opportunities for regional economic growth.

2.1.1.2.3 Ecological Civilization Construction Determines the Backbone Role of Railways

Further data reveals that railways have distinct advantages in terms of land conservation, energy efficiency, and environmental protection. In terms of land use, railways occupy only about one-tenth of the land area compared to roads for the same transportation volume. Regarding energy utilization, China's railways consume less than one-sixth of the energy consumed by the entire transportation sector while handling approximately half of the sector's workload. In environmental protection, railways emit the least amount of pollutants among various transportation modes, especially electrified railways, which are recognized as clean and environmentally friendly modes of transportation.

2.1.1.3 The Current Status of China's Railway Connections with Other Countries

China shares borders with 14 countries, but there are only five neighboring countries with railway connections to China: Russia, Mongolia, Kazakhstan, North Korea, and Vietnam.

Railway connections between different countries are typically established at border stations, also known as railway ports. Currently operational railway ports include: Manzhouli Port in Inner Mongolia (connecting to Russia), Erenhot Port in Inner Mongolia Autonomous Region (connecting to Mongolia), Tumen Port in Yanbian, Jilin Province (connecting to Russia), Suifenhe Port in Heilongjiang Province (connecting to Russia), Alashankou Port and Horgos Port in Xinjiang Uyghur Autonomous Region (connecting to Kazakhstan), Dandong Port in Liaoning Province, Ji'an Port in Jilin Province (connecting to DPRK), Pingxiang Port in Guangxi Zhuang Autonomous Region, and Hekou Port in Yunnan Province (connecting to Vietnam). Furthermore, railway gauges in different countries may not be uniform. There are three main railway gauges in use: standard gauge (1435 mm), broad gauge (greater than 1435 mm), and narrow gauge (less than 1435 mm). The

Table 2.1 China's railway network connectivity with various countries and corresponding track gauges

Connected countries to China's railway	*Border ports*	*Province/city of port location*	*Track gauges of both countries*
Russia	Manzhouli Port	Inner Mongolia	Chinese: 1435 mm Russian: 1520 mm
	Suifenhe Port	Helongjiang	
	Tumen Port	Yanbian, Jilin Province	
Kazakhstan	Alashankou Port	Xinjiang	Chinese: 1435 mm, Kazakh: 1520 mm
	Horgos Port	Xinjiang	
Mongolia	Erenhot Port	Inner Mongolia	Chinese: 1435 mm, Kazakh: 1520 mm
DPRK	Dandong Port	Liaoning	Chinese: 1435 mm, Mongolian: 1520 mm
	Ji'an Port	Jilin	
Vietnam	Pingxiang Port	Guangxi	Chinese: 1435 mm, Vietnamese: 1000 mm
	Hekou Port	Yunna	

compatibility of railway gauges can affect international railway connections (see Table 2.1).

2.1.2 Introduction to CR Express

The CR Express refers to scheduled and fixed-route international rail freight services with predetermined timetables and routes for the entire journey. These services operate between China and Europe, as well as countries along the BRI route. They utilize containers for intermodal rail transportation. The organization of CR Express involves various departments, including domestic and international logistics companies, freight forwarding agencies, customs, and inspection authorities, and CRCT. Among these, CRCT plays a crucial and irreplaceable role as the primary operator of the CR Express. The CR Express has evolved into a pivotal land transportation mode within the realm of international logistics. It plays a crucial role in supporting China's foreign trade development by establishing a land-based trade route connecting China and Europe. This connectivity ensures efficient road connections and seamless logistics operations between these two regions. Furthermore, it contributes significantly to the advancement of the BRI by providing essential transportation capabilities.

Currently, there are three main routes for the CR Express, covering the western, central, and eastern regions. The western route originates from China's central and western areas, passes through the Alashankou (Horgos) Port, and exits to Europe. The central route starts from northern China and exits through Erenhot on the border with Mongolia. The eastern route departs from China's southeastern coastal areas and exits to Europe via Manzhouli or Suifenhe. There are 18 Chinese cities that have opened routes for the China-Europe (Asia) Railway Express. These cities are mainly located in the western, central, and eastern regions. In the western region, the cities include Urumqi, Lanzhou, Xi'an, Chengdu, Chongqing, and Kunming; in the central region, there are Zhengzhou, Wuhan, Changsha, Hefei, and Dongguan; in the eastern region, the cities include Suzhou, Yiwu, Shenyang, Lianyungang, Yingkou, Qingdao, and Jinan. The CR Express has reached 13 cities in eight European countries. These cities include Duisburg and Hamburg in Germany, Warsaw, Łódź, and Malaszewicze in Poland, Pardubice in the Czech Republic, Madrid in Spain, Rotterdam in the Netherlands, Lyon in France, Brest in Belarus, and Cherkessk, Chelyabinsk, and Kaluga in Russia.

2.2 The Exploration Phase and China Railway's Practice (2011–2013)

2.2.1 The Operation of the CR Express from 2011 to 2013 (Key Achievements During the Exploration Phase)

The first China-Europe container train from Chongqing to Duisburg, Germany, was successfully launched by China Railways on March 19, 2011. It departs from Chongqing's Tuanjie Village Container Center Station and travels through the Xiangyang-Chongqing Railway, Lanzhou-Lianyungang Railway, and Lanzhou-Xinjiang Railway. Due to the difference in railway gauges between China and the portion passing through Kazakhstan, the train must undergo a gauge change at the Alashankou Port in Xinjiang before exiting China. It then passes through Kazakhstan, Russia, Belarus, and Poland before reaching Duisburg, Germany, covering a total distance of approximately 11,000 kilometers with a travel time of approximately 15 days. The primary cargo consists of IT products produced locally in Chongqing.

Following the "Chongqing-Xinjiang-Europe Railway" route, the railway line from Wuhan to the Czech Republic and Poland was opened on October 24, 2012. This train departs from Wuhan, goes through Alashankou for gauge change, and passes through Kazakhstan, Russia, Belarus, and other countries before reaching various cities in Poland. The total distance of the journey is 10,700 kilometers, with a travel time of approximately 15 days. It primarily transports electronic products such as laptops produced in Wuhan.

Subsequently, the route from Changsha to Duisburg was opened on October 30, 2012. This route follows a "one main, two auxiliary" configuration: the "main" route goes from Changsha to Duisburg, while the "auxiliary" routes include one that goes to Tashkent in Uzbekistan and another leading to Moscow.

On April 26, 2013, the railway line from Chengdu to Lodz was opened. This train starts in Chengdu, goes through Alashankou for gauge change, and passes through Kazakhstan, Russia, Belarus, and finally arrives at Lodz in Poland, covering a total distance of 9965 kilometers with a travel time of approximately 14 days. It mainly transports IT products and other export goods produced in Chengdu.

On July 18, 2013, a train from Zhengzhou to Hamburg began running. This train departs from Zhengzhou, undergoes gauge change at Alashankou, and passes through Kazakhstan, Russia, Belarus, Poland, and finally reaches Hamburg in Germany. The total distance is 10,245 kilometers with a travel time of approximately 15 days. The cargo includes various items such as tires, high-end clothing, sports and leisure products, handicrafts, and so on.

2.2.2 *Main Issues During the Exploratory Phase*

During the initial two to three years of the operation of the CR Express, there were relatively few domestic cities that had established routes. The primary originating cities during this period included Chengdu, Chongqing, Wuhan, Zhengzhou, among others. During this time, various challenges were encountered, including extended transit times for the trains, multiple operational steps along the route, low efficiency in various operations, a severe shortage of return cargo sources, and limited connectivity of infrastructure. Notably, the handling time at international border stations for the trains was notably prolonged, primarily due to the low efficiency in sorting and customs clearance of container goods within the trains.

2.2.2.1 *Transportation Organization: Punctuality Rates Are Not High, and the Operating Speed Still Requires Further Improvement*

The CR Express shares its domestic route with other freight trains, which can lead to some delays. Additionally, because the cargo transported consists of import and export goods, and railway gauges may differ among countries, the CR Express often requires customs clearance and gauge-changing operations at intermediate stations, particularly at international border stations. During this period, the customs clearance efficiency was relatively low, and the gauge-changing process took a considerable amount of time. The establishment of a continuous route for the entire journey was not yet realized, making it challenging to manage the train's operations outside China. These uncontrollable factors have contributed to a lower punctuality rate for the trains and extended stopover times during the journey, highlighting the need for further improvement in their operating speed.

2.2.2.2 *Customs Clearance: Inspection, Quarantine, and Clearance Efficiency Are Not High*

For the customs clearance, it requires coordination between various departments such as railways, customs, inspection and quarantine, and border inspection. In the customs clearance process from 2011 to 2013, after import and export goods arrived at the port, in addition to railway transshipment operations, import and export companies also needed to go through customs and inspection procedures. This involved providing a substantial amount of documentation and cooperating with port law enforcement agencies to complete a series of on-site customs operations, including declaration, inspection, taxation, and more. This process is time consuming and labor intensive, with many steps and complex procedures, often taking a day or even longer for the train to exit smoothly.

2.2.3 *Key Strategies of China Railway During the Exploratory Phase*

In response to the significant challenges of long processing times at border stations and low operational efficiency of the CR Express, China Railway implemented a series of improvement measures.

2.2.3.1 *Transportation Organization: Enhancing Border Station Operations and the Internal Workflow of Freight Yards*

To optimize the operational processes at border stations and improve the internal workflow, a leadership team was established at the stations. This team is led by the station manager and deputy manager, overseeing coordination among various departments, including station operations, freight operations, and loading/unloading coordination. The main task of the cargo handling department is to coordinate and oversee the internal railway freight operations, specifically the organization of train and container cargo handling operations. The primary task of the freight yard is to monitor and coordinate the internal railway freight operations, collaborate with customs, inspection and quarantine authorities, freight forwarders, and Kazakhstani authorities. They proactively engage with customs and inspection agencies to facilitate the smooth clearance of goods. The primary responsibility of the operation workshop is to oversee and manage the internal railway operational processes. This includes coordinating with locomotive, rolling stock, border inspection, and Kazakh counterparts. They also place a strong emphasis on closely monitoring the operation of the train, with a particular focus on ensuring the efficient organization of the train's transportation and making optimal use of departure lines.

2.2.3.2 *Customs Clearance: Strengthening Coordination Between Port Stations and Customs Authorities*

During this phase, the China Railway lacked comprehensive improvement measures concerning issues related to cargo inspection, quarantine, and customs clearance. The primary focus was on enhancing coordination and communication between the cargo departments at border stations and customs and inspection agencies, with the aim of expediting operational processes.

From the requirements outlined by the China Railway regarding the organization of CR Express operations at border stations, it is evident that their strategy primarily emphasized seamless coordination among various departments and operational phases. By facilitating cooperation between departments such as operations, freight, and cargo handling, China Railway aimed to minimize the time required for activities like container handling and customs clearance at the station, ultimately expediting the release of the train.

2.2.4 *Analysis of the China Railway's Strategies During the Exploration Phrase*

During this phase, which marked the initial stage of China-Europe rail services, there were limited domestic cities offering services, and there were no issues related to competition for freight sources. The primary challenges revolved around improving the efficiency of operations at border stations and streamlining customs inspection and quarantine processes. Therefore, during this stage, the China Railway introduced strategies specifically aimed at addressing these two key issues.

2.3 Flourishing Period of China Railway's Practices (2013–2016)

2.3.1 *The CR Express Guided by the BRI (2013–2016) (Major Achievements During the Vigorous Development Period)*

2.3.1.1 The Proposal and Significance of the BRI

The BRI was officially unveiled during Chinese president Xi Jinping's visit to Kazakhstan in September 2013. In a speech at Kazakhstan's Nazarbayev University on September 7, 2013, he proposed that to make the economic ties closer, mutual cooperation deeper, and space of development broader between the Eurasian countries, we can innovate the mode of cooperation and jointly build the "Silk Road Economic Belt" step by step to gradually form overall regional cooperation. On October 3, 2013, in a speech to Indonesian Parliament, Chinese president Xi Jinping expressed China's willingness to strengthen maritime cooperation with ASEAN countries to make good use of the China-ASEAN Maritime Cooperation Fund set up by the Chinese government and vigorously develop maritime partnership in a joint effort to build the Maritime Silk Road of the twenty-first century.

In terms of regions, the BRI covers an extensive range of areas and cities. The initiative consists of several routes. China-Mongolia-Russia

Economic Corridor (CMREC): it primarily involves transportation and energy corridors connecting China's northeastern regions with Russia and Mongolia. To the east, it connects to Japan and South Korea, and to the west it connects to Europe via Russia; New Eurasian Land Bridge Economic Corridor: it extends westward from the original Eurasian Land Bridge through Xinjiang, connecting Kazakhstan as well as countries in Central Asia, Western Asia, and Central and Eastern Europe; China-South Asia-West Asia Economic Corridor: it connects China's Yunnan and Guangxi with countries such as Pakistan, India, Myanmar, Thailand, Laos, Cambodia, Malaysia, Vietnam, and Singapore. Additionally, it features a southern branch of the Eurasian Land Bridge connecting Pakistan, Afghanistan, Iran, and Turkey; maritime strategic fortresses: they encompass ports, coastal areas, and islands in regions such as the Bohai Economic Rim, Yangtze River Delta, West Coast of the Taiwan Strait, Pearl River Delta, and Beibu Gulf, connecting with coastal countries and regions along the Pacific and Indian Oceans.

BRI proposed by General Secretary Xi Jinping in 2013 holds significant importance in strengthening China's economic and trade relations with neighboring countries in Central Asia, South Asia, and Eurasian nations, fostering regional exchange and cooperation, coordinating domestic and international development, safeguarding the surrounding environment, and expanding opportunities for China Western Development and opening up.

2.3.1.2 The CR Express Guided by the BRI (2013–2016)

On September 29, 2013, a train departed from Suzhou to Warsaw. Starting in Suzhou, the train exited through Manzhouli and traveled through Russia, Belarus, arriving at Warsaw, Poland, covering a total distance of 11,200 kilometers in 15 days. The cargo consisted of IT products such as laptops, LCD screens, hard drives, and chips, primarily sourced from Suzhou and its surrounding areas.

On November 18, 2014, the "Yiwu-Xinjiang-Europe" route was inaugurated. The train departed from Yiwu, Zhejiang Province, passed through the Alashankou border crossing in Xinjiang, and traveled through Kazakhstan, Russia, Belarus, Poland, Germany, and France, ultimately reaching Madrid, Spain, after a journey of 21 days. This route was notable for being the longest in terms of transportation distance, crossing through the most countries, traversing the highest number of provinces, and involving the most track gauge changes. Additionally, Yiwu was the only county-level city to open a China-Europe Railway Express route at that time.

In 2015, the route from Harbin to Russia was launched on February 28. The train traveled a total distance of 6578 kilometers, primarily transporting heavy equipment for oil exploration. On June 13, the route from Harbin to Hamburg was opened, and the train, loaded with electronic products and machinery, embarked on its journey smoothly. This route plans to operate 28 trains this year, with an expected output value of 1.7 billion yuan and a total import and export value of 4.28 billion yuan. The advancement of the BRI has undoubtedly strengthened economic and trade exchanges between China and Europe, as well as the countries along the route. Such economic complementarity and cultural communication require a carrier, an efficient and cost-effective channel for economic and cultural exchanges. The CR Express is unquestionably an important carrier for the Initiative and serves as a link and bridge for mutual communication among the countries along the route.

First and foremost, the CR Express, known for its convenience, speed, efficiency, and cost-effectiveness, has triggered a logistics revolution within the framework of the BRI and on a global scale. It is poised to substantially boost economic and trade cooperation between China and Europe. Simultaneously, it has ushered in fresh economic growth opportunities for the nations and territories along its route, reducing geographical distances, improving the efficiency of economic complementarity, connecting, and unifying an expansive market. This has facilitated the leveraging of complementary advantages and infused significant vitality into the development of market economies.

Secondly, for China, the China-Europe Railway Express has provided a new breakthrough for the opening up of its western regions. Prior to this, the opening up of China was primarily linked through maritime routes along the southeastern coast. However, for the inland western regions of China, the China-Europe Railway Express has undoubtedly represented a significant leap in terms of external opening up. This move holds crucial strategic significance for expanding openness and developing the economy in China's western regions.

Finally, the continuous growth of the global economy has reinforced international linkages, and the CR Express unquestionably intensifies these connections, presenting fresh opportunities for worldwide economic development. Furthermore, it enhances cultural interactions and exchanges between China, Europe, and the countries along the BRI, facilitating deeper mutual understanding and interaction, which plays a vital strategic role. Moreover, it constitutes a significant initiative in support of the two paramount global themes of upholding world peace and fostering development.

In conclusion, the official launch of the CR Express not only brings tremendous benefits and economic development opportunities to China but also offers economic growth prospects for the countries and regions along the BRI. It stands as a remarkable feat in achieving mutually beneficial economic development.

2.3.2 Main Problems During the Period of Vigorous Development

The CR Express routes consist of domestic mainline routes and international border crossing stations. On the one hand, the western corridor in the northwest region of China has limited mainline routes, with only the Lanzhou-Xinjiang Railway available for train departures from Xinjiang. This results in significant capacity constraints on the railway network. On the other hand, there is an issue with insufficient capacity at foreign railway border crossing stations and their subsequent routes. The railways in China and Western Europe use standard gauge (1435 mm), while Russia, the former Soviet Union states in Central Asia, and Mongolia use broad gauge (1520 mm). This difference in track gauges requires the CR Express trains to undergo at least two gauge-changing operations at the border, leading to time-consuming procedures and significantly higher operational costs compared to rail–sea intermodal transport and river–sea intermodal transport. The logistics channel is not well connected, resulting in high operational costs and widespread losses in operations. The long-term one-way transportation of goods has led to overall losses along the CR Express routes. To balance the financial picture, various local governments have resorted to subsidies, creating a chaotic situation in its development. To ensure operations and attract cargo, local governments have introduced subsidy programs, while competition among regions has led to price pressures to secure high-quality cargo sources.

2.3.2.1 Organization of Cargo Sources: Challenges Lie in the Dispersion of Domestic Cargo Sources and the Limited International Return Cargo Sources, Leading to Uneconomical Transportation

Even while many of the China-Europe freight train routes are operating steadily and regularly, overall, there are significantly fewer trains making return trips than there are doing outgoing ones. To make matters worse, the nations bordering the route hardly ever use these trains for freight transportation, which means that container handling at intermediate stations is minimal. It's mostly point-to-point direct transportation instead. This is mostly due to the railway authorities' and logistics businesses' poor cooperation both domestically and internationally. They haven't managed to source items from the nations along the route in an efficient manner.

The domestic supply of goods for the China-Europe freight trains is relatively small and scattered, and almost all "XX to Europe" train services have failed to develop the capacity to attract a significant volume of return cargo. They can only organize one-way freight transport, and there is very little international return cargo. It was only in 2014 that the China-Europe freight trains began to achieve breakthroughs in zero-return cargo. Achieving a balance in two-way transport in the short term remains challenging.

The lack of cargo support from the countries along the China-Europe freight train routes is due to a failure of relevant national departments and entities to incorporate the China-Europe freight trains as part of logistics support in their foreign investments and logistics park construction. There is a significant opportunity to strengthen cooperation with the governments of the countries along the routes, using international production capacity and equipment manufacturing cooperation as a catalyst to extend the China-Europe freight train services to overseas economic and trade cooperation zones established by China in these countries, relevant industrial parks, and free trade zones. This can help attract more sources of cargo for transportation via the China-Europe freight trains. Furthermore, local governments have not fully played their expected roles in supporting regional companies in expanding their capacity cooperation and trade with countries along the China-Europe freight train routes, thereby increasing the sources of cargo for the China-Europe freight trains. Finally, to fully leverage their strengths in cargo consolidation and transportation, the railway department has not properly coordinated with significant domestic and international logistics organizations, port enterprises, and freight forwarders.

2.3.2.2 Brand Development: An Urgent Need for Management Regulations for the China-Europe Railway Express Brand

In June 2016, China Railways officially launched a unified brand for the China-Europe freight trains. CR Express left from a number of cities on that day, including Chongqing, Chengdu, Zhengzhou, Wuhan, Changsha, Suzhou, Dongguan, Yiwu, and more. From then on, all China-Europe freight trains departing from China to Europe would use this unified brand.

As the BRI progressed, there was rapid development in economic and trade exchanges between China, Europe, and the countries along the BRI. This led to significant logistics demand between Asia and Europe. Since China launched the China-Europe freight trains in 2011, they have become a major transportation mode, complementing air and water transportation due to their advantages in safety, speed, environmental friendliness, and minimal susceptibility to natural environmental factors.

The railway authorities greatly expanded their lines and raised the number of train services to accommodate the increasing demand. The railway authorities greatly expanded their lines and raised the number of train services to accommodate the increasing demand. But this growth also brought up problems, like a profusion of train names and logos and erratic market operations, which lessened these freight trains' market power to some extent. It was a smart move on the part of China Railways to integrate mature resources and develop a unified brand for freight trains between China and Europe in response to these issues.

In the construction of the China-Europe freight train brand, a simple and elegant new logo was adopted, and all services were unified under the name "China-Europe Railway Express." Visually appealing logos and memorable names often leave a more profound impression on people, making them easy to remember and inspiring trust. This has significantly boosted the brand's credibility and influence.

The unity of the brand is not just about renaming; it also involves the centralized management of transportation resources. Over the years, China's national railways have operated more than 1700 freight train services, accumulated valuable experience, and established a strong reputation in the China-Europe logistics market, thus gaining extensive influence. The CR Express brand aims to comprehensively optimize and integrate these valuable resources, ensuring better coordination and allocation of tasks among existing train services. This approach enables the brand to handle larger volumes of shipments, unleashing the maximum transportation potential and serving China's foreign trade while ensuring the healthy development of the CR Express logistics corridor.

The rapid development of China's railways has undeniably brought significant promotion to social and economic development, a fact recognized by the international community. Now, by effectively leveraging its existing comprehensive advantages, the railway sector has successfully launched brand-oriented operations for the China-Europe freight trains. This endeavor is bound to create a globally competitive and renowned logistics brand, reshaping the landscape of China-Europe logistics and ensuring smoother trade routes and more stable logistics for the BRI.

2.3.2.3 Operational Network: Insufficient Capacity for Overseas Distribution and Consolidation Centers, Leading to Inadequate Transshipment Capabilities

From the current operation, it can be observed that most are "point-to-point" direct transportation with very few or even no distribution and consolidation points along the route and at the destination. This deficiency in collecting and distributing capacity presents a significant challenge. To address this issue, it is advisable to adopt a "1+N" model for selecting distribution points and organizing the return cargo. The "1+N" model involves extending from existing routes to develop N distribution points and establishing collection points for return cargo. It is essential to conduct in-depth analysis regarding the content, value, and destination of products returning from Europe to China, aiming to identify stable sources of return cargo, especially those with high added value. For example, the "Chongqing-Xinjiang-Europe" route has established distribution and collection points in Russia, and Poland and is responsible for cargo collection there. For routes extending into Germany, new distribution and collection points in Antwerp, Belgium, and Rotterdam, the Netherlands, could be considered. However, the overseas distribution and consolidation centers for other China-Europe freight train routes are still insufficient, and there is an urgent need to expand the construction of distribution centers.

2.3.3 The Key Strategies for China Railways in the Period of Vigorous Development

While maintaining a rational division of labor between maritime and land transportation, a systematic design and organization of the "China-Europe Railway Express" network are established in accordance with the layout of China's economy, the distribution of ports, and international corridor construction. The focus is on the border crossings such as Manzhouli/Suifenhe, Erenhot, and Alashankou/Horgos, constructing three major corridors: the Eastern Line, Central Line, and Western Line. Innovative domestic cargo organization models are employed, with a few key hubs organizing the trains. Various regions shared train numbers and engaged in combined transportation. Cargo was consolidated and fully loaded at these hubs before proceeding to the port for customs clearance, ensuring the high-frequency and regular operation of the freight trains through "group consolidation" of trains and "scattered transshipment" of goods. The roles and functions of local governments in the CR Express network are defined, along with the establishment of a reasonable mechanism for participation and withdrawal. Long-term subsidy policies specific to the originating cities are discouraged. The China-Europe Railway Express Fund has been established, under the management of the China Railway, with joint funding from cities along the route or originating cities, effectively converting local government subsidies into financial contributions.

CRCT, a subsidiary of the China Railway, currently serves as the domestic carrier for various China-Europe freight train routes. It has been noted that there is room for optimization in terms of the operating routes and cargo organization for these freight trains. China Railway is actively developing strategies to reduce costs and enhance efficiency for all stakeholders. During the period from 2013 to 2016, China-Europe freight trains were in a nurturing phase, and their operational costs were relatively high. Sustaining operations without subsidies proved to be a challenge. Nevertheless, with the accumulation of experience in running these trains, the realization of economies of scale, and the expansion of extended services, it is expected that future costs will progressively decrease.

2.3.3.1 Enhancing Multilateral Coordination Mechanisms and Expediting the Development of Overseas Sources of Goods

Bilateral and multilateral communication among the countries along the route is strengthened, and cooperation among railways, customs, national inspections, and logistics service providers is enhanced. The application scope of the China-Europe Smart and Secure Trade Line (SSTL) pilot program is expanded. Customs facilitation is being promoted, and efforts are underway to expedite the harmonization of regulatory and inspection standards along the entire route, with the goal of reducing the transportation time for goods. The CR Express brand is being actively promoted, and initiatives are being undertaken to diversify the sources of return cargo. For longer-distance China-Europe freight trains, like the "Yiwu-Xinjiang-Europe" train, there are plans to introduce trains that handle container cargo at various countries along the route. Moreover, cargo distribution and consolidation centers are being established in transit and European destination countries to facilitate cargo distribution and the consolidation of return cargo.

To better organize sources of trade suitable for China-Europe freight trains, it's important to consider the characteristics of the cargo. Firstly, it's essential to further clarify the characteristics of freight train cargo. These cargoes typically fall between sea and air transportation, gradually attracting high-value goods that were previously shipped by sea and have time-sensitive transportation requirements. Additionally, they attract air cargo with less stringent time constraints.

Secondly, various entities, including overseas Chinese communities, multinational corporations, and others, are actively engaged in promoting and publicizing the China-Europe freight trains. This collaborative effort aims to encourage more trade and cargo transportation through the China-Europe freight train network. Thirdly, initiatives have been launched to explore new sources of cargo. By leveraging the agricultural resources and other commodities available in the countries along the China-Europe freight train route, these initiatives aim to transform foreign raw materials into semifinished products, thereby addressing challenges related to cargo sourcing. In this regard, there are already successful cases. Kazakhstan produces approximately 24 million tons of high-quality wheat each year. They consume about 5 million tons domestically and export another 5 million tons, leaving around 19 million tons that need processing. In China, a company from Ningxia has successfully established a "Ningxia Modern Agricultural Ecological Industrial Park" in Kazakhstan. They utilize Kazakhstan's wheat to refine biobased nylon-56 fibers, effectively solving Kazakhstan's wheat export challenge and addressing the sourcing issue for the domestic market. This is a highly commendable approach that can serve as a valuable model for consideration.

2.3.3.2 Unifying the Organization to Collaboratively Create a Brand

The China-Europe freight trains, as an internationally recognized logistics brand supported by the government, are managed by the China Railway. They have introduced management measures that encompass unified branding, unified transportation organization, unified pricing throughout the journey, unified service standards, unified operational teams, and a unified coordination platform. They have also established rational train routes to create a comprehensive unified timetable, realizing a "public train service" approach. This has resulted in a unified external image and a unified approach to negotiating preferential prices throughout the entire journey. These efforts aim to build a railway international multimodal transportation brand characterized by "fast, punctual, safe, stable, and environmentally friendly" freight transportation.

2.3.4 Analysis of the China Railway's Plan in the Period of Vigorous Development

Since the introduction of the BRI, the China-Europe freight trains have entered a period of vigorous development. The number of domestic originating cities and the operational routes of these trains have increased significantly during this phase. Therefore, the primary challenge during this stage is related to the organization of cargo sources. This includes the competition for cargo sources in foreign originating cities and the shortage of return cargo sources from abroad. During the exploratory phase of robust development, the China Railway's focus shifted away from improving the efficiency of port station operations and towards organizing cargo sources and establishing the China-Europe freight train brand. All the proposed measures and strategies are centered around enhancing the operational efficiency of these trains.

2.4 Outlook for the Standardization and Enhancement Period by China Railway (2016–2020)

2.4.1 1. Development Trends of the CR Express from 2016 to 2020 (Key Concepts for the Standardization and Enhancement Period)

2.4.1.1 Transportation Routes

The CR Express has a total of three exit routes, each departing from different railway border crossings in the eastern, central, and western regions. The details of these three routes are as follows:

1) The western route. Departing from the Alashankou (Horgos) border crossing in Xinjiang, China, it connects with the Trans-Siberian Railway in Kazakhstan and Russia, passing through countries such as Belarus, Poland, and Germany before reaching various European nations. Departing from the Horgos (Alashankou) border crossing, it travels through Kazakhstan, Turkmenistan, Iran, and Turkey, providing access to various European countries. Alternatively, it may pass through Kazakhstan, cross the Caspian Sea, and enter Azerbaijan, Georgia, Bulgaria, and other countries en route to Europe. Departing from Turgat (Erkeshtam) and connected to the planned China-Kyrgyzstan-Uzbekistan railway, it heads toward Kyrgyzstan, Uzbekistan, Turkmenistan, Iran, Turkey, and onward to various European countries.
2) The central route, departing from the Erenhot border crossing in Inner Mongolia, China, connects with the Trans-Siberian Railway through Mongolia and reaches various European countries.
3) The eastern route, departing from Manzhouli in Inner Mongolia (or Suifenhe in Heilongjiang), China, accesses the Trans-Siberian Railway in Russia and provides access to various European countries.

2.4.1.2 Key Hub Cites

Currently, there are over ten originating cities for China-Europe freight trains. These departure points are mainly source nodes, but there are also port nodes. These logistics nodes include Chengdu, Chongqing,

Zhengzhou, Wuhan, Hefei, Yiwu, Suzhou, Nanchang, Linyi, Lanzhou, Kunming, Changsha, Shenyang, Harbin, Xi'an, and Lianyungang.

Following the organizing principle of "integrating main lines and branch lines, and centralizing hubs for consolidation," a number of China-Europe freight train hub nodes are planned to be established in major inland source areas, key railway hubs, important coastal ports, and borderland road ports:

1) Major inland source nodes: these nodes have stable sources of goods, operate two or more direct point-to-point trains per week, possess the capability to organize return trains, and function as consolidation points for China-Europe freight trains.
2) Key railway hub nodes: positioned prominently within the national comprehensive transportation network, these hubs have strong consolidation and marshaling capabilities, handling the aggregation of goods, and facilitating transshipment for China-Europe freight trains.
3) Important coastal port nodes: these nodes play a crucial role in transit transportation, with well-established conditions for intermodal transport between railways and waterways. They operate three or more direct point-to-point trains per week and provide international sea-rail transportation services for China-Europe freight trains.
4) Borderland road port nodes: These are vital railway border checkpoints along the China-Europe freight train route. They serve functions such as customs inspection and clearance, facilitation of transit, and cargo transshipment.

Cities are encouraged to proactively gather sources of goods at China-Europe freight train hub nodes to improve overall efficiency and benefits. China-Europe freight train overseas nodes will be established in a rational manner based on the distribution of overseas sources of goods and railway hub conditions.

2.4.2 Key Problems for the Standardization and Enhancement Period

During the standardization and enhancement period, several key issues emerged: the development of international logistics channels and logistics nodes remained incomplete, with many railway routes in various regions still facing obstacles to smooth operation; China-Europe freight trains faced challenges related to relatively low travel speeds and punctuality; inadequate cargo supply, especially a shortage of return cargo, resulted in instances where China-Europe freight trains often returned empty; the need for further improvements in overseas cargo distribution centers and limited capacity for cargo consolidation and distribution were evident; logistics services were somewhat disconnected, lacking a comprehensive end-to-end service system, leading to low efficiency in coordinating various modes of transportation; the absence of uniform technical standards across various operational phases required attention; port locations experienced suboptimal customs clearance efficiency, disjointed customs inspections, and quarantine procedures, highlighting the need for a coordinated mechanism for seamless customs clearance; the challenge of achieving a better balance of interests between local authorities and China Railway persisted.

2.4.2.1 Transportation: Relatively Low Travel Speed and Punctuality

To ensure the safety of China-Europe freight train operations, each country along the route employs its own train drivers and operates on a relay system. This necessitates crew changes at border stations, and additional activities such as cargo handling, customs inspections, and quarantine checks may also take place at these border stations. These in-transit operations contribute significantly to the relatively low travel speed and punctuality. The lack of comprehensive monitoring and the absence of a mechanism for exchanging real-time operational information, as well as the inability to jointly plan the entire route for these trains, have all led to lower efficiency in organizing China-Europe freight train operations.

2.4.2.2 Customs Clearance: Imperfect Cooperation Mechanism with Customs Authorities in Countries Along the Route Leading to Inefficient Customs Clearance Processes

When it comes to customs clearance for China-Europe freight trains, there are two key aspects to consider: domestic and foreign customs clearance. In the case of domestic clearance, a fully integrated clearance process has not been realized. This means that even though the cargo may have undergone customs inspection and clearance at the departure port, it still goes through a secondary customs inspection and clearance process upon reaching the destination port. These redundant and time-consuming procedures do not contribute to the enhancement of train travel speed. Regarding foreign customs clearance, there is a lack of well-established cooperation, communication, and coordination mechanisms with customs authorities in the countries along the route. This leads to duplicated inspection and clearance procedures, particularly for certain types of goods with unique characteristics, such as meat, fruit, and grains, where dedicated "green lanes" have not been established. In summary, the overall efficiency of customs clearance is not high.

2.4.2.3 Balancing Interests: Challenges in Achieving a Satisfactory Equilibrium Between the Interests of China Railway and Local Governments

Since the launch of the China-Europe freight trains in 2011, many cities in China have become starting points for these trains, such as Chengdu, Chongqing, Wuhan, Zhengzhou, Hefei, Changsha, Yiwu, Suzhou, Changchun, Harbin, and others. As originating stations for these trains, all the cargo is organized by the starting city, and the entire train's cargo is dispatched directly from the starting city without the necessity of consolidation or transshipment at a central hub or center. As a result, the social, economic, and political benefits of running the train are directly attributed to the local government of the starting city, rather than to China Railway. This arrangement has the potential to lead to disputes over interests between local governments and China Railway.

With the increase in domestic cities serving as starting points for China-Europe freight trains, there has been a significant overlap in the operation routes, leading to problems of redundant construction. This situation has prompted various regions to aggressively compete for cargo sources, including engaging in price competition. Such competition has put many train routes in a state of loss, with the primary beneficiaries being European countries. To maintain the normal operation of these trains, local governments often provide subsidies based on different criteria, effectively turning the competition over freight charges into a competition over government subsidies.

China Railway has established China-Europe freight train cargo consolidation facilities at various hub stations along the national border to effectively handle the issue of redundant train route construction and the associated shortage of cargo sources for some trains. Examples include the Western route's Urumqi Consolidation Center, the Central route's Fengtai Consolidation Center, and the Eastern route's Harbin Consolidation Center. Domestic China-Europe freight train cargo can be transported to the consolidation center via express trains, and after reaching full capacity, they are then organized into China-Europe freight trains for departure. In this transportation organization method, the container cargo sources that participate in consolidation at the consolidation center are still organized by the cargo originating city. It appears that the operational performance is attributed to the local government. However, this transportation organization scheme was proposed by China Railway, and, indeed, the results have shown that this approach is economically sound. Consequently, it has created a new challenge of balancing interests between China Railway and local governments.

2.4.3 *Key Strategies for the Standardization and Enhancement Period*

2.4.3.1 Optimizing Transportation Organization

To enhance the organization of China-Europe freight trains, the strategy includes stabilizing existing direct train services and expanding intermodal (transshipment) train services. The goal is to achieve an 80% share of container rail international transport in the total volume by 2020. This effort will be supported by strengthening dispatching, command, and supervision, improving process organization, implementing end-to-end monitoring, enhancing emergency response capabilities, and increasing on-time performance of the trains. In response to market demands, additional train services are introduced. Considering the actual transportation capacity, plans for operating and optimizing China-Europe freight train services have already been formulated. Strengthening collaboration with foreign railways, establishing a mechanism for sharing operational information among the freight trains, jointly developing a comprehensive route plan for the entire journey, reducing overall transit time, and enhancing punctuality and travel speed are initiatives already undertaken to attain an average daily travel distance of approximately 1300 kilometers, thereby improving the level of transportation.

2.4.3.2 Advancing Streamlining Clearance Processes

2.4.3.2.1 Enhancing International Cooperation with Customs Authorities in Countries Along the Route

By establishing an international cooperation mechanism with customs authorities in countries along the China-Europe freight train route, promoting information exchange, mutual recognition of supervision, and law enforcement assistance, expanding mutual recognition of customs supervision outcomes, and signing customs cooperation agreements, we are advancing customs cooperation. We are also implementing mutual recognition of "Authorized Economic Operators" (AEO) between China and Europe to enhance customs clearance efficiency. We support the inclusion of the railway transportation mode in the China-Europe Smart and Secure Trade Lanes pilot program. We are also promoting nationwide customs clearance integration, allowing enterprises to choose any customs office for declaration and tax payment. The strengthening of the construction of multimodal transport supervision centers at crucial logistics nodes' aims to achieve one-time declaration and one-time inspection at the destination, and allows direct release without altering the sealing status at the transshipment point. Customs, quarantine, and other port inspection agencies enhance cooperation, striving to keep the train's stay time at the port within six hours. The acceleration of logistics monitoring informatization aims to enhance the information, intelligence, and standardization levels of multimodal transport control while establishing an efficient, fast, convenient, and secure multimodal transport supervision model.

2.4.3.2.2 Advancing Inspection and Quarantine Integration

We have strengthened international cooperation in inspection and quarantine with countries along the route, successfully promoting regional epidemic management and mutual recognition. A green channel for specific plant and animal disease-free zones has been established along the China-Europe freight train route. Furthermore, "notification, inspection, and release" procedures have been implemented among inspection and quarantine institutions along the train route. This has allowed us to achieve "direct release on export and direct transit on import" along the route and implement policies exempting eligible China-Europe freight train container cargo from opening inspections and port certificate exchanges. We are establishing an international multimodal transportation logistics corridor for railway and maritime (water and land routes) transport and developing a China-Europe freight train inspection and quarantine information system. This system enables comprehensive sharing of entry and exit data for freight trains, streamlines paper documentation, promotes paperless inspection and quarantine processes, and implements a regulatory model of "quarantine at the entry port, continuous monitoring within the country, and direct release at the exit port."

2.4.3.2.3 Further Expanding Port Openness

We support eligible regions in establishing designated national ports for the import of meat, grains, fruits, and complete vehicles. We prioritize the approval and arrangement of inspections for those meeting national requirements. Prior to obtaining the official qualification as a designated port, for those entities that meet the corresponding inspection and quarantine regulatory conditions, they are allowed to serve as import ports for the relevant categories on a trial basis. We strengthen port exchange and cooperation with countries (regions) along the route, and revise and improve bilateral land border port management agreements as needed. We also enhance the construction of border port facilities to improve the customs clearance capacity for inbound and outbound traffic. We strategically plan the placement of inland railway ports to meet the development needs of the China-Europe freight trains. We advance the construction of an "International Trade Single Window" and a shared port management platform, simplify document formats, standardize data, optimize port supervision, law enforcement, and clearance processes, and enhance the intelligence level of ports.

2.4.3.3 Balancing Interests: Maximizing Benefits for Both China Railway and Local Governments

The interests between China Railway and local governments primarily manifest in the economic and social benefits brought about by the operation of China-Europe freight trains. In terms of economic benefits, as it stands, most freight trains are operating at a loss and require subsidies from government and other sectors to continue their operations. This situation is likely to persist for some time. In the transportation scheme using consolidation center stations, the operation of the freight train can be broadly divided into two stages: the transportation stage from the originating city to the consolidation center station and the transportation stage from the consolidation center station to the final destination city of the overseas train. The first transportation stage is generally carried out using express freight trains, and the responsibility for subsidizing the transportation cost deficit during this stage lies with the local government of the originating city. During the second stage, it is the measures implemented by China Railway that generate economic effects, and in this phase, the responsibility for subsidizing the transportation cost deficit can be assumed by the national government. However, as future volumes increase and transportation organization measures improve, it is likely to bring about economies of scale, meaning a significant reduction in average transportation costs, which can ultimately lead to a certain level of profitability. These profits can still be allocated between China Railway and local governments as described above. In terms of social benefits, with the establishment of the China-Europe Freight Train brand, it is poised to become a renowned international logistics brand for container transportation. This will earn China's container train transportation products a prestigious reputation, both domestically and internationally. The brand's value should be shared between China Railway and local governments.

2.4.4 Analysis of the China Railway's Plan for the Standardization and Enhancement Period

Since the inception of the CR Express, similar or identical issues have emerged across three distinct phases, and China Railway has developed corresponding strategies to address the prominent issues in each phase. For instance, in terms of transportation organization, during the exploratory phase, the main challenges were related to the efficiency of operations at the port stations. The corresponding strategy aimed to strengthen station operations and enhance efficiency. In the standardization and improvement phase, the challenges primarily revolved around the entire operational scope of the trains. The corresponding strategy involved developing comprehensive route schedules, intensifying continuous monitoring throughout the entire journey, and improving the punctuality of the trains. Another example is the issues related to customs clearance for cargo. During the exploratory phase, when the number of trains was relatively small, the problem of low customs clearance efficiency was not as prominent. However, during the standardization and improvement phase, with a larger number of trains, efficiency became a critical issue. The corresponding strategy during this period was to enhance cooperation among customs authorities in all countries along the route, adopt advanced customs clearance procedures, and reduce the overall customs clearance time for the trains. Additionally, in terms of organizing the source of goods, both the flourishing development phase and the standardization and improvement phase presented notable challenges. The main issue was the intense competition among domestic originating cities to secure goods sources, coupled with a shortage of overseas return cargo sources. China Railway's strategy to address this challenge was to enhance the construction of domestic and international cargo distribution and transshipment centers. Furthermore, there are specific challenges and corresponding strategies unique to certain phases. One such example is during the standardization and improvement phase when China Railway advocated for the construction of train assembly centers. This initiative brought about a new challenge: balancing the interests between China Railway and local governments. To address this, China Railway developed a series of targeted strategies with the aim of achieving a balanced approach to their respective interests.

2.4.5 *China Railway's Practices Regarding the Standardization and Improvement Period in the Establishment of Assembly Centers*

2.4.5.1 *Reasons for Establishing Urumqi Assembly Center*

Following the introduction of the BRI, there was a surge in enthusiasm among various provinces and cities across the country to operate westbound international freight trains. The opening of westbound international freight train routes saw significant growth. Cities such as Chongqing, Chengdu, Wuhan, Zhengzhou, Xi'an, Changsha, Yiwu, Guangzhou, Suzhou, and others have enthusiastically launched westbound freight train services. Moreover, numerous regions in Xinjiang have also commenced westbound train services destined for Central Asia, Europe, and Russia.

Issues have quickly followed this rapid development. On the one hand, there's intense competition among similar routes. Currently, the Central Route has two lines: Wuhan-Xinjiang-Europe and Zhengzhou-Xinjiang-Europe, while the Western Route has three: Chengdu-Europe, Chongqing-Xinjiang-Europe, and Xin'an-Xinjiang-Europe. With the addition of routes in Xinjiang, this has created fierce regional competition. Despite rapid growth, the Chongqing-Xinjiang-Europe, Chengdu-Europe, and Wuhan-Xinjiang-Europe routes are becoming increasingly homogenized, leading to the wastage of transport capacity along these routes. On the other hand, a common challenge is the shortage of goods. The intensity of competition among regions for goods has exceeded expectations. Some train services are expanding their marketing reach, not only within their provinces or cities but also into the Yangtze River Delta and Pearl River Delta regions, where export goods are concentrated. This widespread behavior of collecting goods began with the opening of the direct Chongqing-to-Europe train service. Chongqing, located in the west, experienced rapid development in the laptop industry but had a limited variety of products, resulting in a shortage of goods. To fill the required transport capacity for a single train service, the government had to subsidize the transportation by transferring goods from regions like the Yangtze River Delta, Pearl River Delta, and even other parts of the country at prices below cost. The fundamental reason for the prevalence of government subsidies is the shortage of goods. Only by achieving the consolidation of goods and ensuring a sufficient supply can we reduce the costs for trading enterprises. This is the fundamental prerequisite for realizing the market-oriented operation of train services.

2.4.5.2 Conditions of Establishing Urumqi Consolidation Center[1]

Timing may not be as crucial as location, and location may not be as critical as collaboration. Xinjiang possesses a threefold advantage of favorable timing, strategic location, and harmonious cooperation, making it a prerequisite for the successful market-oriented operation of westbound trains from Xinjiang.

In terms of timing, with the introduction of the BRI, westward opening has become a new trend in China's economic development, and Xinjiang serves as a natural gateway and a crucial region for this westward opening.

Speaking of geographical advantages, Xinjiang offers the shortest distance for routes heading west. Currently, there are three main routes for CR Express operations in the country, generally categorized into western, central, and eastern corridors. These routes depart from Alashankou (Horgos), Erenhot, and Manzhouli, respectively. When compared to Manzhouli and Erenhot, Xinjiang is uniquely positioned at the intersection of the China-Mongolia-Russia corridor, the China-West Asia corridor, and the China-Pakistan Economic Corridor. Xinjiang has an irreplaceable advantage in the construction of the China-Europe (China-Asia) Railway Express consolidation center. Nationwide, apart from the Northeast region, Xinjiang offers the shortest transportation distance for shipments to Europe. For example, shipping from Chongqing to Europe through Xinjiang is nearly 2000 kilometers shorter than through Erenhot.

[1] The following conditions are derived from "Market-Driven Sustainable Operation of Freight Trains: A Series of Reports on the Urumqi Hub of China-Europe (China-Central Asia) Freight Trains – Part Five."

Xinjiang serves as the "last stop" for westward routes, a distinct advantage that cannot be replicated by any other location.

On April 15, 2016, the China-Europe Freight Train Alliance Conference, hosted by the Xinjiang Uygur Autonomous Region Economic and Information Commission, was held in Urumqi. The conference announced the establishment of the BRI China-Europe Freight Train Alliance, marking the creation of a collaborative platform and coordination mechanism for China's westbound China-Europe international freight train services. Members of the alliance from 11 provinces and cities, including Chongqing, Zhengzhou, Chengdu, Dalian, Xiamen, and Xinjiang, collaborated to establish a public information platform for China-Europe freight train services. Leveraging the advantages of the "Internet +," they jointly collected goods both online and offline and coordinated the operation of China-Europe freight train services.

2.4.5.3 Transportation Organization of the Urumqi Consolidation Center

Cities in the five northwestern provinces and potential exporting cities for westbound cargo can all use the westbound freight trains. These trains depart from various cities, consolidate in Urumqi, and then travel to destinations in Central Asia, Russia, and Europe. Similarly, freight trains coming from Central Asia, Russia, and Europe can be consolidated or transferred in Urumqi before being sent to various destinations across the country.

In terms of transportation organization, the consolidation center can offer three collaboration modes: For fully loaded trains, Xinjiang focuses on providing efficient services to ensure the expedited operation. If there is unused capacity on the train, Xinjiang will organize the supply of additional cargo, collectively contributing to the development of the CR Express brand. Currently, trains from Xinjiang to Central Asia and Russia operate regularly. Enterprises from other regions can organize their cargo to be transported using these trains. For goods that do not meet the conditions for full-train operation, they can first be consolidated in Urumqi. Under the premise of respecting the originating location, after being consolidated into a train, they can then proceed with the journey. This approach helps reduce costs and save time.

2.4.5.4 Achievements of the Urumqi Consolidation Center

Since the inaugural westbound international freight train departed from Xinjiang in March 2014, by the end of November 2016, a total of 328 such trains had been launched. As China's BRI gained momentum, Xinjiang, at the heart of the Silk Road Economic Belt, saw its geographic advantage become increasingly prominent. Although Xinjiang's organization of westbound train services started relatively late, rapid development ensued after May 2016 when the Urumqi consolidation center commenced operations. From the launch of the first train to the 100th train, it took six months, and from the 100th train to the 200th train, it took only three months. On March 15, 2017, at around 17:00, Train X9081, a freight train from the Central Europe (Central Asia) Express, departed from the Urumqi consolidation center for Almaty, Kazakhstan. This marked the 200th train to depart from the Urumqi consolidation center since its opening.

The large-scale and regular operation of freight trains reflects the increasingly smooth coordination between the consolidation centers and various nodes across the country. This improved operational efficiency signifies the ability to provide businesses with comprehensive, multilevel, secure, and efficient logistics services. It can reduce logistics costs, expand profit margins, and enhance competitiveness for enterprises. The concentration of various economic factors also drives rapid economic development in the surrounding regions.

Currently, the coverage mainly consists of Central Asian countries with European countries as supplementary destinations. The primary destinations include Kazakhstan, Tajikistan, Turkmenistan, Kyrgyzstan, and Uzbekistan, comprising five main countries. Additional destinations for train services encompass Eurasian countries such as Georgia, Turkey, Russia, Iran, and Poland. This network effectively achieves full coverage of various railway stations across Central Asia, extending its influence throughout the entire region.

2.5 Summary

2.5.1 Key Tasks

This chapter primarily focuses on China Railway and provides an overview of three of its subsidiary companies. Special attention is given to CRCT, considering its significant role in the operation of the CR Express. The chapter offers a comprehensive analysis of China Railway's involvement since its inception in 2011. The discussion is structured around three distinct phases in the development of the CR Express, which are marked by important milestones, including the launch of the BRI in 2013 and its release of the development plan in 2016. These phases are identified as the exploration period (2011–2013), the vigorous development period (2013–2016), and the standardization and enhancement period (2016 and beyond). Throughout the chapter, the status of CR Express development within each of these phases is outlined, highlighting notable achievements, addressing key challenges faced during each phase, and presenting strategic responses to overcome these challenges.

2.5.2 *Views*

The different phases of the China-Europe Railway Express have achieved significant results, but they also face various pressing issues. During the exploration period, the primary challenges were related to the organization of train transportation and port clearance efficiency. The solution proposed by the China Railway was to strengthen the organization of operations at border stations and control operational processes. In the vigorous development period, the primary problem was the organization of cargo sources, especially for return trips. The solution involved enhancing domestic and foreign trade and establishing distribution points in countries along the route. During the standardization and improvement period, the primary issue was the coordination of interests between local governments and the China Railway. The proposed solution was to formulate comprehensive improvement plans.

2.5.3 *Suggestions*

Firstly, the future emphasis for the CR Express lies in enhancing control and organization throughout its journey. In-transit operations primarily encompass container handling and customs inspection and quarantine. Currently, there is substantial potential for optimization in these aspects, with room to further enhance the timeliness of railway transport. Secondly, in terms of organizing freight sources, the current situation is that there are far more outbound goods than inbound goods, and there is a severe shortage of return cargo sources, leading to low operational efficiency of the railway express. This unfavorable situation can be improved by government initiatives to promote international trade. Thirdly, with the establishment of the CR Express consolidation centers, the issue of balancing interests between the China Railway and local governments has become a new challenge. The losses, profits, and brand value brought about by the operation of the CR Express should be shared or jointly borne by the China Railway and local governments. Their mutual interests need further clarification based on the future operational status of the railway express. In summary, the future of the CR Express requires collaborative efforts between local governments and the China Railway.

CHAPTER 3

China-Europe Railway Express (Chongqing): The Transition from "Yuxin'ou" to "Yaxin'ou"

Jianmei Xiao and Haoyu Wang

3.1 Introduction

Being one of the pivotal strategies in Chongqing's transformation into an inland open highland, the Chongqing-Xinjiang-Europe railway ("Yuxin'ou") International Railway Corridor officially initiated its operations in March 2011. During this inaugural journey, the "Yuxin'ou" railway, loaded with electronic products manufactured in Chongqing, embarked from Chongqing West Railway Station. The domestic leg of this route passed through Dazhou, Ankang, Xi'an, Lanzhou, Urumqi, and Alashankou. The international section extended through Kazakhstan, Russia, Belarus, and Poland, ultimately reaching its destination in Duisburg, Germany. This extensive journey covered a total distance of 11,179 kilometers and took 16 days to complete. This marked the

J. Xiao (✉) • H. Wang
China High-Speed Rail Development Strategy Research Center of Southwest Jiaotong University, Chengdu, China
e-mail: bai.gao@duke.edu

B. Gao, Z. Zhen (eds.), *The China-Europe Railway Express*, China and Globalization 2.0,
https://doi.org/10.1007/978-981-19-2882-6_3

full-scale operation of the "Yuxin'ou" International Railway Corridor. In February 2013, the first return journey train from Duisburg set out, arriving in Chongqing on March 18. This was the first return cargo train for the corridor, two years after its launch. Subsequently, with the relentless efforts of the Chongqing municipal government in various aspects, by October 2013, the "Yuxin'ou" had achieved regular operation. This meant it adhered to a mechanism of "one train per week, and during peak periods, up to three trains per week," effectively addressing the transportation of electronic products during the winter months. In the first half of 2016, the "Yuxin'ou" route operated a total of 164 services, including 112 outbound journeys and 52 return journeys. It transported approximately 140,000 standard containers, marking a 74% year-on-year increase in cargo volume. With the continuous expansion of the "Yuxin'ou" route's operations and its growing influence and reach, the Chongqing municipal government introduced the "Yuxin'ou+" initiative in 2016. This strategic development aims to create a new multimodal logistics corridor that integrates railways, highways, and air transport, known as the Asia-Xinjiang-Europe or "Yaxin'ou" strategy. This strategic upgrade is more optimized than the previous "Yuxin'ou" route, offering broader coverage, reduced transportation costs, and enhanced support for Chongqing's external trade activities.

The fundamental reason for the transformation of "Yuxin'ou" to "Yaxin'ou" lies in a change in Chongqing municipal government's development strategy. Initially, to break through the bottleneck in industrial upgrading and attract major players in the laptop manufacturing industry to establish themselves in Chongqing, the "Yuxin'ou" started its official operations in 2011, thanks to the continuous efforts of the Chongqing government. The establishment of this logistics channel directly catalyzed a transformation in the city's industrial structure, laying the foundation for building a key inland open gateway. However, during the initial stage of "Yuxin'ou" operations, it faced challenges such as different operators, variations in railway transportation services, charges, and customs procedures among different countries, along with issues like high freight rates and a lack of return cargoes due to a shortage of goods. As a result, Chongqing began to seek the formation of a community of shared interests. In this process, Chongqing, with the establishment of the Yuxin'ou (Chongqing) Logistics Co., Ltd., a joint venture between China Railway Group Limited(CREC), Russian Railways, Kazakhstan Railways, Deutsche Bahn AG, and Chongqing Transportation Holdings Group Co Ltd, pioneered a new model for international cooperation in China-Europe railway transportation. This ensured the smooth operation of the "Yuxin'ou" freight train and marked a significant initiative for Chongqing's western opening-up efforts. However, since 2014, with the introduction of the Belt and Road Initiative (BRI) and the increasing competition among various China-Europe freight train routes, especially in the face of the rise of the "Rong'ou Express," Chongqing has felt significant pressure regarding the future development of the "Yuxin'ou" route. Both in terms of the source of goods and the radiation and influence of the train service, Chongqing has been striving to find new breakthroughs in its local development strategy. In response, leveraging the pioneering advantage of the "Yuxin'ou" route and its strategic importance in the BRI, Chongqing actively sought more policy support from the central government, striving to maintain its "leading position" in the competition among freight train routes. In early 2016, Chongqing proposed the "Yuxin'ou+" strategy, namely "Yaxin'ou," to enhance its external openness and establish itself as a logistics hub in the western region. Under this strategy, Chongqing aimed to shift its competitive focus from westward to eastward. It actively collaborated with countries such as Singapore and South Korea, seeking to expand from the western region to Asia. Chongqing strategically aimed to preserve its advantages in terms of cargo sources, the number of train services, and service frequency. The city focused on enhancing the influence and reach of the "Yuxin'ou+" route, infusing new energy into its local development strategy. In line with its objective to expand from the western region to Asia, Chongqing utilized the "Yuxin'ou" route to establish multimodal transportation links with partner countries, including railways, highways, and air routes. The city consistently reinforced the three-dimensional "interconnectedness," comprehensively advancing the construction of logistics channels for external openness.

3.2 From "Yuxin'ou" to "Yaxin'ou"

The "Yuxin'ou" International Railway Intermodal Transportation Corridor refers to the international railway route that utilizes the southern route of the Eurasian Land Bridge. It starts from Chongqing, passes through Xi'an, Lanzhou, Urumqi, proceeds westward via the Northern Xinjiang Railway, and arrives at the border checkpoint of Alashankou, entering Kazakhstan. From there, it continues through Russia, Belarus, Poland, and ultimately reaches Duisburg, Germany. This railway transport corridor is established through the coordination of railway and customs departments in six countries along the route and has a total length of

11,179 kilometers. In the first half of 2016, new border checkpoints at Manzhouli and Khorgos were added, further enhancing its reach to the Central and Eastern European regions.

In October 2010, the Chongqing municipal government and the Ministry of Railways conducted a trial operation of the domestic segment of the "Yuxin'ou" "Five-fixed Trains," including fixed points, fixed routes, fixed time series, fixed schedules, fixed pricing. This domestic segment, running from Chongqing to the border town of Alashankou in Xinjiang, had a length of 3812 kilometers and was designed to operate within a total time of 96 hours and 46 minutes, with a train speed of 40 kilometers per hour. While the train speed was not particularly fast, this trial run confirmed the continuity of the domestic segment, meaning that the train operated without stopping directly to Alashankou. Compared to the existing express services, this train's speed was twice as fast, marking a significant improvement in transportation efficiency.

On November 23, 2010, during a visit by then-Chinese Premier Wen Jiabao to Russia, China, Russia, and Kazakhstan jointly signed two customs facilitation agreements. These agreements stipulated that the three customs authorities would conduct only one customs inspection for goods originating from Chongqing, passing through Alashankou in Xinjiang, and transiting through Kazakhstan and Russia. This streamlined the customs inspection process, eliminating the need for repeated customs inspections, allowing goods to be transported to the Netherlands and Germany more efficiently. On December 7, 2010, the customs authorities of Chongqing and Urumqi signed agreements, including the "Agreement on Establishing an Export Customs Supervision Mechanism for the Yuxin'ou International Railway Corridor" and a "Memorandum of Cooperation on Regional Customs Clearance Reform," laying a solid foundation for the full operation of the "Yuxin'ou" railway corridor.

On January 28, 2011, the "Yuxin'ou" conducted its second test run, which involved transporting Chongqing Lifan Group's motorcycle parts and some electronic products from HP and Acer to two delivery locations in Russia. In contrast to the initial test, this second had two routes: the first route was from Chongqing to Moscow, passing through Urumqi, Alashankou, October City, Sol-Iletsk, and Moscow. This route covered a total distance of 8129 kilometers and had a travel time of 11 days. The second route was from Chongqing to Cherkessk, passing through Urumqi, Alashankou, October City, Astrakhan, and Cherkessk, spanning a total distance of 8340 kilometers and had a travel time of 11 days.

On March 19, 2011, the first "Yuxin'ou" train, loaded with electronic products manufactured in Chongqing, departed from Chongqing West Railway Station. It traveled through Dazhou, Ankang, Xi'an, Lanzhou, Urumqi, and Alashankou, then passed through Kazakhstan, Russia, Belarus, and Poland before reaching its destination, Duisburg, Germany. This marked the full operation of the Yuxin'ou International Railway Corridor. In February 2013, the first return trip (Chang'an Ford Special Train) departed from Duisburg and arrived in Chongqing on March 18. This was the first return freight train on the corridor, two years after its inauguration. By the end of 2013, a total of 96 trains had operated on the route, transporting over 8000 containers. The import and export trade volume reached $3 billion, and the actual travel time was approximately 16 days, saving nearly 30 days compared to maritime transport and costing only one-fifth of air transport.

By the end of 2013, the "Yuxin'ou" achieved regular operation, which included the following: addressing customs issues along the route, establishing a streamlined customs clearance model with a one-time customs declaration, one-time inspection, and clearance for the entire route; successfully resolving the issue of gauge conversion between wide gauge and standard gauge, further clarifying the responsibilities and authorities of railway departments in various countries along the route; developing electronic locks for full-course security monitoring of the "Yuxin'ou" train service's electronic products, enhancing safety while reducing transportation costs; establishing the Yuxin'ou (Chongqing) Logistics Co., Ltd., a joint venture between Deutsche Bahn AG, Russian Railways, Kazakhstan Railways, CREC, and the Chongqing municipal government with the established a communication mechanism and a rapid response mechanism among the railway departments of different countries for swift handling emergencies; implementing a unified transport document for the entire route, further saving transit time, and streamlining procedures; essentially resolving issues related to the winter trial transport of electronic products, among other improvements.

After several years of stable development, the Chongqing municipal government put forward the "Yuxin'ou+" strategy in 2016, also known as the "Yaxin'ou" strategy. The latter strategy relies on the former service to achieve intermodal transportation by rail, road, and air between Europe and Asian countries. For example, in the future, goods from Europe can be transported via the "Yuxin'ou" train to Chongqing and then transferred by air to Asian cities within a four-hour flight radius, such as

Bangkok, Kuala Lumpur, Hong Kong, Osaka, and others. This creates a "Four-Hour Air Economy Circle," centered around Chongqing, significantly reducing transportation costs. In this plan, Chongqing, as a central city connecting the east and west and the north and south in the western region, leverages its geographical advantage to become a key logistics hub linking the "Maritime Silk Road" and the "Silk Road Economic Belt."

3.3 The Upgrade and Transformation of Industries Driven by Logistics

Since the "11th Five-Year Plan" period, Chongqing has been working toward establishing itself as a significant national-level modern manufacturing base, continually adjusting its industrial structure to attract numerous renowned domestic and international companies to set up operations in the city. Simultaneously, the global economic crisis that began in 2008 had a significant impact on the laptop industry in China's eastern regions. Sharply rising costs, including land and labor, squeezed profit margins, prompting companies to seek more profitable growth areas. In this context, Chongqing sought to attract these companies by offering incentives such as policies, funding, labor, and land. From 2009 to 2010, with the efforts of the municipal government, the laptop industry saw rapid development. Enterprises like Inventec Corporation, Quanta Computer, Acer, and ASUS established a presence in Chongqing. During this period, its laptop industry chain began to take shape.

But as an inland city deep in the western region, Chongqing's underdeveloped transportation network and logistics industry made it challenging to meet the demand for laptop products with a requirement for fast inbound and outbound logistics. Relying solely on policy support made it difficult to attract major players in the industry to invest and develop in Chongqing. To address this local development bottleneck, in May 2010, Chongqing opened the "Five-fix" train service to Shenzhen,[1] reducing the total travel time from 116 hours to approximately 58 hours. Through this

[1] The "Five fixed Trains" refer to the rapid freight trains organized to operate on the main railway lines between major cities, ports, and border crossings. The term "Five-fixed" denotes fixed loading points, fixed routes, fixed train numbers, fixed departure and arrival times, and fixed prices. Baidu Baike: https://baike.baidu.com/item/%E8%B4%A7%E8%BF%90%E2%80%9C%E4%BA%94%E5%AE%9A%E2%80%9D%E7%8F%AD%E5%88%97/22503492

sea-rail intermodal route, Chongqing's laptop products could be exported to Europe in around 28 days, saving about 20 days compared to the traditional river-sea intermodal route (through the Yangtze River to Shanghai and then to Europe). During this period, approximately 60% to 70% of Chongqing's laptop products were transported to Europe through sea-rail intermodal means, while the remaining portion still utilized air transport.

However, for laptop products, neither sea-rail intermodal transport nor air transport is the optimal logistics solution. The products have a certain degree of time sensitivity. Shipping from Chongqing to Europe via sea-rail intermodal transport takes around 28 days, and any delay in delivery often results in a decrease in product prices. Furthermore, the low frequency and high cost of flights from Chongqing to Europe do not facilitate the quick and cost-effective transportation of products to European markets. Amid the rapid expansion in the production of diverse laptop products, the Chongqing municipal government realized: relying solely on fiscal subsidies to cover the logistics expenses of these enterprises was not a sustainable approach. This held true for both the city's industrial transformation and the growth of individual enterprise. It became apparent that establishing a more convenient and cost-effective logistics channel was imperative to ensure the industry's sustainable development.

Against this backdrop, based on a Eurasian Land Bridge proposal researched by HP, the then mayor of Chongqing, Huang Qifan, personally led a delegation to Beijing in August 2010. The delegation included prominent figures like HP's senior vice president, Tony Prophet, and other entrepreneurs. They made a request to the General Administration of Customs and the Ministry of Railways (now China State Railway Group Co., Ltd.) to initiate the Chongqing to Europe railway mainline, known as the "Five-fix Trains." The relevant leadership of the General Administration of Customs and the Ministry of Railways expressed strong support for its request.

In August 2010, driven by HP, a Eurasian Rail Conference was held in Berlin, Germany, spearheaded by the DB. This pivotal conference facilitated Chongqing's establishment of connections with Schenker AG, a subsidiary of DB, and TEL (a joint venture between DB and Russian Railways), among other prominent organizations. Following this, Chongqing began contacting railway companies and government entities in Russia, Kazakhstan, and other countries along the railway route, establishing a multilateral negotiation mechanism called the "Five Countries,

Six-Party Joint Meeting."[2] Since then , the opening of the "Yuxin'ou" International Logistics Corridor entered the trial phase.

On the foundation of several successful trial runs, on March 19, 2011, the "Yuxin'ou" officially commenced. Departing from Chongqing West Railway Station, this train, loaded with Chongqing-manufactured laptops, embarked on a journey to Duisburg, Germany. It exited China at the Alashankou Station in Xinjiang and traveled through Kazakhstan, Russia, Belarus, and Poland before reaching its destination in Germany. Covering a total distance of 11,179 kilometers and passing through six countries, the journey took 16 days to complete. This marked the full-scale operation of the "Yuxin'ou" International Railway Corridor. In 2011, a total of 17 train services were operated, transporting 700 40-foot containers, 970,000 Chongqing-manufactured laptops, and 200,000 Chongqing-manufactured monitors. The freight rate for each container was $1 per kilometer.[3]

Subsequently, from 2011 to 2014, public train services were launched on the "Yuxin'ou" route. This expansion extended its influence from Chongqing to other provinces, cities, and regions. Goods from outside of Chongqing could also be transported to Europe via the route, greatly diversifying the types of goods being transported. These goods ranged from traditional IT products to clothing and daily necessities, turning this route into a true international freight corridor. In 2014, Chongqing achieved significant breakthroughs in areas such as the "1+N" distribution system,[4] port qualifications, import of complete vehicles, international postal services, and train speed and cost reduction, further enhancing the development of the corridor.

Undoubtedly, the successful operation of "Yuxin'ou" has provided an additional choice for the import and export of goods in the inland regions, apart from maritime and air transport. It not only establishes a major international railway corridor from China's inland to Europe but significantly reduces the time and cost associated with the import and export of goods. Furthermore, it has facilitated the shift of processing trade to Chongqing and encouraged multinational companies to establish

[2] "The Origin of 'Yuxin'ou'," cqnews.net, https://cq.cqnews.net/cqztlm/node_317750.htm

[3] cqnews.net, https://cq.cqnews.net/cqztlm/node_317750.htm

[4] The "1+N" Distribution System refers to the main line from Chongqing to Duisburg, Germany ("1"), and customers can choose along the line countries as consolidation and distribution points ("N") based on their needs.

outward-oriented industrial bases in the city. This, in turn, led to the Agreement on International Railroad Through Transport of Goods, lifting the "ban on carrying postal parcels by international trains," making Chongqing a vital gateway for inland regions to engage in external trade. It aligns perfectly with the country's grand strategic vision.

3.4 The Construction of the "Yuxin'ou" Community of Shared Interests

During the operation of the "Yuxin'ou" in 2011, several issues became apparent. Firstly, the train service had various operators. Among the 17 train services, 11 were operated by the DB, and the rest were operated by China Railway International Multimodal Transportation Co., Ltd., and other companies. This fragmented approach to operations did not ensure the Yuxin'ou's smooth operation. Secondly, this logistics corridor spanned six countries, and each had significant differences in railway transportation services, fees, customs procedures, and policies. The lack of unified operational standards and information platforms resulted in very low transport efficiency for the train service. Finally, the lack of freight sources has kept transportation rates unreasonably high. In the return journey, over 95% of the cargo consists of IT products manufactured in Chongqing, essentially forming dedicated trains for companies like HP and Acer. The operation schedule is entirely dependent on the production volume of these companies, and there are virtually no return freight sources. Consequently, the advantages of this route are not very prominent.

To address these challenges, Chongqing has initiated efforts to establish a community of shared interests. To promote its regular operation, improve its transportation efficiency and the service level on various sections of the route, further lower transportation costs, and enhance the ability to gather goods, Chongqing convened the "Five Countries, Six-Party Joint Meeting" again in September 2011. During this meeting, the participating parties signed a "Memorandum of Cooperation to Promote the Regular Operation of the 'Chongqing-Xinjiang-Europe' International Railway" and reached a consensus on various issues. The main points included establishing the "Yuxin'ou" platform company to create a mechanism for sharing benefits, increasing train speed and conversion efficiency to achieve a goal of reaching the destination in 12 days, further reducing transportation costs, and striving for return goods. By April 12, 2012, the

"Yuxin'ou (Chongqing) Logistics Co., Ltd.," led by Chongqing Transport Holding (Group) Co., Ltd., was formally established.

The "Yuxin'ou (Chongqing) Logistics Co., Ltd.," established through collaboration between CREC, Russian Railways, Kazakhstan Railways, Deutsche Bahn AG, and Chongqing Transportation Holdings Group, introduced a groundbreaking international railway transportation model between China and Europe. It primarily focuses on two-way "station-to-station" railway freight transport connecting Chongqing with various destinations along the European route. Thanks to the initiatives of the Chongqing municipal government since 2007, multinational and large domestic logistics companies have established their presence in the city. Local logistics firms have also grown significantly, primarily focusing on maritime and air transportation. In contrast, large domestic logistics companies give priority to railway and air transportation. Local logistics companies mainly rely on road, railway, and river transportation. However, based on their operational experiences, none of these entities have been able to effectively tackle the challenges faced by the "Yuxin'ou" International Railway Corridor. In contrast, the joint venture "Yuxin'ou (Chongqing) Logistics Co., Ltd.," established by four countries and five parties, shows great potential in addressing these challenges and furthering the development of the train service.

The "Yuxin'ou" (Chongqing) Logistics Co., Ltd. has five equity investors with a total investment of $6 million and registered capital of $3 million. The first shareholder is Chongqing Transport Holding (Group) Co., Ltd., which holds a 41.1% stake and has subscribed capital of $1.233 million, a large state-owned enterprise group approved by the Chongqing municipal government. Designated as a key supported enterprise for logistics development by both the Chongqing Development and Reform Commission and the Chongqing Economic and Information Commission, it stands as a pivotal player in the realm of modern logistics companies in Chongqing.

The second shareholder is DB Schenker International Freight Forwarding (China) Co., Ltd., a subsidiary of the Deutsche Bahn. They hold a 16.3% stake and have subscribed capital of $489,000. DB is the largest railway transport enterprise in Germany and the leading railway enterprise in Europe. Offering comprehensive railway passenger and freight transport services within Germany and connecting to various European countries, DB has established itself as a world-class integrated logistics service provider. In the context of the "Yuxin'ou" train service, DB Schenker International Freight Forwarding (China) Co., Ltd. plays a pivotal role in ensuring its smooth operation within the European Union segment. Notably, out of the 17 trips conducted in 2011, 11 were exclusively operated by this company, specifically dedicated to transporting HP computers.

The third shareholder is Russian Railways Logistics, a subsidiary of Russian Railways (RZD). They hold a 16.3% stake and have subscribed capital of $489,000. Established on September 18, 2003, Russian Railways stands as a state-owned company with a substantial registered capital exceeding $50 billion. It reigns as the preeminent entity in the Russian transportation sector and holds a distinguished position as one of the globe's largest railway companies. Within the "Yuxin'ou" train service framework, Russian Railways Logistics assumes a pivotal role, dedicated to guaranteeing seamless railway transport services across the Russian, Belarusian, and Ukrainian segments.

The fourth shareholder is Kazakhstan Transportation Services Company, a subsidiary of Kazakhstan Railways (Kazakhstan Temir Zholy). They hold a 16.3% stake and have subscribed capital of $489,000. Kazakhstan Railways holds operational and managerial authority over the primary railway network in Kazakhstan, overseeing new railway initiatives, setting passenger and freight rates, and managing associated tasks. Kazakhstan Transportation Services Company's primary responsibility is to ensure smooth operation of the "Chongqing-Xinjiang-Europe" (Yuxin'ou) train service within Kazakhstan.

The fifth shareholder is CRIMT, a wholly owned subsidiary of CRCTC. They hold a 10% stake and have subscribed capital of $300,000. CRIMT is one of the earliest companies in China engaged in international freight forwarding services. Its core business includes domestic logistics, international (sea-rail) intermodal transportation, and container interchange services.[5] Its primary role is to ensure "Yuxin'ou" railway transport services for the domestic segment.

The highest governing body of "Yuxin'ou" (Chongqing) Logistics Co., Ltd. is the board of directors, with representatives appointed by the

[5] The term "interchange and management of containers" refers to the mutual exchange and use of containers belonging to Russian Railways and Kazakhstan Railways within the territory of China.

five shareholders responsible for the company's management and operations. Additionally, a supervisory board is established to oversee the board of directors. Since July 2012, Thomas Lindy Sorensen, the legal representative of Global International Freight Forwarding (China) Co., Ltd., has served as the Chairman of the Board. In terms of organizational management, the company follows a manager accountability system, with the manager reporting to the board of directors.

In the year of its establishment in 2012, "Yuxin'ou" (Chongqing) Logistics Co., Ltd. operated a total of 41 trips of the "Yuxin'ou" (Chongqing) freight train. The total volume of transported goods amounted to 4501 standard containers, with a total value exceeding $1 billion. The transportation cost per container per kilometer decreased by $0.2 compared to the initial cost of $1 in 2011. Most transported goods remained Chongqing-manufactured products such as laptops, monitors, and printers, with IT products accounting for approximately 92% of the total cargo volume.

By 2013, the number of trips for the "Yuxin'ou" freight train had decreased slightly, with a total of 36 trips throughout the year, including 35 outbound and 1 return trip. The total volume of transported goods exceeded 3000 standard containers, contributing to an import and export trade value of approximately $1.1 billion. The cost of transportation per container per kilometer had decreased to $0.7. In that year, around 13.38 million laptops, with a total value of $531 million, were exported to Europe via the "Yuxin'ou" freight train, with IT products accounting for approximately 90% of the cargo volume. Despite a decrease in the total number of trips in 2013, the freight train welcomed its first return trip after over two years of operation. This trip carried automotive components imported by Chang'an Ford Motor Co., Ltd., consisting of 41 40-foot containers. The successful initiation of the return trip marked a pivotal moment in the evolution of "Yuxin'ou." The return cargo plays a critical role in cost reduction. Furthermore, this facilitates the transportation of a broader array of European products to Chongqing via the train, positioning the city as a burgeoning hub for European-to-Chinese trade. This, in turn, creates favorable conditions for Chongqing's new phase of industrial restructuring.

In July 2013, the "Yuxin'ou" International Railway Corridor officially launched the "China-Europe Safe and Smart Trade Route Pilot Program," or "Anzhimao"[6] project pilot. The implementation of the "Anzhimao" project between China and Europe marked the first time a trial was conducted for transportation methods other than sea freight. The inclusion of railway transport in the "Anzhimao" was of great significance for the comprehensive implementation of "mutual recognition of supervision, information sharing, and mutual law enforcement" for the "Yuxin'ou" international freight train, further enhancing its reach and influence. Additionally, the application of technologies such as electronic locks and temperature-controlled containers for winter ensured that all products suitable for railway transport could be shipped through the "Yuxin'ou" at any time. Starting from October 2013, the "Yuxin'ou" train achieved a regular operation schedule of one trip per week, and during peak times it operated three times a week. This established a solid foundation for the regular operation of the public Yuxin'ou train services.

In 2012 and 2013, more than 90% of the outbound cargo organized by the "Yuxin'ou" (Chongqing) Logistics Co., Ltd. consisted of locally manufactured IT products from Chongqing. The shortage of return cargo became a bottleneck in reducing the costs of operation. Up until 2014, return cargo was not a focal point for the development of the "Yuxin'ou" freight train. However, with the changing circumstances in 2014, relevant departments in Chongqing identified the operation of public return freight trains as a key development focus for the "Yuxin'ou." In the latter half of 2014, Chongqing Minsheng Logistics Co., Ltd., bolstered by the municipal government, assumed complete responsibility for initiating public return freight trains. Meanwhile, the task of coordinating outbound train cargo was entrusted to "Yuxin'ou" (Chongqing) Logistics Co., Ltd.

The "Yuxin'ou" Logistics Corridor represents a significant achievement for the city's westward development. The "Yuxin'ou" (Chongqing)

[6] The full name of "Anzhibao" is the "China-Europe Safe and Smart Trade Route Pilot Program." It is aimed at enhancing the security and convenience of trade supply chains between Asia and Europe. The program involves comprehensive monitoring of shipping containers and their contents throughout the entire journey, establishing a secure, convenient, and intelligent national trade transport chain. This initiative is a collaborative effort between Chinese and European customs authorities and a partnership between customs and businesses. https://baike.baidu.com/item/%E4%B8%AD%E6%AC%A7%E5%AE%89%E5%85%A8%E6%99%BA%E8%83%BD%E8%B4%B8%E6%98%93%E8%88%AA%E7%BA%BF%E8%AF%95%E7%82%B9%E8%AE%A1%E5%88%92/9690083

Logistics Co., Ltd. ensures the secure, stable, and efficient operation of this international trade corridor. Since its establishment in 2012, the company has undergone rapid development under the guidance of the Chongqing Municipal Logistics Office and other relevant departments. This entity has played a pivotal role in enhancing economic and trade interactions between China and the countries along the corridor, fostering mutual economic development, and injecting fresh vitality into global economic recovery efforts. Concurrently, this trade route will aid Chongqing in becoming a prominent western logistics hub, an inland opening-up stronghold, and a bridgehead for China-Europe trade.[7]

3.5 The Introduction of BRI and Competition Among China-Europe Railway Express

Since 2014, with the introduction of the BRI and the continuous development of regional train services like "Rong'ou Express," "Zhengxin'ou," and "Yuxin'ou," competition among China-Europe rail services has been on the rise. This competition has frequently manifested as "price wars," where different train services compete to offer the most competitive rates, resulting in a scenario of escalating competition. For Chongqing, the rise of several China-Europe rail services, particularly the emergence of "Rong'ou Express," has exerted significant pressure on the growth of the "Yuxin'ou." This pressure is evident in the availability of goods and the impact of competing train services in the region.

With the introduction of the BRI, competition between various China-Europe rail services has intensified since 2014. Since the first China-Europe train service (Chongqing to Duisburg) successfully operated on March 19, 2011, cities such as Chengdu, Zhengzhou, Wuhan, Yiwu, and others have also launched container train services to Europe. In 2014, the total number of train services launched throughout the year reached 308, representing a 285% increase compared to the previous year. A total of 26,070 containers were shipped, marking an astounding growth rate. Some data related to these train services are detailed in Table 3.1.

Under the backdrop of the national "Opening to the West" strategy, besides the continuous optimization and development of the "Yuxin'ou" route, other freight trains are also "unwilling to fall behind." The launch

[7]Official website of Chongqing Transport Holding (Group) Co., Ltd: https://cqtransit.com/

Table 3.1 Operation data of China-Europe Railway Express

Train service	*Number of departures*
CRE (Chongqing)	102
CRE (Zhengzhou)	77
CRE (Wuhan)	20
CRE (Wuhan)	1

Source: Zhong Qizhuang, "Analysis of Land Bridge Transportation Situation in 2014," *New Silk Road Horizon*, No.2, 2015

of these train services in different regions is typically initiated by local governments, and as the number of train services increases, the competition in the domestic market has become more intense. For example, the "Zhengzhou-Xinjiang-Europe" (Zhengxin'ou) train service has gained strong momentum. Zhengzhou benefits from its strategic location and well-established transportation infrastructure, which the local government has effectively utilized. Moreover, the implementation of national policies, such as the Central Plain Economic Zone plan, and the strategic importance of Zhengzhou Airport Comprehensive Bonded Zone have contributed to this growth. It is evident that Zhengzhou is strongly committed to consolidating its position as a pivotal transportation and logistics hub within the national network.

Certainly, for Chongqing, the pioneer of these rail services, its first significant competitor is Chengdu, located approximately 300 kilometers away. The commencement of the "Rong'ou Express" has indeed created competitive pressure for the "Yuxin'ou" corridor, particularly concerning the sourcing of goods. Chongqing initiated the "Yuxin'ou" primarily to address the logistics challenges faced by HP when it established its manufacturing operations in Chongqing. The Chongqing municipal government worked diligently to secure support from various parties and navigate complex negotiations to establish the "Yuxin'ou" International Railway Corridor. Indeed, the development of rail services continues to progress. Initially conceived as a supportive venture to attract investments, the "Yuxin'ou" route only operated specialized trains for HP laptops. The departure schedule was tailored based on the production demands of the enterprises. By April 2014, Chongqing expanded its operations to include public freight trains, making the service accessible to the broader market. Simultaneously, with the advancement of the BRI and the shift of national

IT industry to the central and western inland regions, major cities such as Chengdu, Zhengzhou, and Wuhan have launched direct routes to Europe. The "Rong'ou Express" from its inception adopted a development strategy to attract cargo from the public, placing enormous pressure on the source of goods for the service.

The development of various China-Europe rail services in different regions has had a profound impact on the logistics landscape in central and western China, leading to escalating competition among these services. For instance, during the first year of operation of the "Rong'ou Express," its capacity utilization was less than 40%. However, through a year of market cultivation, by 2014, the situation had significantly improved. The railway service achieved a capacity utilization rate of over 90%, and when the 45th service was launched, it experienced overcapacity issues.[8] This transformation underscores the increased demand and competitiveness of China-Europe rail transport services in various regions. In addition, Chengdu Railway Port has also initiated the declaration process for designated import ports for whole vehicles and meat. Furthermore, in the first return trip of the "Yuxin'ou," an import whole vehicle train departed from the Duisburg Port in Germany in March 2014.[9] Prior to this, imported whole vehicles generally came from coastal ports such as Tianjin and Shenzhen. Against this backdrop, the central and western regions have transformed from secluded hinterlands into the forefront of China's westward opening.

In May 2014, the Chengdu municipal government held a press conference, where it was revealed that the sources of goods for the "Rong'ou Express" extended to various regions, including Southwest, South, and East China. Particularly, goods from ten national special customs supervision areas such as Shanghai Pudong Airport, Suzhou Industrial Park, Wuxi High-tech Comprehensive Bonded Zone, and Jiangsu Wujiang Export Processing Zone accounted for 51% of its total cargo volume.[10] In the second half of 2014, both Chengdu and Łódź, Poland, initiated the establishment of transfer centers. Chengdu also planned to build a 275-*mu* (about 18 acres) railway bonded logistics center (Zone B). In this context,

[8] Xiuzhong Li, "Chengdu-Zhengzhou Subsidizes China-Europe Railway Express and Engages in Price Wars with Chongqing, Unwilling to Let It Enjoy Exclusive Benefits," sina.com: https://finance.sina.com.cn/360desktop/roll/20140820/022820060227.shtml

[9] China News Network, https://www.chinanews.com/cj/2014/08-19/6506794.shtml

[10] China.org.cn, https://finance.china.com.cn/roll/20140826/2637626.shtml

Chongqing actively applied for the comprehensive bonded area for railways in the same year. The intense competition between China-Europe freight trains, especially the development and growth of the "Rong'ou Express," exerted significant competitive pressure on the operation of the "Yuxin'ou" route.

Price wars remain the predominant means of competition among different China-Europe rail services. This rivalry encompasses tactics like departure frequency, transportation efficiency, stability in departures, operational convenience, and measures like the temporary opening of new ports and enhancements in customs supervision efficiency. However, the most direct and frequently the most fiercely contested approach is through pivotal price wars. For example, being the "trailblazer" in China-Europe rail services and faced with numerous "imitators," Chongqing has previously proposed to relevant national authorities that only the "Yuxin'ou" services should be operated, restricting the operation of other rail services to Europe. This proposal aims to prevent redundant construction and cut-throat competition. Implementing this concept would designate Chongqing as the sole originating point for rail routes from China to Europe. It implies that goods from across China would be centralized and dispatched from Chongqing, presenting a distinct advantage for the city. Nevertheless, other cities hosting competing rail routes might incur substantial losses and are unlikely to endorse a scenario where exclusive benefits favor Chongqing.

To secure more cargo, various rail services have offered competitive prices. Zhengzhou, in particular, has been proactive by providing free transportation to goods originating within a 1500-kilometer radius, encompassing over 80% of major cities, including Guangzhou. In the initial phase of the "Rong'ou Express" operation, Chengdu established a container price of $7000 to maintain competitiveness in the market. As the operational situation evolves, there will be a gradual increase in prices, with the intermediate costs covered by financial subsidies. Simultaneously, there have been instances where specific regions, overlooking actual market conditions, prematurely initiated international rail services for the sake of "showcase projects" and "political performance." In certain regions, certain departments or companies have also exaggerated the status, quantity, value, and efficiency of their China-Europe rail services for promotional and political purposes, occasionally manipulating data.

Nevertheless, amid the fierce and unregulated competition, it is crucial to acknowledge the positive impact of these train services on local economies. Despite some experts and media expressing concerns about the reliance on government subsidies for train service operations, labeling it as significant financial waste, a different perspective reveals the inherent logic behind the competition and rivalry among China-Europe train services. Local governments have been savvy in recognizing their substantial potential to spur regional economic development. Particularly within the BRI framework, the allure of "market dividends" and "policy dividends" serves as a driving force sustaining the intense competition among these train services. Various factors contributing to this competition include the following.

Firstly, it has enhanced the local investment environment. By 2014, the frequency of China-Europe train departures had increased approximately 15 times. This surge in departure frequency is attributed to the rapid growth in export and production volumes, stimulating local economic development and employment. Taking Chongqing as an example, since the launch of the "Yuxin'ou" route, Chongqing's foreign trade volume skyrocketed from $6 billion to $95.5 billion in 2014, achieving a remarkable fourfold increase in just six years. Chongqing's total import and export value propelled it to the top position among western provinces and cities, with the European market share surpassing the national average. Leveraging the "Yuxin'ou" route, Chongqing, ranking first in foreign trade among western provinces and cities, took the lead in reaching the pinnacle of western openness. The "Yuxin'ou" also propelled the development of logistics and commerce in Chongqing, laying the foundation for the creation of the largest logistics park in the western region. Simultaneously, it provided the conditions for Chongqing to establish the only multimodal transportation base (rail, water, air, etc.) in the western region. In March 2015, the then mayor Huang Qifan stated in an interview, "With this train service, we can directly reach Europe through Xinjiang. Therefore, we have become a vanguard. We were originally at a disadvantage, and now we have turned it into an advantage."

Secondly, there is the acquisition of "market dividends." The fierce competition ultimately aims to gain an advantage and secure "dividends" in regional competition. Logistics is an industry with highly apparent economies of scale, especially for international rail services. For localities and carriers, the larger the quantity of shipments per unit of time, the greater the negotiating leverage with railway companies along the route, leading to more significant price reduction space. Hence, the "gambling agreement" between the Chongqing municipal government and China

Railway is, in essence, akin to offering a wholesale price with quantity discounts by the railway corporation. This incentivizes Chongqing to organize more shipments, leading to a reduction in its unit costs. Therefore, the "gambling agreement" is beneficial for both parties, but it can pose a challenge for other regions operating China-Europe rail services, further reinforcing competitive mechanisms.

Thirdly, gaining "policy dividends" is evident. When a particular rail service performs notably well in the market, it attracts attention from the central government and relevant ministries. As a result, these regions become more qualified to apply for special preferential policies. These policies encompass inland railway ports, ports for importing complete vehicles, comprehensive bonded zones, container central stations, and other relevant measures. Upon receiving these policy incentives, the local appeal to the market undergoes a qualitative enhancement, creating a virtuous cycle. For instance, during President Xi Jinping's visit to Germany on March 29, 2014, he personally welcomed the "Yuxin'ou" rail service at Duisburg railway station. This garnered increased attention, importance, and support for the development of the route from national ministries, recognizing it as a crucial component of the "Silk Road Economic Belt" initiative. This significantly boosted Chongqing's confidence in accelerating the development of "Yuxin'ou." Similarly, since the inception of the "Zhengxin'ou" service in Henan Province, there has been a continuous increase in investment, coupled with substantial discounts through preferential policies. Particularly noteworthy is the province's heightened commitment to "Zhengxin'ou," especially after President Xi Jinping inspected the inaugural cargo site, elevating it to a key priority for the entire province.

It is evident that the competition among China-Europe rail services stems from intense local development rivalry. Taking the competition between Chengdu and Chongqing as an example, the Chengdu municipal government has been striving to establish itself as the key logistics hub in the western region, aiming to evolve into the largest comprehensive logistics center in the west. Chengdu media has reported, "By 2017, Chengdu will essentially become the logistics center for the western region."[11] However, Chengdu faces challenges, primarily in terms of railways and water transport. To address these shortcomings, Chengdu, with the support of Sichuan Province, is adopting indirect measures. Firstly, by utilizing the container terminal at Luzhou Port in the province, Chengdu is

[11] CNR News, https://sc.cnr.cn/sc/2014cd/20150423/t20150423_518381025.shtml

promoting the integration of rail and water transport and providing subsidies for highway transportation costs. Secondly, there are plans for future construction, expansion of railways, and high-speed rail networks. The "Rong'ou Express" is also expected to gradually increase its departure frequency to a high-frequency service of one train per day. A series of actions clearly indicate Chengdu's ambition to become the largest comprehensive logistics center in the western region, with its primary competitor being Chongqing. Additionally, Zhengzhou, another major player in the "China-Europe Railway Express" competition, plans to attract consulates from countries along the rail route to establish diplomatic and trade connections. "Zhengxin'ou" is a crucial selling point in this strategy.

By the end of 2014, the development momentum of China-Europe rail services such as "Yuxin'ou," "Zhengxin'ou," "Hanxin'ou," and "Rong'ou" had become quite robust(see Table 3.2). These services

Table 3.2 Operation status of selected China-Europe Railway Express in 2014

Name	*Main cargo types*	*Main source locations*	*Government subsidy (USD)*	*Frequency (2014)*
Yuxin'ou	IT products, automotive parts, home appliances, clothing, and footwear	Chongqing and coastal provinces (more than half from other regions)	3500–4000	3–4 trains per week
Hanxin'ou	Electronics, clothing, machinery, and medical products	Goods from Hubei and Wuhan (accounting for about 70%)	4000–5000	1–2 trains per week
Rong'ou	IT products, automotive parts, home appliances, clothing, and footwear	Mainly local sources, extended to Xiamen, Shenzhen, Kunming	3000–3500	1–2 trains per week
Zhengxin'ou	Electronics, high-end clothing, light industrial consumer goods, mechanical and electrical products, etc.	Zhengzhou and surrounding within 1500 km	3000–7000	2 trains per week
Yixin'ou	Small commodities, hardware tools, etc.	Local goods in Yiwu	No subsidy	Not regularized

Data Source: Wang Yangkun, "Current Status, Issues, and Suggestions for the Development of China-Europe Railway Express," *Comprehensive Transportation*, Special Issue, Volume 1, 2015.

showcased their unique strengths in the domestic market, forming a competitive landscape with multiple players coexisting.[12]

3.6 Leveraging the "Trailblazer" Advantage to Seek National Policy Support

As the "trailblazer" of China-Europe rail services, the initial development of "Yuxin'ou" made significant strides with the support of national policies. Beginning with specialized trains catering to laptops, it has transformed into a crucial hub for Chongqing's external trade. Moreover, it stands as a noteworthy example for other Chinese cities to follow in the realm of international rail services. As of 2014, "Yuxin'ou" encountered both new opportunities and challenges. The intensifying competition among cities launching the rail services, along with highly homogenized routes, created a competitive market landscape. Against this backdrop of intense competition among rail services, Chongqing actively seized the significant opportunity presented by the BRI. Leveraging the advantage of being the "trailblazer" in China-Europe rail services, Chongqing sought enhanced national policy support to maintain its leading position in the evolving landscape of rail service competition.

In the broader spectrum, the inception of the BRI has presented substantial developmental prospects for the western regions. Chongqing, strategically positioned as a pivotal linkage for both the BRI and the "Yangtze River Economic Belt" strategies, occupies an unparalleled status. As the sole municipality directly under the central government in China's inland territories and a designated national central city, Chongqing inherently spearheads the realm of openness within the BRI framework. In terms of its geographic location, Chongqing enjoys a unique position as a bridge between eastern and western regions and a connector of north and south. The government has clearly designated it as a key support for western development and openness, "a pivotal hub of the Yangtze River Economic Belt in the western region," and "an inland opening-up highland." In recent years, Chongqing has accelerated the establishment of collaborative mechanisms to align customs clearance procedures along various routes and develop international logistics networks. This effort has resulted in a distinctive open structure characterized by the three "Three

[12] Yangkun Wang, "Current Status, Issues, and Suggestions for the Development of China-Europe Railway Express," *Comprehensive Transportation*, Special Issue, Volume 1, 2015.

in One" concept. It indicates that Chongqing stands out with comprehensive transportation hubs encompassing water, land, and air routes, featuring three nationally top-tier ports, and equipped with three specialized customs supervision areas for imports and exports. This unique combination sets Chongqing apart and solidifies its position as one of the most open inland regions in China.

It's worth noting that Chongqing's growth plans are highly aligned with national strategies, enabling it to leverage its advantage as a pioneer in rail services to seek support for national policies. As outlined in Chongqing's 2014 government report, the city is actively aligning itself with the BRI and the comprehensive development initiatives of the "Yangtze River Economic Belt." Chongqing is proactively advancing the construction of an open cooperative mechanism characterized by streamlined customs clearance procedures and the establishment of international logistics gateways. This initiative has resulted in the establishment of three pivotal open ports: Cuntan Port, Jiangbei Airport, and Tuanjie Village Railway Station, complemented by various bonded open platforms.[13] Chongqing's implementation of BRI and the "Yangtze River Economic Belt" development can be summarized as "Three major goals, Five principles, and Six tasks." One of the "Three major goals" entails a substantial strengthening of support capabilities for the Western Development and Opening-up Strategy. This necessitates maximizing Chongqing's strategic pivotal role, expediting the development of an inland opening-up highland, and establishing comprehensive east-west external channels. The objective is to augment openness across various dimensions—scope, breadth, and depth—both internally and externally. This encompasses expediting enhancements to the customs supervision system, continuously innovating, and broadening the scope and methods of trade. As part of the "Six tasks," there is a clear directive to "facilitating international logistics channels." This entails vigorously expanding the functions of the "Yuxin'ou International Railway Corridor," ensuring the regular and stable operation of international trains on the route.[14] The "Yuxin'ou," as a trailblazer in the realm of China-Europe freight trains and a vital support for Chongqing's response to the BRI, seized a new development opportunity

[13]Referring to the Chongqing Municipal People's Government Work Report (Third Session of the Fourth Municipal People's Congress), dated January 18, 2015

[14]Chongqing's Implementation of the BRI Press Conference. https://www.cq.gov.cn/igixmj/gkzxft/202310/tInterview_2329.html

in 2014. With support from several policies related to the BRI, the "Yuxin'ou" made significant breakthroughs in terms of operation frequency, cargo organization, speed enhancement, and cost reduction.

In 2014, with strong support from central government relevant departments, "Yuxin'ou" received five new functional designations: the Tuanjie Village Railway Port was approved as a national first-class port; the automobile whole vehicle import port passed national acceptance; approval was granted for the establishment of a railway bonded logistics center (Type B), allowing it to conduct activities such as import bonded warehousing, export tax refund, transit trade, and international procurement distribution; it was designated as a fruit import port and a meat import port; a trial operation for international postal containers was launched.[15]

In September 2015, the then mayor of Chongqing, Huang Qifan, emphasized "the significance of adopting 'Yuxin'ou' as a platform to expand the inland open gateway" during the annual meeting of the Chongqing mayor's International Economic Advisory Council. He also highlighted that infrastructure connectivity was a top priority for the BRI and "Yangtze River Economic Belt" initiatives.[16] In alignment with this, since the BRI was introduced and with the backing of relevant departments, Chongqing has actively worked toward optimizing the Yuxin'ou International Railway Transportation Corridor. This optimization is pursued through five key strategies: coordinating and innovating customs clearance integration mechanisms[17] with countries along the route, establishing cross-border joint venture operating companies, launching "Five-fixed Trains," facilitating international coordination of freight rates with an overall reduction, and addressing technical issues related to transportation security, thereby achieving standardized operation under the "Yuxin'ou" framework.

Against this backdrop and driven by steadfast efforts at both the national and municipal levels, the number of departures for the "Yuxin'ou" freight train grew rapidly in 2015. Throughout the year, a total of 257 trains were

[15] China Today. http://www.chinatoday.com.cn/chinese/sz/dskzg/201506/t20150615_800034155.html

[16] cqnews.net. https://cq.cqnews.net/cqztlm/node_324969.htm

[17] "Customs-Inspection Integration" refers to the integration of the previously separate customs declaration and inspection processes into a single entry, where customs declaration and inspection are done simultaneously. This achieves the integration of "one-time declaration," "one-time inspection," and "one-time release," commonly known as the "three-one integration."

operated, including 156 outbound and 101 inbound trains, transporting 210,000 standard containers, marking a 97% year-on-year increase. Additionally, around April 2015, according to reports from the Ministry of Commerce website, the freight rate for each container per kilometer on the route had decreased from the initial $1 to $0.55, making it nearly equivalent to maritime shipping rates. Meanwhile, the total transit time was reduced from 16 days to 13 days. In 2015, the commodities carried by the "Yuxin'ou" became increasingly diverse, with IT products and non-IT products each accounting for about 50% of the cargo volume, respectively. Outbound goods included a variety of categories such as laptops, clothing and home goods, communication equipment, machinery, automotive spare parts, daily necessities, and coffee beans. On the return journey, goods included complete cars and automotive components, cosmetics, machinery, beer, and baby products. Notably, precision instruments, chemical raw materials, and cold chain foods also appeared in the cargo list for the route. The sources of goods spanned regions including North China, East China, South China, and Southwest China. Approximately 40% of the goods originated locally in Chongqing, while goods from other regions increased to around 60%.

3.7 From the West to Asia

Since 2014, the competitive landscape among different China-Europe train services has become increasingly evident. The initial advantage of the "Yuxin'ou" has gradually diminished, prompting Chongqing to adjust its strategic planning. This led to the introduction of the "Yaxin'ou" strategy in early 2016. To drive the strategy forward, Chongqing shifted its focus from the previous "westward" competition mindset of the "Yuxin'ou" era to seeking breakthroughs "eastward." The aim was to maintain their advantages in terms of goods sourcing, train services, and frequency while expanding their reach from the western region toward Asia. Concurrently, they began restructuring their trade dynamics and introduced the slogan of "financial innovation" to inject more vitality into the "Yaxin'ou" strategy. Throughout this transition, Chongqing actively bolstered collaborations with Asian countries, particularly with nations like Singapore and South Korea, striving to forge strategic agreements. These efforts amplified the impact and reach of the "Yaxin'ou" strategy, enhancing overall connectivity within the initiative.

In line with the local strategy of Chongqing and in response to the declining numbers of "Yuxin'ou," the city has implemented measures to preserve the quantity and value advantage of its rail services amid intense market competition. Despite these efforts, the outcomes have not yielded significant results. Historically, Chongqing enjoyed a substantial advantage over other cities in providing rail services, particularly for high-value goods. In 2013, Chongqing Customs oversaw 36 rail services with a total value of $1.1 billion, averaging around $30.56 million per service.[18] By the end of February 2016, statistics showed that "Yuxin'ou" had operated 530 services, accounting for about 50% of the total number of China-Europe rail services. The import and export value had exceeded $10 billion, representing 80% of the total goods value of China-Europe rail services passing through the Alashankou border crossing.[19] This data suggests that by the conclusion of February 2016, the average cargo value per train for "Yuxin'ou" had declined to approximately $18.86 million. According to statistics from Chongqing Customs covering the period from January to September 2016, they supervised 286 "Yuxin'ou" rail services, involving 21,800 TEUs of containers and cargo valued at approximately 10.2 billion yuan ($1.4 billion).[20] This data indicates that the average cargo value per train in Chongqing since 2016 had decreased to around $5.13 million. Intense market competition has not only constrained the growth of "Yuxin'ou" train services but also compelled efforts to maintain their quantity and frequency. In the face of such competition, the operators have resorted to transporting low-value-added goods and even attaching empty containers to increase the frequency of train operations. This strategy, while sustaining the number of train services, has led to a continual reduction in the average cargo value per train. Given these circumstances, Chongqing initiated the "Yaxin'ou" strategy in 2016 as a comprehensive approach to break through the competition in the rail services market. This strategic pivot aimed to explore a wider market in Asia, steering away from the fierce competition in the western markets. The strategy was crafted not just to overcome existing challenges but to enhance the city's strategic standing in foreign trade within the western

[18] Chongqing Customs. http://chongqing.customs.gov.cn/chongqing_customs/515855/515856/518111/index.html

[19] China Express Association. http://www.cea.org.cn/content/details_10_9622.html

[20] Chongqing Customs. http://chongqing.customs.gov.cn/chongqing_customs/515855/515856/1082790/index.html

region. It served as the cornerstone for the city's advancement in this domain.

On April 16, 2016, with the aim of advancing the strategic shift from "Yuxin'ou" to "Yaxin'ou," the Chongqing municipal government organized the "Promotion of China-Singapore (Chongqing) Demonstration Initiative on Strategic Connectivity." This project marked the third government-level cooperation between China and Singapore. However, unlike the previous two projects—Suzhou Industrial Park and Tianjin Eco-City—the China-Singapore (Chongqing) Demonstration Initiative on Strategic Connectivity was not focused on developing and constructing a specific location. Instead, it aimed to collaboratively create a comprehensive "connectivity" network, with Chongqing as the operational hub of this extensive network. During the conference, Mr. Chan Chun Sing, minister in the Prime Minister's Office of Singapore, highlighted, "If we can establish a new lifeline through Chongqing to connect with Southeast Asia, including ASEAN, and link the west to Europe, we could unlock two-thirds of China's potential."[21] This statement resonates with the core focus of the "Yaxin'ou" strategy, emphasizing the shift from the west to Asia. The city's initiatives to extend the railway network to industrial parks, ports, and airports effectively address the last-mile connectivity challenge. Simultaneously, Chongqing explores multimodal transportation options, building upon the foundation of the "Yuxin'ou" route to create an integrated network of railways, highways, and air transport with Singapore.

Chongqing has forged a strategic partnership with Singapore's airlines and is proactively engaging with domestic airlines to explore the potential establishment of a major airline company base in the city. This approach entails collaborating closely with Singapore's airlines to position Chongqing as a central hub for their operations. Concurrently, discussions are underway with prominent domestic airlines, including China Southern Airlines, China Eastern Airlines, and Hainan Airlines, with the objective of making the city the preferred choice for these airlines to establish operational bases and facilities. The overarching objective of the "Yaxin'ou" strategy is to utilize the existing "Yuxin'ou" rail services to transport European goods to Chongqing. Collaborations with airlines, including Singapore's airlines, enable efficient transshipment of these goods to various Asian cities such as Bangkok, Kuala Lumpur, Hong Kong, Taiwan

[21] Chinadaily.com. https://cnews.chinadaily.com.cn/2016-04/18/content_24624544.htm

region, Tokyo, Osaka, and Seoul. These Asian metropolises are all within a four to five-hour air radius of Chongqing. The strategic vision is to establish Chongqing as a pivotal hub for intermodal rail-air transport between Europe and Asia, streamlining transshipment trade processes and fostering seamless connectivity between continents.

Moreover, the local outbound source has experienced sluggish growth, underscoring Chongqing's imperative to expand logistics channels for more efficient gathering of return source goods. In 2015, outbound sources for "Yuxin'ou" exhibited a balanced distribution between IT and non-IT products, with approximately 40% originating locally. Among local source goods, IT products remained predominant. In 2016, with fierce competition for source goods from other regions, according to an interview with the Chongqing Municipal Logistics Office in late October, the person in charge anticipated that the proportion of local source goods would increase in 2017. According to the statistics released by the Chongqing Municipal Bureau of Statistics in early December, the production of some large-scale industrial products from January to November 2016 is as follows: automobiles: 2.8657 million units, a 3.9% increase; motorcycles: 7.1581 million units, a 5.7% decrease; microcomputer equipment: 61.2302 million units, an 8.2% increase; printers: 12.5176 million units, a 6.7% decrease; mobiles: 261.6239 million units, a 60.5% increase; liquid crystal displays: 31.1389 million units, a remarkable 586.8% increase.[22] Among these sources, the laptop industry has been a significant driver of Chongqing's rapid foreign trade growth in recent years. However, after a period of rapid expansion, the sector's growth appears to have slowed down. Despite a continuous rise in production, the export value has consistently declined, falling significantly below the figures from the same period in the previous year (see Table 3.3).

The slowing growth of Chongqing's laptop industry inevitably implies a decrease in its support for the outbound freight sources of the "Yuxin'ou." Another major outbound freight source, printers, has also experienced a significant decline in production. However, the production of mobiles has surged by 60.5%, accounting for approximately 20% of the country's total mobile production. Additionally, the production of liquid crystal displays has skyrocketed by 586.8%. These two industries are poised to emerge as

[22] Chongqing Statistics Information Website. https://data.tjj.cq.gov.cn/cqtjjfbk/#/publishingIndicatorSearch/ndsj?themeCode=sjydsjFbk&folderId=e0aa3196e53944718a12eb6aa0ef8ea5

Table 3.3 Chongqing laptop exports from January to September 2016 (Unit: 100 million yuan)

Month	*1*	*2*	*3*	*4*	*5*	*6*	*7*	*8*	*9*
Cumulative growth in export value		124.22	206.02	283.48	349.18	439.93	537.31	630.35	720.14
		−43.1%	−34.5%	−30.3%	−28.4%	−23.8%	−19.5%	−15.7%	−15.0%

Note: Data for January is unavailable on the official website of Chongqing Municipal Statistics Bureau

Source: https://data.tjj.cq.gov.cn/cqtjjfbk/#/publishingIndicatorSearch/ndsj?themeCode=sjydsjFbk&folderId=e0aa3196e53944718a12eb6aa0ef8ea5

vital local freight sources supporting outbound "Yuxin'ou." Despite Chongqing's continuous efforts in industrial restructuring, its "6+1" pillar industries[23] sustain robust growth. However, the escalating frequency poses challenges in maintaining local supply to meet demand. Attracting return freight sources has become a new focal point of competition. In this scenario, expanding market reach is the sole means to maintain a leading edge amid intense market competition. Thus, Chongqing has proactively expanded its target market to East Asia and Southeast Asia, necessitating the urgent construction of a new logistics corridor.

In the context of sluggish export growth and strong import expansion in Chongqing's foreign trade, the city has pivoted toward linking East Asia and Southeast Asia through the "Yuxin'ou" International Logistics Corridor, thereby accessing broader markets. This strategic move has established Chongqing as a crucial hub for import and export trade on the Chinese mainland. The BRI has provided a valuable development opportunity for Chongqing. It has not only injected more vitality into the "Yuxin'ou" rail services within the "Belt" region but also facilitated the integration of Chongqing into both the "Belt" and the "Road." This connectivity has forged a new and comprehensive maritime and land trade route, representing a strategic breakthrough that promises extensive developmental prospects for the city in the future.

Therefore, unlike the "Yuxin'ou," the "Yaxin'ou" route has a broader and more comprehensive goal of "connectivity." Taking the example of

[23] "6+1" pillar industries in Chongqing include electronic information industry, automobile industry, equipment manufacturing industry, integrated chemical industry, materials industry, energy industry, and consumer manufacturing industry.

the China-Singapore project, Xu Qiang, the then director of Chongqing Municipal Commission of Commerce, stated:

> The achievement of goals for the China-Singapore Initiative in Chongqing is measured against a set of criteria known as 'Two Reductions, Two Increases, Four Possessions.' 'Two Reductions' refer to reducing logistics costs and financing costs in the western region; 'Two Increases' refer to enhancing Chongqing's radiation capacity and increasing the replicability of various mechanisms as an operational center, which can be extended to other areas outside of Chongqing; 'Four Enhancements' refer to having efficient operational mechanisms, a scientific planning blueprint, innovative institutional mechanisms and policies, and active participation of market entities benefiting from project cooperation.[24]

Huang Qifan, the then mayor of Chongqing, described the future vision and path, revealing its intangible and tangible architecture. He also revealed plans to leverage cooperation with the "Yuxin'ou" and collaborate with Singapore to transform Chongqing into a global hub for finance, logistics, modern services, and cloud computing. He emphasized that a key feature is its operational center in Chongqing, radiating to the surrounding areas and promoting comprehensive trade cooperation between China and Singapore. In his words, "these projects serve Chongqing, but they can also serve Southwest China, other parts of China, the BRI, and Southeast Asia."[25]

3.8 Transition from Railroad Transport to Multimodal Connectivity

To ensure the smooth implementation of Chongqing's local development strategy and cope with the intense competition from the China-Europe freight trains, Chongqing must find new breakthroughs in the "Yaxin'ou" strategy. By the end of 2015, the "Yuxin'ou" freight trains had made a significant impact, accounting for 45% of the total number of China-Europe Railway Express and contributing to 80% of the total import and export value through Alashankou.[26] However, a drastic change occurred in 2016. Examining data from cities with partial operations of China-

[24] chinanews.com. https://www.chinanews.com/df/2016/04-16/7836838.shtml

[25] huanqiu.com. https://society.huanqiu.com/article/9CaKrnJT0Qv

[26] *ceweekly.cn*. https://www.ceweekly.cn/finance/macro/2016/0306/143397.html

Europe freight trains, Chengdu, situated only 300 kilometers from Chongqing, aimed to launch 400 trains in 2016, surpassing Chongqing's plan by 50 trains. Chengdu not only achieved this target but did so before November's conclusion, establishing itself as the leading city in China for China-Europe freight train operations. In contrast, the total number of "Rong'ou Express" trains in 2015 was a mere 103, less than half of Chongqing's operations. Faced with intense competition, Chongqing is now pivoting the development of the "Yaxin'ou" route from a singular focus on railways to a more comprehensive and interconnected strategy.

Firstly, garnering active support and response from other Asian countries forms the basis for the three-dimensional construction of "connectivity." In November 2015, China and Singapore signed the framework agreement for the "China-Singapore (Chongqing) Demonstration Initiative on Strategic Connectivity," marking the commencement of the third intergovernmental cooperation project. Chongqing serves as the operational center, concentrating on "modern connectivity and modern service economy." Chongqing is strategically utilizing the "Yuxin'ou" route to establish a comprehensive multimodal transportation network integrating railways, highways, and air transport with Singapore. This initiative has garnered positive responses from the country. For example, luxury goods transported from Europe to Singapore currently face air freight costs five times higher than rail transport. By adopting a rail-air intermodal transportation approach through the "Yuxin'ou" route, goods can be swiftly transported from Europe to Chongqing within 12 days by rail. Upon arrival, these goods enter the bonded zone without customs clearance procedures. Following packaging and sorting, the goods are promptly transported to Singapore, taking merely five hours by air. While this approach adds 12 days to the transportation time, it substantially reduces overall costs. For Singapore, this approach opens up a more cost-effective transportation method between Europe and the country, carrying significant strategic importance for its economic development. Additionally, in May 2015, the mayor of Incheon, South Korea, Yoo Jeong-bok, expressed strong interest in the "Yaxin'ou" corridor during his first visit to Chongqing. The city proposed that Incheon utilize the international railway interconnection corridor, starting from Chongqing, to facilitate European goods bound for South Korea to be transshipped through the "Yuxin'ou" route. This rail-air intermodal transport system would reduce costs by more than half. Yoo found this suggestion highly feasible, believing it to be a "win-win solution" for both South Korea and Chongqing.

Secondly, to enhance the influence of the "Yaxin'ou" route, the strategic upgrade of the "Yuxin'ou" route extends southward through "rail-road intermodal transportation," transforming the "segments" into an interconnected "network." Currently, the eastern route of the International Land-Sea Trade Corridor departs from Chongqing for ASEAN has been established. Goods departing from Chongqing, passing through the Pingxiang Port in Guangxi, can reach Hanoi, Vietnam. This transportation route reduces the shipping time by over 20 days compared to sea transport and costs only one-fifth of air transport. In the forthcoming years, Chongqing envisions the establishment of two additional routes to Southeast Asia, namely the central route (Chongqing–Mohan in Yunnan–Singapore) and the western route (Chongqing–Ruili in Yunnan–Yangon, Myanmar). The anticipated annual value of goods transported by Chongqing-ASEAN highway buses is set to reach 20 billion yuan ($2.79 billion) by 2020, propelling the city's industrial economy. For instance, Chongqing Lifan Group, leveraging the "Yuxin'ou" route, has strategically expanded its automotive market northward, emerging as a prominent brand for taxis in Russia. Simultaneously, it capitalizes on southern markets, reaching countries like Vietnam more cost-effectively for motorcycle sales.

Thirdly, the establishment and enhancement of multimodal transportation systems, including rail-road, rail-water, and rail-air intermodal transport, play a pivotal role in attracting both outbound and inbound freight sources. This strategic focus forms the bedrock for advancing the "Yaxin'ou" route. In response to formidable competition, Chongqing is strategically allocating substantial resources to propel the development of the route. For Chongqing, the significance of "Yuxin'ou" extends beyond being a mere international logistics corridor; it stands as a transformative catalyst, propelling this inland city toward heightened openness and global connectivity. Hence, Chongqing is pursuing a dual strategy. Firstly, it aims to secure more favorable national policies, such as becoming the exclusive pilot city in the western region for international mail delivery. Simultaneously, the city actively nurtures relationships with existing major clients and expands outbound freight sources by establishing rail-road, rail-water, and rail-air intermodal transport connections with neighboring provinces and cities. Crucially, Chongqing recognizes that perpetual regional competition for outbound China-Europe freight sources would result in a zero-sum game, ultimately benefiting Europe. Moreover, if China maintains a long-term trade surplus with Europe, it could be detrimental to the sustained development of both economies. Looking at its trade data in 2016, there is a significant increase in imports, while exports continue to decline (see Table 3.4).

In conclusion, Chongqing's pursuit of a three-dimensional interconnected network extends to the financial sector as well. It has raised the banner of "financial innovation," aiming to create a robust financial corridor under the BRI, thereby strengthening the implementation of the "Yaxin'ou" strategy. Like Chengdu, which has positioned itself as the "Western Financial Center," Chongqing, too, aspires to excel. In recent years, it has consistently advocated for "financial innovation," hoping to ride the wave of the BRI and become a financing hub for both the western regions and Central Asia. The "Two Reductions," driven by the "Yaxin'ou" route, focuses on two essential aspects: reducing logistics costs and lowering financing expenses. Evidently, the introduction of the strategy not only transformed Chongqing's geographical disadvantage within China but established a major artery connecting Europe to the Asian continent. Within this framework, logistics, finance, and trade are integral components. Similar developmental strategies and goals have been pursued and diligently implemented by Chengdu as well. From the operation of the China-Europe freight train to logistics development, and then to economic development strategies, the competition between these two cities has continually escalated. From the current standpoint, leveraging the operation of the China-Europe freight train as a breakthrough point and comprehensively integrating relevant resources to construct an international railway intermodal transportation corridor under the BRI will undoubtedly be one of the most crucial aspects in the competition between these "competitors."

Chongqing's efforts to promote the development of modern service economies within the "Yaxin'ou" strategy include strengthening collaborations in areas like finance, big data, and cloud computing with relevant countries. The partnership with Singapore is a noteworthy example. Chongqing has enhanced various aspects of connectivity between the two regions, such as settlement systems for offshore and onshore RMB transactions, as well as cross-border e-commerce and big data and cloud computing communications, promoting, for example, the formation of cross-border e-commerce by certain Internet terminals. Chongqing has actively encouraged various financial institutions from Singapore,

Table 3.4 Chongqing's overall import and export trade value from January to September 2016 (Unit: billion yuan)

Month	*1*	*2*	*3*	*4*	*5*	*6*	*7*	*8*	*9*
Total import and export value		976.46	1390.58	1718.27	2072.29	2280.32	2552.26	2824.13	3153.70
Cumulative growth		−4.9%	−0.6%	−7.0%	−6.7%	−10.2%	−11.8%	−11.3%	−12.6%
Total export value		803.83	1121.40	1353.15	1602.87	1691.76	1833.83	1973.25	2158.51
Cumulative growth		−3.7%	0.7%	−7.3%	−8.5%	−13.4%	−17.0%	−18.3%	−20.7%
Total import value		163.63	269.18	365.12	469.42	588.56	718.43	850.88	995.19
Cumulative growth		−10.2%	−5.9%	−5.7%	−0.4%	0.7%	5.0%	10.4%	12.2%

Note: Data for January is unavailable on the official website of Chongqing Municipal Statistics Bureau

Source: https://data.tjj.cq.gov.cn/cqtjjfbk/#/home.

including securities firms, insurance companies, and leasing companies, to establish branch offices in Chongqing and participate in its market development. In the aviation sector, for example, aircraft financial leasing is one of the key development areas that the government pays close attention to. Former Chongqing mayor Huang Qifan highlighted the significance of this market, stating that "aircraft leasing is crucial because airlines typically lease aircraft rather than investing in direct purchases. Given the interconnected cooperation between Chongqing and Singapore in this regard, financial and aviation sectors have converged, emphasizing the importance of aircraft leasing. Chongqing is committed to making breakthroughs in this area in collaboration with Singaporean companies."[27]

[27] chinanews.com, https://www.chinanews.com/cj/2016/04-16/7836868.shtml

CHAPTER 4

China-Europe Railway Express (Yiwu): Evolution of the "Yiwu-Xinjiang-Europe" Freight Train Operation Model

Zhihong Zhen, Ying Ma, and Shuxing Han

Yiwu, known for hosting the world's largest small commodity market, has emerged as a bustling hub of commerce in China. Today, in the new era of the Belt and Road Initiative (BRI), it has once again captured the spotlight due to the "Yiwu-Xinjiang-Europe" route, known as Yixin'ou in

Z. Zhen (✉)
Shanghai University, Shanghai, China

Shanghai University of International Business and Economics, Shanghai, China
e-mail: bai.gao@duke.edu

Y. Ma
Shanghai University, Shanghai, China

S. Han
Shanghai University of International Business and Economics, Shanghai, China

B. Gao, Z. Zhen (eds.), *The China-Europe Railway Express*, China and Globalization 2.0,
https://doi.org/10.1007/978-981-19-2882-6_4

Chinese. Since its inauguration on April 23, 2013, connecting Yiwu to five Central Asian countries, Yiwu has rapidly expanded its reach by launching eight international railway freight train routes to Central Asia, Europe, and the Middle East within just four years. It now stands as the sole county-level city in China offering China-Europe freight train services and boasts the highest number of international railway freight train routes in the country. Consequently, its development model has garnered widespread attention, with a growing body of research seeking to elucidate the remarkable growth of Yiwu's China-Europe freight trains, despite its status as a county-level city.

Many reports and studies attribute the rapid development of the Yixin'ou route to its successful market operation model. However, the research has found that the route's development is not solely a result of market construction; in fact, it owes much of its success to the policy initiatives of the Yiwu municipal government. With the Chinese government's BRI serving as a pivotal catalyst, the evolution of Yiwu's CR Express has unfolded in two distinct phases: market-driven construction and government-led development. This shift in development paradigms can be traced back to the transformation of Yiwu's strategic approach to development. Across these two distinct phases, changes have reshaped the role and significance of the Yixin'ou route within the city's development landscape, consequently influencing the government's functions in this context, ultimately resulting in the emergence of two distinct models.

Before the introduction of the BRI, Yiwu's goal was centered around establishing itself as an international trade and commerce hub. To realize its strategic positioning of "buying global goods, selling global goods," a mature logistics industry was needed to support this vision. Thus, at this juncture, the Yixin'ou route became a crucial logistical infrastructure for Yiwu's market development. Private enterprise, Yiwu Tianmeng Industrial Investment Co Ltd. (hereinafter referred to as Tianmeng Company), took the lead in responding to market demand and initiated the opening of freight train services from Yiwu to five Central Asian countries, providing railway logistics support for the small commodity market. During this period, the Yixin'ou route operated in a fragmented transit mode, with a relatively small scale, shorter distances, and an unstable operational frequency.

However, following the initiation of the BRI, Yiwu's development strategy underwent a notable transformation, moving away from a market-centered approach and shifting its focus toward urban development.

During this phase, Yiwu pivoted from its previous objective of establishing itself as an international trade and commerce hub to assuming a pivotal role within the framework of the BRI. The city aimed to "go west by land and go east by sea," effectively bridging the "Silk Road Economic Belt" with the "21st Century Maritime Silk Road." In this broader context, the Yixin'ou route emerged as a critical component of Yiwu's "going west by land" strategy, playing a central role in advancing the goals of the Belt and Road Initiative. The development model of the Yixin'ou route also underwent a transition, shifting from market-driven construction to government-led development. The Yiwu municipal government assumed a prominent role, supplanting Tianmeng Company as the primary driver behind the construction and operation of the Yixin'ou route. On the one hand, the government ensured the supply of goods for the railway through various means such as government subsidies, establishing foundations, and promoting market procurement trade methods. On the other hand, the government initiated specific reforms within local state-owned enterprises, establishing Yiwu International Land Port Group Co., Ltd. (hereinafter referred to as Land Port Group) to oversee logistics park operations. They also established the "One Customs, Two Inspections, CR Express Green Channel," creating a specialized platform to facilitate the development of the Yixin'ou route.

In the following sections, the chapter will expand on the development phases of the Yixin'ou route. This will provide the basis for a closer examination of how the shift in Yiwu's strategic objectives, both before and after the introduction of the BRI, has impacted the role of Yixin'ou route in the city's development. Additionally, it will delve into how these shifts in strategic goals have driven changes in its development model.

4.1 Development Journey of the China-Europe Railway Express (Yiwu)

The export of small commodities has always been a crucial pillar of Yiwu's economic growth. Before the introduction of international freight trains, land and sea transport were the primary means for small commodity exports. Since the opening of the first Yiwu to Central Asian countries freight train service in 2013, the Yiwu international freight trains industry has experienced rapid growth. Looking at the historical context of its development, the evolution of the Yixin'ou route can be divided into two phases. As shown in Table 4.1, the period before 2014 marked the initial stage of Yiwu's freight trains' development. During this period, Yiwu had only one freight route to the five Central Asian countries, operating in a fragmented transit mode. Furthermore, this route had not achieved regular operations, with unstable operating times severely hampering its development. After 2014, its freight train service entered a phase of rapid expansion. Between 2014 and 2017, Yiwu successively opened seven routes to the five Central Asian countries, Madrid in Spain, Tehran in Iran, Mazar-i-Sharif in Russia, Riga in Latvia, and London in the United Kingdom. Yiwu became the city with the highest number of international railway freight routes. During this period, the operational model of the routes shifted from fragmented transit to full-train direct services, achieving stable and regular operations.

On April 23, 2013, Yiwu inaugurated its first international freight railway route to the five Central Asian countries, operating under the railway customs clearance model, also known as the secondary customs clearance model. This route commenced from Yiwu, traversed the Alashankou border port in Xinjiang for customs clearance, and proceeded to Almaty in Kazakhstan. Subsequently, it was further distributed to other cities in Central Asian countries, including Kazakhstan, Uzbekistan, Kyrgyzstan, Turkmenistan, and Tajikistan. Over the years, the Central Asian region, positioned at the heart of the Eurasian continent and lacking direct access to the sea, predominantly relied on railways or roadways for the import and export of goods. Conversely, Yiwu's primary mode of exporting small commodities was through sea transport. This disparity in export channels severely hindered Yiwu's ability to reach the markets of the five Central Asian countries effectively. The launch of this train route addressed a crucial gap in Yiwu's international freight trains system. It significantly

Table 4.1 Two phases of development of CR Express (Yiwu)

	Before 2014	*2014–2017*
Route scale	One route	Eight routes
Coverage	Central Aisa	Central Asia, Europe, and the Middle East
Operational mode	Fragmented transit, nonstandardized	Full-train direct services, two-way regular operations

Data Source: Compiled by the author based on relevant literature

bolstered the city's exports to the Central Asian region, establishing Central Asia as a vital destination for Yiwu's foreign trade exports.

According to statistical data from Yiwu Customs, in 2013, the export value of small commodities from Yiwu to the five Central Asian countries reached $67.23 million, representing a year-on-year growth of 50.87%. Yiwu Customs also reported a significant surge in container volume, monitoring containers bound for the five Central Asian countries, which increased from 52 containers in 2012 to a remarkable 618 containers[1] in 2013. During this phase, while Yiwu had established freight routes extending westward to Central Asia, the Yixin'ou route still operated in a fragmented transit mode. The transportation of goods primarily involved bulk cargo. After departing from Yiwu, goods were transported alongside other Central Asian-bound trains within China, arriving at the Alashankou border crossing in Xinjiang. Subsequently, the goods underwent transshipment upon exiting Alashankou.[2] This transshipment process led to inconsistent freight transit times and uncertain scheduling frequencies. Hence, this phase represented an exploratory period in the development of the Yixin'ou route, rather than the establishment of a fully standardized international freight trains logistics industry with stable and consistent operations.

After 2014, Yiwu's China-Europe freight train entered a rapid development phase, marked by significant changes in the number of routes, operational scope, and modes. On January 20, 2014, Yiwu introduced a specialized cargo train service connecting the city with Central Asian countries. Unlike previous routes, this service achieved regular operation and, crucially, shifted from fragmented transshipment to direct whole-train transportation. Goods on the domestic segment were no longer mixed with other cargo destined for Central Asia. Instead, they were transported directly from Yiwu to the Alashankou border crossing in Xinjiang, streamlining the process significantly. After passing customs, there was no longer a need for cargo transfer; it was directly dispatched to the Almaty distribution center in Kazakhstan. Over the following three years, Yiwu subsequently opened seven container freight dedicated lines to Europe and the Middle East. Among these, the Yiwu to Madrid in Spain and Yiwu

[1] Xu Xiao'en: "Yiwu's 'New Silk Road' Inaugurates International Container Express to Central Asian Countries," *Zhejiang Daily*, January 21, 2014, p. 3.

[2] Jianli Yao, Yiyi Zhu, "Yiwu to Madrid Direct: The Normalization of the 'Yixin'ou' Train Service," *21st Century Business Herald*, May 20, 2015, 5th Edition.

to Tehran in Iran routes were even included in the "Construction and Development Plan of China-Europe Railway Express (2016–2020)." Within a short period, Yiwu surpassed cities like Chongqing and Chengdu, which had started developing such freight train services earlier, making it the Chinese city with the most railway freight dedicated lines (see Table 4.2).

On November 18, 2014, the freight train service between Yiwu and Madrid, Spain was launched, marking the inaugural Yixin'ou route. This train operates twice a week on the outbound journey and once a month on the return journey, covering a total distance of 13,052 kilometers and taking 21 days to complete. It traverses eight countries, including Russia, Belarus, Ukraine, Poland, Germany, France, and others, making it the world's longest international freight train route currently in operation.

In 2016, following the establishment of the Central Asia and Central Europe freight train services, Yiwu inaugurated the Middle East train service bound for Tehran, Iran, becoming China's first freight train service to the Middle East. The "Yiwu to Tehran" train departs from Yiwu, exits China through the Alashankou Port in Xinjiang, traverses Kazakhstan and Turkmenistan, and reaches its destination in Tehran, covering a total of four countries. During its journey, it undergoes two gauge changes and

Table 4.2 Yiwu China-Europe freight container dedicated routes

Serial number	*Name*	*Departure date*	*Duration*	*Frequency*
1	Yiwu to Central Asian Countries	January 20, 2014	12 days	2 trains per week
2	Yiwu to Madrid, Spain	November 18, 2014	21 days	
3	Yiwu to Tehran, Iran	January 28, 2016	14 days	
4	Yiwu to Chelyabinsk, Russia	August 13, 2016	8 days	1 train per week
5	Yiwu to Mazar-i-Sharif, Afghanistan	August 28, 2016	15 days	1 train per week
6	Yiwu to Riga, Latvia	October 20, 2016	15 days	
7	Yiwu to London, United Kingdom	January 1, 2017	18 days	

Source: Compiled by the author based on interview data from Yiwu Land Port Affairs and Port Management Bureau on January 18, 2017

takes 14 days to arrive at the Salahes Border Freight Terminal in northeastern Iran, near the Turkmenistan border. Afterward, it continues its journey within Iran for several more days, reaching its destination in Tehran, covering a total distance of 10,399 kilometers.[3] The launch served as a crucial bridge connecting the "China-Central Asia-West Asia Economic Corridor," establishing a convenient route for trade between China and the Middle East. This development further strengthened economic and trade ties between China and Iran, as well as other countries in the Middle East, signifying a significant milestone. In the same year, Yiwu also initiated two additional freight routes to Mazar-i-Sharif in Afghanistan and Chelyabinsk in Russia, with regular weekly operations. Furthermore, a trial operation was launched for a route to Riga, the capital of Latvia, expanding the reach of the Yixin'ou route.

In the beginning of 2017, Yiwu expanded its train service to London, the capital of the UK. This marked the first freight train service to reach the British Isles by crossing the English Channel. The route covered 15 cities in 10 European countries, starting from Alashankou and passing through Kazakhstan, Russia, Belarus, Poland, Germany, Belgium, France, and others. It also traversed the English Channel via the tunnel and ultimately arrived at London's Barking station, covering a total distance of over 12,000 kilometers, and taking 18 days.[4] The commencement of the Yiwu to London route not only expanded the export route for the city's small commodities but also, of greater significance, elevated Yiwu's international standing. This railway service played a pivotal role in establishing global recognition for Yiwu, a county-level city, and generated a wealth of business opportunities. Consequently, it bolstered Yiwu's position as a prominent international trade hub.

As of March 27, 2017, the Yixin'ou route had completed 160 round trips, transporting 12,414 standard containers. On the outbound journey, the train made 134 trips, carrying 11,540 standard containers. Among these, the Yiwu to Madrid train ran 110 times, transporting 9360 standard containers; the Yiwu to Russia train ran 6 times, carrying 580 standard containers; the Yiwu to Belarus train ran three times, carrying 286

[3] Zongzhi Huang. "The Latest Silk Road Train Arrives in Tehran Following the Opening of China-Europe and China-Central Asia Trains." *People's Daily* (Overseas Edition), February 19, 2016, p. 1.

[4] Xuqian Mao. "The First China-Europe Train from Yiwu to London Departs on New Year's Day," *China Yiwu News*, December 23, 2016, http://news.zgyww.cn/system/2016/12/31/010090108.shtml, Last accessed on April 10, 2017.

standard containers; the Yiwu to Afghanistan train ran 12 times, carrying 1086 standard containers; the Yiwu to Iran train ran once, carrying 64 standard containers; the Yiwu to Latvia train ran once, carrying 84 standard containers, and the Yiwu to London train ran once, carrying 88 standard containers. On the return journey, the train made a total of 26 trips, transporting 866 standard containers. Several China-Europe freight train routes not only continuously exported Chinese manufactured goods but also facilitated the development of import trade in Yiwu. According to statistics, in 2016, Yiwu's imports and exports with BRI countries reached 114.543 billion yuan ($15.6 billion), a year-on-year increase of 4.89%. Of this, exports accounted for 113.99 billion yuan ($15.5 billion), with a year-on-year growth of 4.86%, while imports were 5.52 billion yuan ($0.75 billion), reflecting a year-on-year growth of 10.97%.[5] So, why has the Yixin'ou container freight line experienced rapid development since 2014? What factors have influenced the evolution of Yiwu's freight train services into different operational models over time? In the following section, we will delve into how the development model of Yiwu's China-Europe freight trains has undergone transformation from the perspective of the city's changing development strategy. We will explore how the evolution of Yiwu's development strategy has influenced the shifting dynamics and strategies of the Yiwu to Europe freight train services.

4.2 Development Strategy: From "Trade Metropolis" to "Strategic Pivot City"

In most of the existing research on the development model of the Yixin'ou route, it is overwhelmingly considered that the rapid development of the Yiwu freight trains is the outcome of market construction. However, this research finds that the evolution of the Yixin'ou route is not solely attributable to market forces but, of greater significance, to government-led initiatives throughout its construction process. Before 2014, the emergence of the first Yiwu freight train was indeed a result of market-driven

[5] The author compiled this information based on interviews conducted by the research team at the Yiwu Land Port Affairs and Port Management Bureau on January 18, 2017. Additionally, reference was made to an article titled, "The Timing, Geographical Advantage, and Human Effort: Zhejiang Yiwu Competing to Be at the Forefront of BRI" by Xijinyan and Zhang Yuhuan, China News on March 24, 2017. The article can be accessed at http://www.chinanews.com/cj/2017/03-24/818232.shtml. The last access date for this source was April 29, 2017.

construction. The private enterprise, Tianmeng Company, organized the Yiwu to Central Asia five-country freight train in response to the substantial market demand for railway logistics in Yiwu. However, the rapid development of the Yiwu to Europe container freight train after 2014 was facilitated by government promotion, and this shift in the model was driven by Yiwu's evolving development strategy. As indicated in Table 4.3, during the market construction phase, Yiwu's development strategy aimed at establishing an international trade metropolis with the objective of "buying global goods and selling global goods." The Yixin'ou route served as the logistics infrastructure that facilitated market internationalization and was operated independently by private enterprises in response to market demands. However, after President Xi Jinping proposed the BRI in September and October 2013, Yiwu shifted its development center from building an international trade metropolis to becoming a BRI pivot city, expanding westward via land and eastward via sea. In the new economic situation, especially in the face of the impact of e-commerce and the opportunities for vigorously developing the import market, Yiwu began to shift its focus from operating physical markets to operating the city to enhance its competitiveness. The concept of operating the city was summarized by our research team through field research in Yiwu. Its essence lies in its development planning no longer revolving around the operational logic of its physical markets. The concept is mainly manifested in two aspects. First, Yiwu is no longer focused on the small commodity market in its industrial layout. In recent years, the city has adjusted its industrial layout, focusing on the development of four categories of

Table 4.3 Yixin'ou market building vs. government building

	Market	*Government*
Development strategy	Build an international trade metropolis	Establish a pivotal city for the Belt and Road Initiative
Strategic goals	Buying and selling global goods	Connect to the west by land and to the east by sea
Strategic leverage	Market-driven, private enterprise operation	Driving force
Key actors	Market-driven, private enterprise operation	Government-driven, private enterprise operation

Source: Compiled based on relevant literature and interview data with the Yiwu Land and Port Affairs and Port Management Bureau on January 18, 2017

industries: fashion industry, information industry, health industry, and equipment manufacturing industry. Second, Yiwu places importance on the environment and talent. "Five Waters Co-governance," namely five areas of water governance: pollution control, flood prevention, drainage management, water supply security, and water conservation, and "Three Changes and One Demolition," namely the renovation of old residential areas, old industrial zones, urban villages, and the demolition of illegal constructions, summarize the environmental governance policy of the Yiwu city government. In addition, Yiwu has promoted initiatives such as "Zhejiang Merchants Returning" and the creation of a civilized city, reflecting its emphasis on environmental governance. Its fundamental goal is to bring about a fundamental change in Yiwu by improving the environment and quality of life, attracting more high-quality industries and high-end elements to enhance Yiwu's competitiveness. At this juncture, the Yixin'ou route has transformed into a crucial means for Yiwu to link up with the "Silk Road Economic Belt" in the west. With this new strategic orientation, the route's model has also shifted from the initial market-driven model run by private enterprises to a government-backed construction model with private enterprise operation (see Table 4.3).

4.2.1 Market Development

Export trade has always been a crucial pillar driving the economic development of Yiwu. However, the global financial crisis in 2008 had varying impacts on major developed countries worldwide, directly affecting the city's export trade. In 2009, Yiwu's GDP growth rate dropped from its previous double-digit growth to 9%, and the growth rate of foreign exports decreased from 25% to 12%.[6] To improve this situation, the Yiwu municipal government, while adhering to the existing principle of "promoting commerce and building the city," further enhanced its internationalization. They proposed a development strategy to build an international trade metropolis, aiming to transform Yiwu into an international city where all three major trade modes—export, import, and re-export—are developed simultaneously, with the goal of achieving "buying global goods and selling global goods."

[6] Data source: "Yiwu National Economic and Social Development Statistical Bulletin" (2008–2010).

During the 11th Five-Year Plan period, Yiwu put forward the development principle of "strengthening one positioning and deepening one strategy."[7] The "strengthening one positioning" referred to the positioning of an international trade city. Under the development orientation of an international trade metropolis, Yiwu optimized its urban layout and integrated urban development space. The "deepening one strategy" referred to the internationalization-driven strategy. The Yiwu municipal government stated that internationalization strategy was the deepening and development of "thriving business and building the city" strategy in the new era. It emphasized the internationalization of the market as its guiding principle, driving the internationalization of small commodity manufacturing and research and development, enhancing the internationalization of urban service functions, continuously improving the level of internal and external openness, and strengthening its ability to participate in domestic and international economic cooperation and competition on a larger scale, in broader fields, and at a higher level, by utilizing both domestic and international markets and resources.[8]

The "Decision of the Yiwu Municipal Committee of the Communist Party of China on Building an International Trade City," issued in 2008, outlines Yiwu's future development strategy with a focus on both domestic and international markets. It emphasizes the principles of "introducing in" and "going out" simultaneously to build a core consisting of "Three Centers" and "Two High grounds" to construct an international trade city. The "Three Centers" refer to the International Small Commodities Trade Center, the International Small Commodities Innovation Center, and the International Small Commodities Exhibition Center. The "Two High grounds" refer to the regional logistics high ground and the regional financial high ground. Specifically, building the International Small Commodities Trade Center aims to adhere to and deepen the development strategy of "promoting business and building the city," establish and improve the market system, innovate, and enhance market functions,

[7]Yiwu municipal government: "The 11th Five-Year Plan Outline for National Economic and Social Development of Yiwu," Official Website of "China Yiwu," May 9, 2008, http://www.yw.gov.cn/zfmhzxxgk/001/03/01/201106/t20110630_233092.shtml, last accessed on April 21, 2017.

[8]Yiwu municipal government: "The 11th Five-Year Plan Outline for National Economic and Social Development of Yiwu," Official Website of "China Yiwu," May 9, 2008, http://www.yw.gov.cn/zfmhzxxgk/001/03/01/201106/t20110630_233092.shtml, last accessed on April 21, 2017.

attract domestic and international suppliers, importers, wholesalers, and large retailers, and strive to make Yiwu the world's most influential hub for small commodities distribution, information, and pricing. The goal is to achieve "buying global goods and selling global goods" and become a significant platform for Chinese small commodities to enter the world market and for global small commodities to enter China. Building the International Small Commodities Innovation Center involves vigorously developing the small commodities creative industry, continuously enhancing the comprehensive strength, independent innovation capability, and international competitiveness of the small commodity manufacturing industry. It aims to make Yiwu the global center for small commodities research and design, as well as the center for intellectual property trading, attracting numerous enterprises or individual studios specializing in small commodities design and research to cluster in Yiwu. This effort promotes the prosperity of creative industries based on small commodities and improves the intellectual property protection system, achieving "small commodities innovated in Yiwu." The construction of the International Small Commodities Exhibition Center revolves around the "China Yiwu International Commodities (Standards) Fair" as a typical symbol to lead the global trend in small commodities development. It involves constructing and improving exhibition facilities, enhancing exhibition service functions, nurturing, and attracting renowned domestic and international exhibition organizations, and regularly hosting high-level international and domestic conferences and brand exhibitions. The aim is to develop Yiwu's exhibitions into comprehensive platforms for commodity trading, information dissemination, product innovation, and price formation, guiding the global trend in small commodities development. Creating the regional logistics high ground entails establishing a comprehensive transportation network encompassing road, rail, and air transport, with fully functional logistics information and service platforms. This effort involves cultivating and attracting a batch of modern logistics enterprises with international competitiveness, constructing a comprehensive customs clearance system, and making Yiwu a pivotal hub for small commodities distribution with significant influence both nationally and globally. Building the regional financial high ground, epitomized by the establishment of the Yiwu Financial Cluster, seeks to attract numerous domestic and international bank branches, securities, insurance, and trust companies, ensuring convenient international settlement and rapid development of intermediary businesses such as consulting, evaluation, wealth management, and investment. The goal is to transform Yiwu into a regional hub for investment and financing, financial services, and financial innovation.

When establishing an International Trade City, "international" signifies the global orientation, "trade" represents the central focus, and "city" denotes the quantity. In essence, creating an International Trade City means addressing both international and domestic markets, consolidating diverse resources, emphasizing small commodities, and balancing import-export and domestic trade. The core framework includes the International Small Commodities Trade Center, International Small Commodities Innovation Center, International Small Commodities Exhibition Center, regional logistics hub, and regional financial center. This core framework, known as the "Three Centers and Two High grounds," aims for harmonious development in politics, economics, society, culture, and ecology. It strives for comprehensive strength, well-developed urban functions, harmonious social order, efficient management systems, rich cultural heritage, beautiful ecological environments, affluent people's lives, and high global recognition and reputation as a trade city.[9]

Under such a guidance, the Yiwu people realized that trade cannot be one-sided, and the city needed to transform from its existing world small commodity wholesale market into a global trade center. To truly achieve the goal of "buying global goods and selling global goods," it was essential to strengthen the "imports" and "transshipment" aspects. Hence, Yiwu established a new trade pattern known as "the three links of exports, imports, and transshipment," emphasizing a balanced approach to trade. In this way, the international logistics industry became a vital auxiliary industry supporting the development of the small commodity market and driving the "three-links" trade pattern. In fact, Yiwu has long been committed to the development of logistics-related industries to complement its small commodity exports. However, for an extended period, Yiwu predominantly emphasized maritime and land transport, and even air transport, while railway transportation remained a weak link in its logistics development. Prior to the commencement of international freight trains, Yiwu's goods primarily found their way to Europe via three methods: maritime, sea-rail intermodal, or air transport. Maritime transport entailed

[9] Xiangyang Fang, Chunqiu Lou. "Yiwu's Comprehensive Construction of an International Trade Metropolis – Initiating a New Leap in Building the 'Three Centers and Two High Grounds,'" *Jinhua Daily*, July 23, 2008, p. 1.

the movement of goods from Yiwu to the ports of Ningbo or Shanghai using land transport, followed by a southbound sea voyage after departing from Ningbo or Shanghai. This route involved crossing the Malacca Strait into the Indian Ocean and subsequently undergoing multiple transshipments to reach Europe. This approach was the most time consuming, typically taking over two months for goods to reach Europe. Sea-rail intermodal transport, on the other hand, involved goods departing from Ningbo or Shanghai ports and traveling northward, passing through the Korean Strait between the Korean Peninsula and Kyushu Island in Japan, reaching Vladivostok in Russia, and then being transported to Europe via the existing railway lines of the Eurasian Land Bridge through Russia. Although faster than pure maritime transport, it still required approximately one and a half months and included multiple transshipments along the way. Air transport was the quickest method, entailing the direct airlift of small commodities from Yiwu to Europe. However, it was also the most expensive alternative. Therefore, considering market demand, Yiwu held significant market potential in the realm of railway transportation.

Yiwu is a hub for China's small commodity market, with a vast quantity of goods shipped from Yiwu to destinations worldwide every day. Faced with significant market demand and the absence of international freight railway transportation, Tianmeng Company, as a private enterprise, was the first to identify this potential logistics market. Feng Xubin, chairman of Tianmeng Company, explained, "Every day, numerous container trucks depart from Yiwu to the Alashankou in Xinjiang. At that time, an average of 17 trucks transported Yiwu's small commodities to the border of Xinjiang or Urumqi for customs clearance. However, for such long-distance transportation of over 4000 kilometers, rail transport had its advantages.[10] Therefore, we came up with the idea of opening an international intermodal railway route from Yiwu to Central Asia." In 2010, Tianmeng Company began preparations to establish a CR Express operation company and simultaneously applied for Yiwu's first railway customs supervision site.[11] In 2013, the first freight train service from Yiwu to five Central Asian countries was opened, marking the first time that the city's

[10] Wei Zhang. "Yixin'ou's Manipulator Feng Xubin," *Decision-Making*, No. 1, 2016.

[11] Based on the interview data with the Yiwu Land Port Affairs and Port Management Bureau conducted by the research team on January 18, 2017, we found that initially the Yiwu Municipal government did not provide clear support and assistance in customs applications. It can be said that Tianmeng negotiated separately with customs and railway authorities, with Tianmeng being responsible for organizing the source of goods, and then using the

small commodities were exported to the Central Asian market using a railway customs clearance mode. Railway customs clearance, in this context, refers to the transportation of goods using different modes of transport with the approval of customs authorities. The customs clearance export mode primarily targets small commodities exported to the Eurasian continent. After customs clearance at Yiwu Customs, these goods are transported via the Lanzhou-Xinjiang Railway to customs checkpoints like Alashankou, where they undergo customs clearance for export to foreign countries. For instance, small commodities within containers that have completed customs clearance at Yiwu Customs can arrive at Almaty, Kazakhstan, just 15 days after leaving, compared to the traditional route where they would be transported by road to ports like Ningbo and then shipped to Russian ports before being transported further to Russia's hinterlands and the five Central Asian countries, which would take about 40 to 45 days.[12] The head inspector from the Yiwu Railway Freight West Station Customs Supervision Office explained, "Shipping from Yiwu to Central Asia by sea takes 40 to 45 days, while shipping via the Yixin'ou route to Central Asia generally takes 12 days.[13] The transportation cost for this part is roughly equivalent to sea freight." Although long-distance railway transportation doesn't have the lowest transportation costs like sea shipping, it saves more than half of the time compared to sea shipping and is more cost-effective than air transportation. This makes it suitable for products that are perishable, have high added value, and require a certain level of timeliness. Therefore, the Yiwu to Central Asia freight train service, promoted by Tianmeng Company, primarily targets international transportation of such products, filling a gap in Yiwu's freight train market.

Yiwu's development strategy for building an international trade metropolis is centered around the goal of "buying global goods and selling global goods." Following the principle of "categorizing by type, managing by category, and aggregating for development," the city has defined the functional positioning of its markets. It aims to optimize the layout of the urban commercial center and the international trade city blocks. Additionally, the strategy seeks to further enhance the market system, with

railway transportation channel provided by the China Railway Corporation and paying the transportation fees.

[12] Kai Xu, Jianya He, Hongcan Shi. "New Policy for 'Railway Customs Clearance' Shortens Freight Transit Time by Half," *Hangzhou Daily*, November 18, 2013, 1st Edition.

[13] Jianli Yao, Yiyi Zhu. "Direct Train from Yiwu to Madrid: Regularization of the 'Yixin'ou' Freight Train Service," *21st Century Business Herald*, May 20, 2015, 5th Edition.

the small commodity market as the leader, complemented by specialized markets and supported by factor markets. Within this strategy, the Yixin'ou international freight railway has become a crucial supporting element for market development. Tianmeng Company recognized the market demand and opened the Yiwu to Central Asia freight train service. This not only expanded the export routes for Yiwu's small commodities but also brought new business opportunities for Tianmeng Company.

4.2.2 Government-Led Building

However, after the Chinese government introduced the BRI, Yiwu shifted its focus to become a key city in this initiative. Consequently, the development of the Yixin'ou route gained strategic significance, and the government became a crucial driving force behind its development.

In September and October 2013, during his visits to Central Asian and Southeast Asian countries, Chinese president Xi Jinping proposed two major initiatives, namely the "Silk Road Economic Belt" and the "21st Century Maritime Silk Road" (referred to as Belt and Road Initiative, or BRI for short). The key directions of the "Silk Road Economic Belt" are as follows: from China through Central Asia to Europe (the Baltic Sea); from China through Central Asia to the Persian Gulf and the Mediterranean; and from China to Southeast Asia, South Asia, and the Indian Ocean. The key directions of the "21st Century Maritime Silk Road" are as follows: from Chinese coastal ports through the South China Sea to the Indian Ocean, extending to Europe; and from Chinese coastal ports through the South China Sea to the South Pacific. According to the BRI, on land, it relies on international corridors, supported by central cities along the route and cooperation platforms in key economic and trade industrial parks. Together, they aim to create international economic cooperation corridors such as the New Eurasian Land Bridge, China-Mongolia-Russia, China-Central Asia-West Asia, and China-Indochina Peninsula. At sea, it focuses on key ports and aims to jointly build efficient and secure transportation channels.

To align with the BRI, Yiwu has put forward a strategic concept to become a pivotal city along the route. Leveraging its strategic advantage as an international trade comprehensive reform pilot zone, Yiwu aims to seize the significant opportunities presented by the BRI construction, enhance its position in international division of labor, promote the transformation and upgrade of traditional commerce, and establish itself as a commanding point in global small commodity trade. Yiwu aims to be a cornerstone for the BRI economic and trade cooperation, creating a global hub for small commodity trade. With a favorable position within the United Nations Economic and Social Commission for Asia and the Pacific's Intergovernmental Agreement on Dry Ports, Yiwu plans to cultivate and develop a modern logistics system, improve inland port services, drive the growth of high-end services such as finance and settlement, and build an international land-port city.[14] In its specific development process, Yiwu is strategically prioritizing the development of two key open transportation routes, namely the "Yiwu-Xin-Europe" and the "Yiwu-Ningbo-Zhoushan" Grand Open Channel. It is integrating these routes into the BRI plans to enhance its overall openness and connectivity. To the west, Yiwu is concentrating its efforts on ensuring the smooth and regular operation of the Yixin'ou route, establishing reliable land connections between Yiwu and Central Asia, Europe, and other regions. It actively participates in the construction of the New Silk Road Economic Belt in this direction. To the east, Yiwu is planning to integrate with the "Yiwu-Ningbo-Zhoushan Grand Open Channel," which forms a transcontinental land–sea logistics artery linking Asia, Europe, and Africa. Yiwu is actively engaging in the development of this channel, aligning itself with the construction of the Twenty-First Century Maritime Silk Road. These strategic initiatives aim to enhance Yiwu's role as a crucial hub for trade and logistics, facilitating the seamless flow of goods and connectivity between different regions, and contributing to the broader goals of the BRI.[15]

The new strategy bestows a new strategic position upon the Yixin'ou route. During its initial market development phase, Yixin'ou existed solely as logistics infrastructure to support the growth of the small commodity market. Today, Yixin'ou has become a strategic lever in the effort to transform Yiwu into a pivotal city along the BRI route. Yixin'ou not only provides Yiwu with multiple outbound channels but serves as a link for bringing opportunities inward. What's even more crucial is that through

[14] Communist Party of Yiwu Municipal Committee, "Decision of the Communist Party of Yiwu Municipal Committee on Accelerating Urban Transformation and Development," "China Yiwu" Government Official Website, September 10, 2014, http://hzjd.yw.gov.cn/zcfg/201409/t20140910__591262.html, last accessed on April 21, 2017.

[15] Yiwu municipal government, "13th Five-Year Plan for National Economic and Social Development of Yiwu City," "China Yiwu" Government Official Website, March 11, 2016, http://www.yw.gov.cn/wap/mbzfzx/mbmryw/201603/t20160311_883442.html, last accessed on April 21, 2017.

the Yixin'ou it enhances the international visibility of Yiwu, a county-level city, and strengthens its economic and trade cooperation with cities along the Silk Road Economic Belt. Therefore, in this strategic positioning, the government naturally takes the place of private enterprises as the key driving force behind the development of Yixin'ou route. The Yiwu to Madrid container freight train, which was inaugurated on November 18, 2014, is a typical example of government-led initiatives. The planning and launch of this route were the result of direct collaboration between the leaders of China and Spain. On September 26, 2014, during a meeting with then Spanish prime minister Mariano Rajoy, Chinese president Xi Jinping proposed the operation of the Yixin'ou, which departs from Yiwu, Zhejiang, and arrives in Madrid. Xi pointed out that, Yiwu stands as the world's largest small commodity market, while Madrid serves as Europe's primary distribution hub for small commodities. The establishment of this trade route has the potential to significantly elevate the level of economic and trade collaboration between China and Spanish markets.

The strategic importance of the Yixin'ou route lies not only in the market opportunities it provides for Yiwu but also, more importantly, in the strategic dimension as it strengthens economic and trade cooperation between Yiwu and Europe. From a market perspective, taking the Yiwu to Madrid route as an example, the opening fills a gap in the railway connections between Yiwu and Europe. It offers advantages in terms of time cost, transit cost, and freight cost for the internationalization of Yiwu's small commodities. Firstly, in terms of time, a typical journey from Yiwu to Madrid by train takes only around 21 days, which is at least half the time saved compared to traditional shipping or a combination of shipping and railways. The most significant advantage of this time reduction is the acceleration of capital turnover and the alleviation of upfront financing pressures. Secondly, in terms of the transit process, once the train departs from Yiwu West Railway Station, it can go directly to Madrid, eliminating the need for multiple modes of transportation such as road, rail, and sea. Lastly, regarding transportation costs, although the Yixin'ou is slightly more expensive than shipping or a combination of shipping and railways, it is only 25% of the cost of air freight. This makes it highly suitable for the export of high–value added and time-sensitive Yiwu small commodities to Europe. Zhejiang Mengde Import and Export Co. in Yiwu primarily engaged in import and export trade, with Spain as its main export destination. The company's annual export trade volume to countries like Spain, Morocco, North Africa, and Syria amounts to €15 million. Previously,

Mengde's goods were either shipped via "Rail-Sea Intermodal Transportation" from Ningbo Port or loaded onto ships near the Guangzhou branch. After the opening of the Yixin'ou route, 30% of the company's export business shifted to rail transport. A Mengde company representative explained:

> Our company has signed a long-term strategic cooperation agreement with Yiwu Tianmeng Company, the operator of the Yixin'ou route. All goods imported by Mengde are transported via the Yixin'ou freight train, and Tianmeng provides us with preferential pricing. The selling price of the first return shipment of goods has been reduced by approximately 15% compared to before, thereby lowering the import costs of our products and enhancing Mengde's price advantage. For example, Spanish Castillod Clavijo Red Wine, which used to be priced at 188 yuan ($25.6)per bottle, can now be reduced to 150 yuan ($20) through railway transportation via the Yixin'ou route. Furthermore, in the past, red wine was mainly shipped by sea, taking at least 65 days to clear customs. Due to the rough sea journey, in order not to affect the taste, it generally needed to be stored for 2–6 months before it could be put on the market. Now, after clearing customs in Madrid, the red wine is sealed in containers. Since the products meet the legal requirements for the return journey, they are unlikely to be inspected upon opening the containers. They can be directly transported to Yiwu, and within one month, they can be on the market. The overall cost of the products has decreased by 15% to 20%. For example, Dinastla Vivanco red wine has decreased from 425 yuan ($58) to 320 yuan ($43.4), 750ml "Heinu" olive oil has decreased from 125 yuan ($17) to 99 yuan ($13.5), and sparkling water has decreased from 40 yuan ($5.4)to 26 yuan ($3.5).[16]

On a strategic level, the Yixin'ou route has become a powerful ambassador for Yiwu and serves as its distinctive symbol. The Yiwu to Madrid international freight train covers a total distance of 13,052 kilometers, passing through six countries: China (departing from Alashankou in Xinjiang), Kazakhstan, Russia, Belarus, Poland, Germany, and France, ultimately reaching Madrid, Spain. It is currently the world's longest railway freight route, crossing the most number of countries. This extensive

[16]Qi Dong. "What Has the Yixin'ou Freight Train Brought to Yiwu in Its Two Years of Operation," *Urban Express*, November 18, 2016, 13th Edition. You may also refer to: Yiping Gao. "After the Opening of Yixin'ou, 30% of Mengde's Export Business Shifting to Railway Transportation." Zhejiang Private Enterprises Website, April 24, 2015, http://www.zj123.com/info/detail-d304097.htm. Last accessed on April 12, 2017.

railway not only serves as a transport corridor for goods but also acts as a promotional ambassador for Yiwu. Leveraging the Yixin'ou railway, Yiwu not only markets its small commodities to countries along the Silk Road Economic Belt but also promotes the city itself globally, significantly enhancing Yiwu's reputation on a global scale. Furthermore, this route includes four stopover points for loading and unloading cargo in Warsaw, Poland, Berlin and Duisburg in Germany, and Paris, France. This further strengthens Yiwu's economic and trade cooperation with various European countries. Yiwu is now China's only city with direct freight lines to the Middle East. These routes, such as the Yiwu-Afghanistan and Yiwu-Iran lines, have enhanced China's ties with Middle Eastern countries. Officials from the Yiwu Land Port Affairs and Port Administration Bureau emphasized the significance of the Yixin'ou route:

> After the launch of the Yixin'ou route, Yiwu has established very high-frequency economic and cultural cooperation with countries along the route. Initiating projects in Spain, Belarus, Germany, and others is a direct result of the benefits brought about by the opening of these freight train services. These benefits are intangible and cannot be measured in terms of just thousands or millions of dollars. This includes our cooperation with the Barcelona Free Trade Zone, cooperation with Aragon, and the potential construction of a Spanish-style town in Yiwu—all of which are dividends brought about by the operation of the freight train services.

The Yiwu municipal government, driven by both market demand and strategic significance, shifted its focus toward enhancing the opening of the Yixin'ou route.[17] The transition from market-driven development to government-led growth significantly reduced the preparation time for launching these train routes. During the market-driven phase, it took three full years from the proposal to the launch of the Yiwu to Central Asia five-country freight railway, promoted by the Tianmeng Corporation. In

[17] On May 11, 2015, the publicly listed company Zhejiang China Commodity City Group Co., Ltd. issued an announcement titled "Commodity City: Letter of Intent for Cooperation." The announcement stated that Commodity City intended to increase its investment in Yiwu Tianmeng Industrial Investment Co., Ltd. through equity participation. The validity period of this letter of intent was one year. However, as of April 11, 2017, Commodity City had not reached a formal agreement on cooperation with Tianmeng. According to information gathered from interviews conducted by the research team, the Yiwu municipal government expressed its intention to assist Tianmeng Company in jointly developing freight train services through equity participation and increased capital investment.

contrast, the Yiwu to Madrid freight train service, after receiving personal attention from the Chinese president, went from planning to official operation in less than two months. In September 2014, President Xi Jinping discussed the opening of the Yiwu to Madrid freight train with the Spanish prime minister. In October, the secretary of the Yiwu Municipal Party Committee and the Spanish ambassador to China jointly promoted cooperation on the Yixin'ou China-Europe freight train. On November 18, the Yiwu to Madrid container freight train was officially launched. Concurrently, the local government undertook a series of initiatives to promote the Yixin'ou route, further increasing its visibility and helping it fulfill its role as a strategic component of the BRI. Within China, Yiwu Customs tailored a comprehensive support package for the Yixin'ou freight train services, including the specialized train brochures and targeted guidance to interested enterprises.[18] Internationally, Yiwu signed friendly city memorandums with the government of Fuente la Higuera in Spain and the Smarhon District of Minsk Oblast in Belarus. Agreements for strategic cooperation related to the Yixin'ou railway were signed with the government of Aragon Autonomous Community in Spain and the region of Smarhon in Belarus, jointly advancing the regular operations of the train routes. Additionally, Yiwu government strengthened cooperation with countries along the BRI route by hosting international forums and constructing international trading centers to promote the line. Since 2014, Yiwu has hosted various economic forums, including the "China-West Asia North Africa Development Vision Dialogue," "China-Central Asia Cooperation Forum," and the "New Silk Road Forum." The city has also undertaken the construction of the "China-ASEAN Commodity Trading Center," further enhancing the visibility of Yixin'ou route and Yiwu itself on the international stage.[19]

[18] Xin He. "First 'Yiwu to Madrid' Freight Train Reaches Spain," Official Website of the General Administration of Customs of the People's Republic of China, December 11, 2014, http://www.customs.gov.cn/publish/portal0/tab1/info726896.htm, last accessed on April 22, 2017.

[19] Lingling He, Zuohua Hu, "Observations on Yiwu's Proactive Integration into National Strategies for Transformation and Development," "China Yiwu" Government Official Website, February 8, 2015, http://www.yw.gov.cn/zfzx/ztbd/sdxqjs/201502/t20150206_674650.shtml. Last accessed on April 12, 2017.

You may also refer to: Mao Libo, "Yiwu: Toward Internationalization, Building a New Paradigm," Economic and Trade Practice, Issue 3, 2015.

During the market development phase, the Yixin'ou route, serving as a crucial logistics element in the establishment of an international trade and logistics hub, was predominantly influenced by market dynamics throughout its entire setup and operation. Tianmeng Company was the pioneer in recognizing the potential for an international freight railway linking Yiwu. After three years of dedicated efforts, they successfully inaugurated the Yiwu to Central Asia international freight railway. However, during the government-led development phase, the Yixin'ou route attained a strategic significance. It became a focal point in Yiwu's commitment to supporting the BRI. The government began to devote substantial attention to the railway project, supplanting private enterprises as the primary driving force behind its advancement. This shift resulted in rapid development, with the government actively facilitating the opening of eight new China-Europe freight train routes within a mere three-year span.

4.3 Government Support Across the Entire Industry Chain to Propel the Development of the "Yixin'ou" Route

During the government development phase, the Yiwu municipal government provided "full industry chain" policy support for the Yixin'ou route. When looking at the operation process of the China-Europe freight train from the perspective of the industry chain concept, the full industry chain of a China-Europe freight train route includes seven components: cargo consolidation, operation, operation platform, customs clearance, customs, border checkpoints, and inspection and quarantine bureaus, overseas transportation, overseas storage, and distribution. During the market phase, Tianmeng Company was solely responsible for various aspects of the route, from cargo consolidation and route operation to overseas storage and distribution, all of which were market-driven based on demand. However, as the railway gained strategic importance during the government-led development phase, the government began to participate comprehensively in various stages of the railway project, becoming a significant actor in driving its operation and development. During the cargo consolidation stage, although the sources of goods still came from local foreign trade companies or freight forwarding companies in Yiwu, the government provided source security for the railway's operation through means like financial subsidies. In the operational phase, facing competition from multiple China-Europe freight train routes domestically, the Yiwu municipal government leveraged the advantage of local small commodities to enhance the competitiveness. Additionally, they provided subsidies to Tianmeng Company in support of maintaining the railway's operation. In terms of constructing the operational platform, Yiwu strategically incorporated the development of a dedicated functional zone for the Yixin'ou route into the city's urban planning. They also shifted their focus away from constructing all-encompassing logistics platforms and instead prioritized the development of specialized logistics platforms. This approach led to the creation of specialized railway logistics zones tailored specifically to meet the transportation requirements of the Yixin'ou route.

4.3.1 Government Provides Source Security

Adequate cargo supply is essential to the operation of the Yixin'ou route. During interviews with relevant officials from the Yiwu Municipal Bureau of Land and Port Affairs, we learned that "as long as we can keep goods in Yiwu, the route will have something to transport." The operation of a China-Europe freight train is divided into outbound cargo (goods exported from China) and inbound cargo (goods imported to China from abroad). For Yiwu, the assurance of outbound cargo supply is rooted in its expansive small commodity market. The Yixin'ou freight train transports Chinese-manufactured small commodities to countries along the Silk Road Economic Belt. On the other hand, the guarantee of inbound cargo supply is facilitated by Zhejiang merchants located worldwide. They utilize the railway to transport items such as Spanish wine, olive oil, German milk powder, and more back to China. During the government-led development phase, the Yiwu municipal government, while upholding the existing market-based cargo consolidation, harnessed the influence of overseas Chinese entrepreneurs through reforms in export trade practices. This included providing customs clearance facilitation, government subsidies, and establishing overseas exchange foundations. These endeavors ensured a steady and abundant supply of cargo for the route and firmly established Yiwu as a pivotal source of goods along the BRI.

In the realm of export trade practice reforms, Yiwu took significant steps following its designation as an experimental city for international trade reform in 2011. The local government formulated a comprehensive reform plan aimed at promoting the Market Procurement Trade Mode. After three years of trials and promotional efforts, Yiwu officially and fully implemented this mode in November 2014. The Market Procurement Trade Mode represents a foreign trade approach that has emerged within the context of professional market internationalization. This mode entails eligible domestic and foreign enterprises and individuals purchasing goods within market aggregation areas duly recognized by relevant national authorities. Subsequently, these goods are declared for export through the customs authorities responsible for the main customs or port customs corresponding to these market areas.[20] Compared to other trade modes, the Mode is more suitable for the characteristics of Yiwu's small commodity industry, which is diverse, deals in a wide variety of products, operates in multiple batches, handles small quantities, and involves group shipments for export. It can be seen as an upgraded version of the existing tourist shopping trade mode. Currently, small commodity exports mainly rely on general trade or tourist shopping trade methods. For general trade, due to the wide variety of small commodities and the tendency to export them in group shipments, customs inspections are relatively slow and complex. Moreover, small commodities exported through general trade do not enjoy the preferential policies offered by the government for small commodity exports. The other option, exporting small commodities under the tourist shopping trade mode, does offer policy benefits and customs facilitation but has a limited single export quota. Each batch of goods cannot exceed $50,000. For a city like Yiwu, whose pillar industry is small commodity trade, this quota is insufficient to meet the daily demand for large-scale small commodity exports. The new market procurement trade mode introduced after the reform raised the maximum limit for the declared value of goods per shipment to $150,000. Additionally, it provided preferential policies such as value-added tax exemptions for goods exported under the mode. These changes encouraged more traders to choose Yiwu as a source for their exports, ensuring an abundant supply of goods for the Yixin'ou China-Europe freight train service.

In the development of the import market, on February 9, 2015, the Yiwu Municipal Committee issued the "Several Opinions on Accelerating Import Trade" (Yiwu Committee Document [2015] No. 5). It was outlined that by 2020 Yiwu aimed to become a leading gateway for global daily consumer goods entering China, a significant hub for the

[20] Zuohua Hu, Guowei Jiang. "Yiwu 'New Special Zone': China's Foreign Trade Transformation Is Timely," Xinhuanet.com, May 8, 2011, http://www.zj.xinhuanet.com/newscenter/2011-05/08/content_22709363.html, last accessed on April 12, 2017.

distribution of imported daily consumer goods nationwide, a crucial base for cross-border e-commerce imports, and achieve an import commodity sales volume of 100 billion yuan ($13.6 billion), forming a comprehensive trade pattern of "buying and selling global goods." On May 27, 2016, to further expand imports, optimize the trade structure, and promote industrial upgrading, the Yiwu Municipal People's Government Office issued the "Notice on the Ten Measures to Promote the Development of Import Trade (Trial Implementation)" (Yiwu Government Office [2016] No. 68). These measures included fostering and strengthening import entities, supporting marketing platform construction, improving public import services, expanding corporate financing channels, enhancing customs clearance services, improving inspection and quarantine efficiency, supporting the development of cross-border e-commerce, encouraging the introduction of foreign brands, supporting companies in participating in import exhibitions, and cultivating imported talent. These measures were designed to boost the development of the city's import market. Currently, Yiwu is in the process of establishing significant import platforms, such as the Silk Road New Area, Import Commodity Expo, and Import Commodity Pavilion, and expanding activities in cross-border e-commerce and import wholesale. It is also working on expanding international airports, the Yixin'ou route, sea-rail intermodal transportation, and bonded logistics centers as major import channels. Leveraging a global network of traders, a vast array of goods, and a conducive environment, Yiwu has the potential to become a key gateway for global daily consumer goods entering China. As cross-border e-commerce has emerged as a new format of "Internet + Foreign Trade," it has experienced rapid growth in recent years, with growth rates exceeding 30%. Compared to traditional foreign trade, cross-border e-commerce has shown remarkable potential. According to statistics from the Yiwu E-commerce Office, from January to October 2016, the local cross-border e-commerce transaction volume reached 55.66 billion yuan ($7.6 billion), marking a year-on-year increase of 15.7%. On May 31, 2016, the first shipment of cross-border e-commerce goods carried by the Yixin'ou freight train arrived at the China (Hangzhou) Cross-border E-commerce Comprehensive Pilot Zone Airport Park after undergoing secondary customs clearance. This marked the successful collaboration between the Yixin'ou China-Europe freight train and the cross-border e-commerce import model, ushering in the "Railway Era" for cross-border e-commerce.[21]

In terms of customs clearance facilitation, the Yiwu municipal government, through the signing of cooperation memorandums with Xinjiang ports, implemented a "one-time inspection" service for goods transported via the Yixin'ou route. This shifted the previous "inspection first, then customs declaration" model to a "customs-inspection collaboration, one-time clearance" model. The ease of customs clearance is a crucial factor influencing many businesses 'choice of using the Yixin'ou route as a transportation method. The Chief Procurement Representative of Spain's Amate Company once stated, "As long as customs clearance is convenient, we will definitely choose railway transportation for exporting goods."[22] To facilitate this, in 2014, Yiwu signed memorandums of cooperation with Urumqi Customs, including the "Local Declaration and Port Inspection and Release" memorandum with Hangzhou Customs and the "Enhanced Coordination Measures for Railway Transfer Cargo Supervision" with Alashankou Customs. These agreements collectively created an effective and smooth customs environment. In accordance with the characteristics of local small commodity exports, a "one-time inspection" policy was implemented for Yiwu's railway-transferred small commodities for export. Port customs provided priority services to Yixin'ou freight trains in international railway transshipment and customs clearance procedures, creating a streamlined "green channel" for swift clearance at the port. With the adoption of the new operational model, the previous sequential customs clearance process, involving inspection before customs declaration, transitioned into a parallel model where both inspection and customs declaration occur simultaneously. This transformation significantly reduced the waiting and processing time between inspection and customs declaration. It is estimated that the "one-time declaration" policy can save more than 30% of the time typically spent on inspection and customs declaration operations.[23] Government-led customs clearance facilitation has motivated

[21] Guojin Chen, Bo Zheng, "Successful Collaboration Between Yixin'ou route and Cross-Border E-commerce for the First Time," Official Website of the General Administration of Customs of the People's Republic of China, June 2016, http://www.customs.gov.cn/publish/portal0/ta65602/info802141htm, last accessed on April 12, 2017.

[22] Hongsheng Chen, Chenlu Zhang, "The New Silk Road Opens a New Journey of Trade between China and Europe," *Yiwu Business Daily*, 16 December 2014, p.1.

[23] Yue Guan. "New Customs Clearance Model in Guangdong Achieves Declaration, Inspection, and Release in One Step," Guangzhou Customs Official Website, May 24, 2012,

a growing number of traders to opt for Yiwu as their preferred customs clearance location and to choose Yixin'ou freight trains as their primary goods transportation channel.

The Yiwu municipal government provided subsidies to the operating company, Tianmeng Company, to facilitate their regular operations and offered financial incentives to businesses that chose international freight railway transportation, aiming to attract more cargo sources. When it was launched, the Yixin'ou route faced competition from other modes of transportation such as maritime and air transport, as well as competition from other China-Europe freight train routes such as "Chongqing-Xinjiang-Europe," "Chengdu-Europe," "Wuhan-Europe," and "Zhengzhou-Xinjiang-Europe." To attract more business and cargo sources, the Yiwu government provided a subsidy of 3.6 million yuan ($0.5 million) to the Tianmeng Company, ensuring that the Yixin'ou container train route could offer rates comparable to regular freight rail transport.[24] In addition to that, the Yiwu municipal government also provided financial subsidies to the carriers engaged in international freight transport via the Yixin'ou route based on the actual number of loaded containers arriving and departing from the west railway station. For containers destined for the Asian region, the subsidy standard was 1620 yuan ($221) per standard container (equivalent to two 20-foot containers), and the subsidy amount was calculated as the carrier's actual completed container volume (standard containers) for that year multiplied by 1620 yuan ($221). For containers destined for the European region, the subsidy standard was 3240 yuan ($443) per standard container (equivalent to two 20-foot containers), and the subsidy amount was calculated as the carrier's actual completed container volume (standard containers) for that year multiplied by 3240 yuan ($443).[25]

http://guangzhou.customs.gov.cn/publish/portal31/tab560/module24791/info371921.htm, Last accessed on March 28, 2017. Also refer to Hong Xinian, He Jianya. "Yiwu Customs: Innovative Services Supporting 'Yixin'ou'," China Yiwu Government Portal, November 19, 2014.

[24] Jianli Yao and Yiyi Zhu. "Yiwu Direct to Madrid: The Normalization of the Yixin'ou Freight Train," *21st Century Economic Report*, May 20, 2015, 5th Edition.

[25] Yiwu municipal government: "Several Opinions of Yiwu Municipal People's Government on Accelerating the Development of Modern Logistics Industry," Government of Yiwu, China, May 4, 2014, http://www.yw.gov.cn/smyg/tz/zsyz/zszc/201504/t20150413_699545.shtml, last accessed on April 21, 2017.

In terms of international engagement, the Yiwu municipal government has harnessed the strength of overseas Chinese entrepreneurs by establishing overseas foundations to ensure a stable supply of goods for the route. One of the major distinctions between the route and other domestic freight train routes lies in the type of goods transported. While routes like "Chongqing-Xinjiang-Europe," "Chengdu-Europe," and "Wuhan-Europe" primarily transport electronic products produced by multinational companies in China, the Yixin'ou route sources a variety of small commodities manufactured in China, including textiles such as socks, scarves, and leggings. As the world's largest distribution center for small commodities, Yiwu not only exports a significant volume of locally produced goods to over 200 countries and regions worldwide but also serves as a transshipment point for goods from neighboring countries like India. The bulk of this market demand comes from overseas Zhejiang merchants. Yiwu is one of the most economically outward-oriented cities in China, with more than 10,000 foreign businessmen from over 100 countries and regions residing in the city. Especially in Europe, Spain hosts a significant number of Zhejiang entrepreneurs. According to statistics, there are over 100,000 Qingtian people from Zhejiang in Spain, most of whom engage in international trade. Furthermore, 80% of their merchandise is sourced from Yiwu. This underscores the importance of rallying overseas Chinese business forces as a vital source of supply for the Yixin'ou railway transport. On March 15, 2016, the Yiwu-Spain Exchange Foundation was formally established under the guidance of the Yiwu municipal government. Its primary role is to serve as the representative of the Yiwu government, facilitating extensive exchanges and cooperation between Yiwu and Spain. Additionally, it works to harness the collective efforts of overseas Chinese entrepreneurs, further enhancing the development of the Yixin'ou route.

During the construction phase, whether it's the reform of trade methods, the development of import markets, the promotion of customs facilitation, the implementation of fiscal subsidies, or the establishment of overseas foundations, a central goal of these measures by the Yiwu municipal government is to provide ample supply guarantees for the route and maintain the stable operation of the railway line.

4.3.2 *Government Drives Specialized Railway Logistics Operation Platform Construction*

Throughout its history, the logistics industry has been a key development focus for the Yiwu municipal government, with logistics operation platforms serving as hubs for industrial resources. During the market development phase, the Yiwu municipal government placed a greater emphasis on creating comprehensive logistics platforms, particularly focusing on three transportation modes: aviation, road, and maritime. This emphasis was since, during this phase, the Yixin'ou freight railway primarily served as a complementary support industry for the development of Yiwu's small commodity market. However, with the introduction of the BRI, the Yixin'ou railway route was endowed with strategic significance. Consequently, the Yiwu municipal government began to focus on building a specialized international freight railway operation platform. Firstly, there was a specialized reform of the state-owned enterprises responsible for platform operation, shifting from the original "1+4" model to a "1+8" model. This involved restructuring the existing comprehensive transportation development limited liability company and establishing a specialized logistics platform operation company, known as the Land-Port Group, which was responsible for the operation of major logistics and bonded zones in Yiwu. Secondly, in terms of logistics platform construction, the focus shifted from comprehensive logistics platform development to the establishment of a specialized railway logistics platform, including the setting up of railway customs supervision facilities to support the operation of the Yixin'ou route.

In December 2013, the Yiwu municipal government introduced the "Opinions on Deepening Government Investment and Financing System Reform and State-owned Enterprise Management System Reform" (referred to as the "Opinions" below). The "Opinions" outlined the adjustment of the structural layout of Yiwu's existing local state-owned enterprises, shifting from the original "1+4" model to a "1+8" model. Under the original "1+4" model, the "1" referred to the State-owned Assets Supervision and Administration Commission, and the "4" referred to state-owned Assets Operation Limited Liability Company, Yiwu Small Commodity City Hengda Development Limited Liability Company, Yiwu City Transportation Development Limited Liability Company, and Yiwu City Public Utilities Limited Liability Company. Among these, the Yiwu City Transportation Development Limited Liability Company had comprehensive responsibility for the city's logistics, passenger transport, road construction, and airport management. After the reform, Yiwu City adopted a new layout for state-owned assets and enterprises known as "One Center, Eight Groups." The "One Center" referred to the Yiwu state-owned capital operation center, serving as the centralized and unified investment and financing platform for city-owned enterprises, providing financing and fund management services to city-owned enterprise groups. The "Eight Groups" consisted of Yiwu City Urban Investment Construction Group Co., Ltd., Yiwu City Transportation Investment Construction Group Co., Ltd., Yiwu City Urban and Rural New Community Investment Construction Group Co., Ltd., Yiwu City International Land Port Group Co., Ltd., Yiwu City Market Development Group Co., Ltd., Yiwu City Water Construction Group Co., Ltd., Zhejiang China Small Commodities City Group Co., Ltd., and Zhejiang Hopeful Group Co., Ltd. The transition from the original four major groups to eight major groups allowed for a more detailed allocation of functions among Yiwu's state-owned enterprises. The newly established Land Port Group, which resulted from the restructuring of the Yiwu City Transportation Development Limited Liability Company, specialized in the operation and management of major logistics platforms in Yiwu. Other functions such as passenger transport and road construction were undertaken by other specialized state-owned enterprises. This new layout of state-owned assets and enterprises was more conducive to improving the government's investment and financing system. On the one hand, specialized roles facilitated the dedicated use of funds and the establishment of state-owned enterprise project ownership, promoting specialized centralized construction and delegated construction. On the other hand, leveraging the corporate functions of state-owned enterprises activated and expanded investment efforts, utilized financial leverage, diversified financing for public projects, and provided more specialized logistical resources for the Yixin'ou freight train service.

During the government construction phase to support the development of the Yixin'ou route, the Yiwu municipal government, through the Land Port Group, made significant efforts to establish two specialized logistics platforms with distinct functions. Firstly, concerning imports, Yiwu established a bonded logistics center to ensure that return cargo could directly enter the bonded zone. This provided policy convenience for the import of return cargo. Secondly, regarding exports, Yiwu activated new railway customs supervision facilities and concurrently established a railway logistics center. These initiatives ensured the smooth export of goods from the China-Europe freight trains on their outbound journeys. These measures were implemented to support the efficient operation and development of the Yixin'ou route.

On January 29, 2014, the General Administration of Customs, the Ministry of Finance, the State Taxation Administration, and the State Administration of Foreign Exchange jointly issued a document approving the establishment of the Yiwu Bonded Logistics Center (Type B). On November 18, 2014, the Yiwu Bonded Logistics Center officially commenced operations, becoming the third in Zhejiang Province and the only one in the central and western regions of Zhejiang. Prior to the establishment of the bonded logistics center, imported goods had to go through customs clearance and tax payment procedures before entering Yiwu. With the completion of the bonded logistics center, goods imported to Yiwu could be distributed and reported collectively, meaning they could be sold first, and the declaration process could be centralized afterward. This significantly reduced the time required for importing goods. In the context of importing return cargo via the Yixin'ou route, Yiwu Customs actively supported the storage of return cargo in the Yiwu Bonded Logistics Center. By making full use of the functions such as in-bond warehousing, tax deferment, and customs cooperation, the center provided hardware support for the development of import trade in the inland regions using the Yixin'ou China-Europe freight trains. This played a crucial role in creating the necessary conditions for the normalized development of import trade in Yiwu.[26]

At the same time, the Yiwu municipal government organized the construction of a new railway port customs supervision site operated by the Land Port Group. During the market development phase, as Tianmeng Company was the first to organize the development of the China-Europe freight train service, the railway customs supervision site had been operated by Tianmeng Company. On November 16, 2016, the new Yiwu railway port customs supervision site, led by the Yiwu municipal government, was officially put into use. The operation of this newly inaugurated site was no longer handled by Tianmeng Company but was transferred to the

[26] Lingling He, Zuohua Hu. "Observations on Yiwu's Proactive Integration into National Strategies for Transformation and Development," Government of Yiwu, China, February 8, 2015, http://www.yw.gov.cn/zfzx/ztbd/sdxqjs/201502/t20150206_674650.shtml. Last accessed on April 12, 2017.

state-owned enterprise, the Land Port Group. The new customs supervision area covered an area of over 70,000 square meters, more than three times larger than the old site, and the number of customs inspection platforms increased from the original 5 to 13. This expansion significantly improved overall logistics efficiency. Yiwu Customs established dedicated service windows for the Yixin'ou route at both the railway customs supervision site and the Yiwu Port, implementing a "24/7" appointment-based customs clearance mode. On March 11, 2015, the Yiwu municipal government also signed a strategic cooperation agreement with the Shanghai Railway Bureau to jointly promote the construction of the Yiwu West Railway Logistics Center. This project had a construction scale of 1,344.54 acres and included the construction of a railway port to complement the road network-based logistics center, fulfilling functions such as international container dispatch transportation, railway international intermodal transportation, and sea-rail intermodal transportation.[27]

During the government construction phase, the Yiwu municipal government, through the Land Port Group, provided specialized logistics support services for the operation of the Yixin'ou railway.

4.3.3 Government Cultivates Strategically Functional Urban Area

During the government construction phase, the Yixin'ou route, serving as a crucial component of Yiwu's alignment with the national BRI, saw significant development. The Yiwu municipal government played a pivotal role not only in establishing a specialized logistics platform and providing supporting services for the railway's operation but also in strategically planning and constructing three major functional zones within the city to align with the national-level BRI.

In August 2014, Yiwu City issued the "Decision of the Yiwu Municipal Committee of the Communist Party of China on Accelerating the Promotion of Urban Transformation and Development." This decision outlined the future urban development plan for Yiwu, which focuses on the concept of "One Core and Three Zones." Building upon the existing central urban area, the plan includes the development of three new areas:

[27] Shuangshuang Li. "Sheng Qiuping Attends the Signing Ceremony of Cooperation for the Construction of Yiwu West Railway Logistics Center," Yiwu Business News, March 12, 2015, 1st Edition.

the Silk Road New Zone, the Land Port New Zone, and the Science and Innovation New Zone. The Silk Road New Zone, located in the northeastern part, capitalizes on advantages related to global trade and international services. It leverages the concentration of people, information, and capital flows, along with a relatively well-developed commercial network. This zone integrates and enhances functions such as the International Trade City, the Financial Business District, the International Cultural Center, and the Exhibition Center. It also focuses on hosting projects related to the BRI, trade transformation and upgrading, and foreign investment services. The Land Port New Zone, situated in the western part, revolves around the facilitation of logistics and port functions. Leveraging transportation advantages like airports, railways, and highways, it centralizes the development of domestic logistics, intelligent warehousing, express logistics, railway logistics, airport logistics, and comprehensive bonded areas. The Science and Innovation New Zone, located in the northern part, emphasizes talent aggregation and innovation-driven development. It capitalizes on the convenient transportation hub provided by high-speed railways and the city's beautiful ecological environment. This zone hosts functions related to higher education, technological research and development, innovative design, innovation services, and technology incubation.[28]

In this phase, Yiwu utilized the development of its three major strategic functional zones to leverage its strategic role in the BRI. Taking advantage of the development of the Yixin'ou China-Europe freight trains, Yiwu aimed to establish a national-level platform for the route. Starting with the Silk Road New Zone, Yiwu sought to connect with initiatives such as the Silk Road Fund, the Asian Infrastructure Investment Bank, the China-Latin America Cooperation Forum, and the Shanghai Cooperation Organization. The city hosted international events like the Silk Road Economic Belt Cities Forum, the China-Japan-Korea Sister Cities Exchange Conference, and the China-Africa Civil Forum. These efforts aimed to strengthen communication and exchanges between Yiwu and countries along the BRI route. In the Land Port New Zone, Yiwu promoted the construction of railway logistics centers and comprehensive

[28]Yiwu municipal government. "Decision of the Yiwu Municipal Committee of the Communist Party of China on Accelerating Urban Transformation and Development." 'China Yiwu Government Portal, September 10, 2014, http://hzjdyw.gov.cn/zcfg/201409/t20140910_591262.html, Last accessed on April 21, 2017.

transportation hubs. It also worked to secure temporary openings of railway ports and sought approval for importing goods like meat and complete vehicles through these ports.[29]

4.4 Conclusion

Yixin'ou route has undergone a shift from market-based development to government-led construction, driven by a change in Yiwu's development strategy. After the 2008 financial crisis, Yiwu aimed to become an international trade and commerce hub. To mitigate the impact of the crisis on its export industry, Yiwu adopted a market positioning of "buying globally and selling globally," focusing on both domestic and international markets. It developed three trade modes: export, import, and reexport, with international railway transport serving as a logistics carrier to facilitate the integration of these three modes. Similar to other logistics modes like maritime and air transport, market demand became the main driving force behind the development of international freight train services. Consolidation, route operations, customs clearance, and overseas distribution were market controlled, allowing companies to operate independently. Therefore, during this period, Yiwu-Europe freight trains mainly operated in a scattered transit mode, with irregular schedules and limited route coverage.

After China proposed the BRI in September and October of 2013, the market-driven Yixin'ou route model began to undergo transformation. Under this new strategy, Yiwu set its sights on becoming a pivotal city in the construction of the BRI, seeking land connections to the west and maritime routes to the east. During this period, the Yixin'ou route emerged as a strategic focal point for Yiwu's alignment with the "Silk Road Economic Belt," and the government assumed a pivotal role in orchestrating its development. The Yiwu municipal government effectively utilized government policy regulation to allocate resources across the entire industry chain for the development of the Yixin'ou route. Initially, the government assumed the role of primary planners for the route, replacing private enterprises. Secondly, they provided essential market support in the form of financial subsidies. Lastly, they harnessed

[29] Yiwu municipal government. "Yiwu Government Work Report for the Year 2015," Government of Yiwu, China, February 1, 2015, http://www.yw.gov.cn/zfmhw-zxxgk/001/05/02/201502/t20150202_671480.shtml. Last accessed on April 21, 2017.

state-owned enterprises to establish a specialized operational platform for the railway. Under the government's guidance, Yiwu successfully launched eight China-Europe freight train routes within just four years. These routes expanded their operations to multiple countries in Central Asia, Europe, and the Middle East, with three of them achieving regular, consistent operations.

References

Guojin Chen, Bo Zheng. "The First Successful Collaboration between 'Yiwu to Europe' and Cross-Border E-Commerce," General Administration of Customs of the People's Republic of China Official Website, June 2016, Link, accessed on April 12, 2017.

Hongsheng Chen, Chenlu Zhang. "New Silk Road Opens a New Journey for China-Europe Trade," *Yiwu Business Daily*, December 16, 2014, p1.

Qi Dong. "Two Years After Opening: What Yiwu to Europe Railway Has Brought to Yiwu," *Metropolitan Express*, November 18, 2016, p13.

Xiangyang Fang, Chunqiu Lou, "Yiwu's Comprehensive Construction of an International Trade and Business City - Starting a New Round of Transformation and Development with 'Three Centers and Two High Grounds,'" *Jinhua Daily*, July 23, 2008, p1.

Yiping Gao. "After Two Years of Operation, 30% of Mengde's Export Business Has Shifted to Railway Transport." Zhejiang Private Enterprises Network, April 24, 2015, Link, accessed on April 12, 2017.

Yue Guan. "Guangdong's New Customs Clearance Model: Declaring, Inspecting, and Releasing in One Go." Guangzhou Customs Official Website, May 24, 2012, Link, accessed on March 28, 2017.

Zuohua Hu, Guocheng Jiang. "Yiwu's 'New Special Zone': China's Foreign Trade Transformation Is Just Right." Xinhuanet, May 8, 2011, Link, accessed on April 12, 2017.

Jianya He."Yiwu Customs: Innovative Services to Support 'Yiwu to Europe.'" Government Portal of Yiwu, November 19, 2014a, Link, accessed on March 28, 2017.

Lingling He, Zuohua Hu. "Yiwu Actively Integrates into National Strategies to Promote Transformation and Development." Government Portal of Yiwu, February 8, 2015, Link, accessed on April 12, 2017.

Xin He. "First 'Yiwu to Madrid' Train Arrives in Spain," General Administration of Customs of the People's Republic of China Official Website, December 11, 2014b, Link, accessed on April 22, 2017.

Zongzhi Huang. "After the Opening of China-Europe Trains and Central Asian Trains, the Latest Silk Road Train Arrives in Tehran," *People's Daily* (Overseas Edition), February 19, 2016, 1st Edition.

Shuangshuang Li. "Sheng Qiuping Attends the Signing Ceremony for the Construction of Yiwu West Railway Logistics Center." *Yiwu Business Daily*, March 12, 2015, p1.

Libo Mao. "Yiwu: Towards Internationalization, Building a New Paradigm," *Economic and Trade Practice*, No.3, 2015.

Xuqian Mao. "The First 'Yiwu to London' China-Europe Railway Express Departs on New Year's Day," Government Portal of Yiwu, December 23, 2016, Link, accessed on April 10, 2017.

Xiao'en Xu. "Yiwu Sets off on a New Silk Road, Opening an International Container Special Train to Five Central Asian Countries," *Zhejiang Daily*, January 21, 2014, 3rd Editon.

Jianli Yao, Yiyi Zhu. "Direct Yiwu to Madrid: 'Yiwu to Europe' Railway Becomes Regular." *21st Century Business Herald*, May 20, 2015, 5th Edition.

Yuhuan Zhang. "Yiwu in Zhejiang Seizes the Opportunity to be at the Forefront of the Belt and Road Initiative." China News Network, March 24, 2017, Link, accessed on April 29, 2017.

Wei Zhang. "Feng Xubin: The Operator of Yiwu to Europe," *Decision Magazine*, No. 1, 2016.

Kai Xu, Jianya He, Hongcan Shi. "New Policy for Railway Customs Clearance Reduces Freight Time by Half," *Hangzhou Daily*, November 18, 2013, 1st Edition.

CHAPTER 5

China-Europe Railway Express (Chengdu): Changes in the Operation Mechanism of the "Rong'ou+" Freight Trains

Lihua Wang

The "Rong'ou" freight trains went through a transition from being privately operated to state owned. In 2013, at its inception, the "Rong'ou" were operated by the Sino-foreign joint venture company Chengdu Eurasia Rail Logistics Co., Ltd., which was responsible for providing end-to-end logistics services following a market-oriented model. This joint venture company was formed through voluntary contributions from Poland's HATRANS Logistics Ltd., Jiangsu Feiliks International Logistics Inc., and Shenzhen YH Global Logistics Co., Ltd. It integrated the respective strengths of domestic and international partners and was responsible for services such as sourcing, warehousing, and transportation. Starting from April 1, 2016, "Rong'ou" was operated and managed by Chengdu International Railway Service Co., Ltd, a wholly owned subsidiary of Chengdu International Railway Port Investment and Development

L. Wang (✉)
Center on China High-Speed Rail Development Strategy Research, Southwest Jiaotong University, Chengdu, China
e-mail: bai.gao@duke.edu

B. Gao, Z. Zhen (eds.), *The China-Europe Railway Express*, China and Globalization 2.0,
https://doi.org/10.1007/978-981-19-2882-6_5

(Group) Co., Ltd., which, in turn, is a subsidiary of Chengdu Industrial Investment Group Co., Ltd. The factors that led to this change are worth exploring and discussing. This chapter asserts that the transformation of the "Rong'ou"'s operational mechanism is a result of ongoing reconciliation between national strategies and the economic development planning of the Chengdu municipal government. Among these factors, a crucial element influencing the change in its operational mechanism is the shift in Chengdu's urban positioning. In the "12th Five-Year Plan" for Chengdu, the municipal government's urban positioning was defined as the central city in the western region. In this context, despite the government's response to the Belt and Road Initiative (BRI) by establishing the "Rong'ou" freight train service, its precise role was unclear, and the management was not given high priority. It was managed through a joint venture company from a market-oriented perspective. Moreover, the market-oriented operation requires a solid industrial foundation, effective policy guidance, and financial support. Compared to the "Yuxin'ou" (Chongqing-Xinjiang-Europe) route, the "Rong'ou" started with a weaker foundation, lacking the necessary conditions for market-oriented operation, which made its operation exceptionally challenging. After Chengdu formulated its "13th Five-Year Plan," it specifically proposed to develop Chengdu as a "national central city." In this context, the government recognized the crucial role played by the "Rong'ou" route in driving the city's development. The train service underwent repositioning, driven by the recognition that aligning the development of the "Rong'ou" with the city's strategic positioning required harnessing the government's predominant role in its operation and transitioning its operational model from private to state owned. This chapter attempts to explain the changes in Chengdu's positioning and the impact on the operation mechanism of the "Rong'ou" train service under different national strategies at different times.

5.1 Changes in the Operational Mechanism of the "Rong'ou" Freight Train

In recent years, the development of China-Europe Railway Express has experienced rapid growth, yielding remarkable results. The number of routes has expanded, and one such route is "Rong'ou." Originating from Chengdu, it traverses the Alashankou border, spans various countries, including Russia and Belarus, before reaching its destination in Łódź, Poland. The total length of this route is 9826 kilometers, with 3511 kilometers from Chengdu to Alashankou and 6315 kilometers from Alashankou to Łódź. On April 26, 2013, the train commenced operations, and its transit time has gradually decreased from 15 days to 11 days, making it the fastest-running China-Europe express train currently in operation. For information on the operating mileage and source locations of various routes, please refer to Table 5.1.

However, the China-Europe Railway Express experienced an evolving process in its formation and operation as a relatively new initiative under the backdrop of the BRI. The operation mechanism of the "Rong'ou" differs from other China-Europe railways, and it underwent a transition

Table 5.1 Statistics on the running mileage and source locations of China-Europe Railway Express

Name	*Inauguration date*	*Route*	*Operating distance*	*Travel time*	*Major source locations*
Rong'ou	April 26, 2013	Chengdu–Baoji–Lanzhou–Łódź	9826 kilometers	11 days	Southwest China, East China, South China
Suman'ou	September 30, 2013	Suzhou–Manzhouli–Warsaw	11,200 kilometers	12 days, once a week	East China
Yuxin'ou	March 19, 2013	Chongqing–Xi'an–Duisburg	111,79 kilometers	13 days, three times a week	HP, Acer, ASUS, Foxconn
Hanxin'ou	April 25, 2014	Wuhan–Xi'an–Duisburg	10,963 kilometers	15 days, 1 to 2 trips per month	Central China, Southwest, South China
Yuxin'ou	November 22, 2013	Guangzhou–Xinjiang–Russia	20,000 千米 20,000 kilometers	15 days, twice a week	Pearl River Delta
Zhengxin'ou	July 28, 2013	Zhengzhou–Xi'an–Hamburg	10,214 kilometers	Twice a week	North China

Source: Compiled from the article "Analysis of Indicators for Land Bridge Transport in 2016 and Related Data on China-Europe Railway Express and Forecast for the Development of China-Europe and China-Central Asia Railway Express in 2017" by Wang Dezhan (*New Silk Road Horizon*, No.2. 2017)

from being privately operated to state owned. In its initial stages, in 2013, the "Rong'ou" was operated by private companies such as HATRANS Logistics Ltd in Poland, Jiangsu Feiliks International Logistics Inc., and Shenzhen YH Global Logistics Co., Ltd. However, starting from early 2016, a state-owned company established by the Chengdu Industrial Investment Group Co., Ltd. took over its management. At different stages, the "Rong'ou" adopted various operational models, with governments and businesses playing different roles in its operation. The modifications to its operational mechanism can be broadly categorized into two phases based on the varying operators involved.

The first phase spanned from April 26, 2013, to March 31, 2016. During this period, the "Rong'ou" operated under a "Government Guidance – Private Enterprise Operation" model. According to research conducted by the Chengdu Municipal Logistics Office, the establishment of the "Rong'ou" was modeled after the "Yuxin'ou," employing a "Government Guidance – Enterprise Management" operational mechanism. However, the two differed slightly in their operational structure, with the former being managed by a joint venture company and the latter by a state-owned enterprise. The Chengdu municipal government allowed private enterprises to operate with the aim of maximizing the market-oriented operation of the "Rong'ou," leveraging market mechanisms to facilitate its rapid development. In this context, the government and the Chengdu Eurasia Rail Logistics Co., Ltd. clearly delineated their roles. The government was responsible for policy guidance and platform construction, while the Chengdu Eurasia Rail Logistics Co., Ltd. handled the day-to-day operations of the railway. They attempted to implement market-oriented management in terms of the source of goods, warehousing, and transportation.

The Chengdu municipal government plays a leading role in the operation of the "Rong'ou" railway. This includes aspects such as the formation, improvement of the operating environment, and coordination of external relationships. Specific units under the government, including the Chengdu Municipal Commission of Commerce, Chengdu Logistics Office, and the Qingbaijiang District People's Government, provide services for the operation. In addition, Chengdu Customs plays a crucial role in facilitating the customs clearance of goods in the process.

The Chengdu municipal government orchestrated a range of activities to establish a platform for the development of the "Rong'ou" railway. On October 25, 2014, during the 15th Western China International Fair

(WCIF), the Chengdu Municipal People's Government hosted the "Silk Road Rong'ou – Success Worldwide" event, also known as the "2014 China-Europe Railway Express (Chengdu) and Chengdu Railway Port Promotion Conference" at the banquet hall on the fifth floor of Chengdu New Convention and Exhibition Center. Around 300 participants attended this event, including consuls from foreign consulates in Chengdu, representatives from domestic and foreign business associations in Chengdu, leaders of central government units based in Chengdu, delegates from various provinces, autonomous regions, municipalities directly under the central government participating in the WCIF, as well as leaders from well-known domestic and international logistics companies, foreign trade manufacturers, and freight forwarding companies. During the conference, participants collaborated on the strategic utilization of the China-Europe Railway Express (Chengdu) and strengthened communication and exchange between foreign trade companies, manufacturing enterprises, international freight forwarders, and railway companies, utilizing the international platform of the China Western International Fair.[1]

To address the issue of "grouping cargo difficulty" for the "Roug'ou" route, the Chengdu municipal government has strengthened economic cooperation with other regional core cities through its intermediary role, creating a favorable economic environment for the operation of the train. In 2014, Chengdu signed framework agreements with Kunming and Guiyang, respectively, titled "Cooperation Agreement between the Chengdu Municipal People's Government and the Kunming Municipal People's Government Using the China-Europe Railway Express (Chengdu)" and "Cooperation Agreement between the Chengdu Municipal People's Government and the Guiyang Municipal People's Government Using the China-Europe Railway Express (Chengdu)." These agreements leverage the strengths of each city to jointly use the China-Europe Railway Express (Chengdu) and extend the route to Kunming and Guiyang. This initiative aims to promote economic and

[1] At the promotion conference, Chen Zhongwei, director of Chengdu Municipal Logistics Office, representing the Chengdu municipal government, delivered a special presentation on the China-Europe Railway Express (Chengdu). Fu Xuekun, deputy secretary of the Qingbaijiang District Committee, provided an overview of the logistics park and railway port construction and operation. Mr. Tomasz Grzelak, chairman of the China Europe Railway Express (Chengdu) Co. Ltd., promoted and recommended the train service. Representatives from major customers of the train service, such as DHL and DELL, were also present at the meeting and gave speeches.

trade exchanges between the western regions of China and various European countries, facilitating the shared development of Chengdu, Kunming, and Guiyang In addition to these efforts, the Chengdu Municipal Logistics Office also signed a "Chengdu-Shenzhen Railway Express Cooperation Framework Agreement" with China Logistics Group Co., Ltd. This agreement aims to attract cargo from the Pearl River Delta region to utilize the China-Europe Railway Express (Chengdu) for transportation via the China-Europe railway freight corridor to and from Europe, thereby enhancing its overall competitiveness.

The Chengdu Municipal Commission of Commerce spearheads the development of the "Rong'ou" platform, focusing on accelerating the completion of the Qingbaijiang Container Center Station and broadening international market presence. In 2014, the Qingbaijiang Railway Container Center Station, facilitated by the Chengdu Municipal Commerce Commission, was granted provisional approval as an external open port and a designated port for meat imports. In the realm of global market expansion, notable strides have been made in constructing the "Imported Food Trading Center" within the Chengdu Comprehensive Bonded Zone. The operational trial phase of the "International Commodity Exhibition Center" is already underway. The Chengdu Municipal Commission of Commerce has orchestrated a series of promotional initiatives for the China-Europe Railway Express (Chengdu), vigorously expanding both domestic and international markets. These efforts have significantly bolstered the momentum of open economic development. In 2015, the Chengdu Municipal Commission of Commerce strategically prioritized the "port economy" as a pivotal focus in Chengdu's foreign trade endeavors. Their annual objectives for that year specifically emphasized the imperative to robustly develop port and hub economies. This included supporting the return transportation business of the "China-Europe Railway Express" and "China-Asia Railway Express" dual golden channels, expanding imports, actively pursuing recognition as a "port of entry for complete vehicle imports," "designated fruit import port," and "designated meat import port." Additionally, efforts were intensified to fortify the functions of port services, marking a decisive step toward the city's economic advancement.

To offer precise policy direction for the "Rong'ou" railway project, the Chengdu municipal government has entrusted the Chengdu Port and Logistics Office with direct coordination responsibilities. This office is mandated with crafting strategic development blueprints and establishing essential platforms for the route's advancement. Originating in 2003, this office emerged from the government's initial Logistics Office. Its fundamental objective was to cater to the external connectivity requirements vital for the economic progress of Sichuan Province. It was also charged with setting up essential logistics infrastructure to enhance investment allure. In 2005, it was placed under the purview of the Transport Commission. Taking a strategic approach, it was mandated with forging a comprehensive logistics system, creating specialized port divisions to bolster port construction, thereby ensuring the harmonious growth of both ports and logistics. In response to the BRI in 2012, the planning for the "Rong'ou" project commenced. To optimize its governmental functions, align with the BRI objectives, and expedite the route's development, the Chengdu Port and Logistics Office underwent internal restructuring. This restructuring resulted in the establishment of five specialized divisions, each meticulously allocated specific functions concerning planning, policies, and industrial development. The distinct roles of each division are outlined in Table 5.2 for clear delineation.

From the departmental structure of the Chengdu Port and Logistics Office, the responsibilities of each department are quite clear. The Planning and Policy Division is primarily responsible for the development planning and policy formulation related to ports and logistics. The Port and Civil Aviation Division mainly focuses on port construction, while the Industrial Development Division primarily handles logistics industry development. The Multimodal Transportation Division is mainly responsible for building the multimodal transportation system.

The simplification of customs procedures and protective measures for the "Rong'ou" is managed by the Chengdu Customs. Throughout the operation, Chengdu Customs actively coordinates with ports to implement a convenient customs transit mode. When the train arrives at the Alashankou Customs, goods can be inspected without the need for further transit, saving at least two days in customs clearance time for businesses. Additionally, Electronic Data Interchange (EDI) transmission[2] is used

[2] The term EDI stands for Electronic Data Interchange, which is a standardized data format internationally recognized. It is used for structuring transactional messages related to various industries, including trade, transportation, insurance, banking, and customs. These structured data messages are transmitted through computer communication networks, facilitating data exchange and processing among different departments, companies, and enterprises. This process enables the seamless execution of various business operations centered around trade.

Table 5.2 Functional departments and responsibilities of the Chengdu Port and Logistics Office

Functional departments	*Responsibilities*
Comprehensive Affairs Division	Responsible for the daily operation of government agencies, handling tasks such as goal setting, document management, conference management, confidential communications, and record-keeping. They are also responsible for tasks related to information management, security, confidentiality, public petitions, government transparency, logistics, and fixed asset management. This department oversees organizing government agency structures, human resource management, and the administration of retirees. Additionally, they handle suggestions from members of the local National People's Congress and proposals from members of the local Chinese People's Political Consultative Conference.
Planning and Policy Division	Responsible for formulating the development strategies, medium to long-term development plans, and policy measures for the logistics industry and port construction throughout the city. They analyze and research major issues related to logistics industry development and provide recommendations. Additionally, they take the lead in regional logistics cooperation efforts. This department is responsible for conducting legal reviews and filing regulatory documents. They also handle the drafting of comprehensive documents and prepare for important meetings.
Industrial Development Division	Responsible for providing guidance in the formulation of detailed control plans for logistics concentration development areas and city-level strategic functional areas. They also formulate related policies and systems for the construction and management of logistics concentration development areas and oversee their implementation. This department handles the registration and filing of key logistics projects throughout the city, and it provides guidance to promote the development of key logistics enterprises. Additionally, they formulate policy measures to promote the development of urban common distribution and organize their implementation.
Multimodal Transport Division	Responsible for coordinating and promoting the establishment of a multimodal transportation system with Chengdu as the hub. This system encompasses various transportation modes, including road, rail, aviation, and water transport. They also work on advancing the construction of railway and highway freight stations, coordinating the opening of railway and highway logistics channels, and spearheading the promotion of advanced transportation methods and modern logistics technologies.

(*continued*)

Table 5.2 (continued)

Functional departments	*Responsibilities*
Port and Civil Aviation Division	Responsible for coordinating the advancement of the public port system and customs special supervision area construction. They organize and coordinate port management efforts, handle port policy approval tasks, and oversee the construction of Chengdu Electronic Port. Additionally, they promote streamlined customs clearance procedures, formulate plans for the development of Chengdu's aviation hub, and implement policies to boost passenger and cargo transportation at the airport. The department is also involved in coordinating the launch of international scheduled direct flights, guiding the development of airlines based in Chengdu, and advancing significant aerospace industry projects. They manage the daily operations of the Municipal Port Service Leadership Office.

Source: Chengdu Municipal Port and Logistics Office. Website, http://www.cdwl.gov.cn/

throughout the entire process, allowing for the advance submission of transit data to the customs EDI systems of countries along the route, ensuring a seamless transit process. Considering issues such as severe wind conditions in Xinjiang, congestion at the Alashankou Port, and rising transportation costs along the route, Chengdu Customs has actively signed a Memorandum of Cooperation with Hohhot Customs on regional customs cooperation. This has opened a second domestic transportation route for the China Europe Railway Express (Chengdu), ensuring that the newly established route can smoothly clear customs and exit through the Erenhot Port. This greatly enhances customs clearance efficiency and boosts the route's market competitiveness.[3]

The Qingbaijiang District Government, overseeing the logistics park crucial for the "Rong'ou" project, has consistently upgraded its infrastructure. Collaborating closely with other ports and relevant departments, they initiated key improvements. Notably, the government spearheaded the Railway Port Project within the container logistics park. This endeavor encompassed the construction of pivotal structures like the port's joint inspection building and international business area, enhancing the park's overall functionality and efficiency. The Port Joint Inspection Building

[3] Bihong Chen. "Opening New Routes for China Europe Railway Express (Chengdu)." *Sichuan Daily*, September 18, 2013.

stands as a cutting-edge facility, seamlessly integrating intelligence and advanced information technology. Its multifaceted design serves as an external gateway, streamlining customs and inspection processes to create a seamless "one-stop clearance" platform for businesses engaged in international trade. This facility not only houses the offices of major logistics companies, freight forwarders, customs clearance firms, and trade enterprises but also provides essential support services, including communication, information management, and business and tax agency services, enhancing operational efficiency for resident businesses. The international business area encompasses inspection areas, supervision yards, bonded warehouses, inspection and quarantine fields, laboratories, and fumigation facilities. It serves as the region for international goods clearance and inspection operations and is the first modernized supervision area in the country that achieves seamless integration with the railway central station. Furthermore, the Qingbaijiang District Government has engaged in deep cooperation with major coastal ports such as Yantian Port in Shenzhen, Yangshan Port in Zhejiang, and the Port of Xingang in Tianjin, establishing an information data exchange platform that ensures "seamless integration" with these ports. The Qingbaijiang District Government has proactively facilitated collaboration among Chengdu Customs, port customs, and border trade port customs. Through signed agreements, swift cargo transfer and customs cooperation have been enabled between these regions. This initiative has empowered the Chengdu railway freight hub to assume vital port functions, including Chengdu customs clearance, port release, and maritime linkage, effectively realizing the "inland shift" of port functions. Consequently, the region has established the largest railway cargo distribution center and maritime information exchange hub in western China. At the same time, active efforts have been made to connect with other regions such as Lanzhou, Shanghai, and Kunming, to establish a strategic transportation network extending to Central Asia, East Asia, the Pacific region, South Asia, West Asia, Southeast Asia, and even Europe. This ultimately positions the logistics industry in Qingbaijiang as an international and hub-type inland port in the western region, anchored in Chengdu, serving Sichuan, radiating across the western region, and connecting globally.

The daily operation of the China-Europe Railway Express (Chengdu) is managed by a joint venture company. In 2013, Chengdu Eurasia Rail Logistics Co., Ltd., a Sino-foreign joint venture, assumed responsibility for providing end-to-end logistics services following a market-oriented approach. The joint venture company was established through voluntary cooperation and investments from Poland's HATRANS Logistics Ltd., Jiangsu Feiliks International Logistics Co., Ltd., and Shenzhen YH Global Logistics Co., Ltd. It brings together their respective strengths to offer services such as cargo sourcing, storage, and transportation. Research findings reveal that Chengdu Eurasia Rail Logistics Co., Ltd. faced operational challenges and encountered difficulties in sustaining its activities. An announcement by China Railway Tielong Container Logistics Co., Ltd. on August 8, 2014, disclosed that the relevant shareholders of Chengdu Eurasia Rail Logistics Co., Ltd. agreed to authorize its subsidiary, Shanghai Tieyang Multimodal Transportation Co., Ltd. (TMT) (in which Chengdu Eurasia Rail Logistics Co., Ltd. held a 51% stake), for the comprehensive management of Chengdu Eurasia Rail Logistics Co., Ltd. The enterprises involved signed an "Enterprise Entrusted Management Agreement." The board of directors of Chengdu Eurasia Rail Logistics Co., Ltd. also passed a resolution to appoint relevant personnel from TMT as the general manager of the railway service company, who would be fully responsible for the actual operation and management of the company on behalf of TMT.

In the second phase commencing after April 1, 2016, the "Rong'ou" underwent management by a government-led state-owned entity. Chengdu International Railway Service Co., Ltd., a wholly owned subsidiary with a registered capital of 30 million yuan ($4 million), was established by Chengdu International Railway Port Investment and Development (Group) Co., Ltd., a subsidiary of Chengdu Industrial Investment Group Co., Ltd., starting from April 1, 2016. This subsidiary took charge of the comprehensive operation and management of the "Rong'ou" express train. During this period, the Chengdu city government significantly enhanced its support for the "Rong'ou" express train. This involved the establishment of new government departments, increased financial investments, and the full utilization of the government's pivotal role in the operation of the "Rong'ou" initiative.

Following the nationalization of the "Rong'ou" and in alignment with the evolving needs of national strategies and regional economic development plans, the Chengdu Port and Logistics Office established the "International Capacity Cooperation Division." This specialized division is dedicated to issues pertaining to international capacity cooperation and the establishment of foreign logistics parks within the framework of railway service development. Its key responsibilities encompass devising strategic work plans and policy measures to advance international capacity cooperation under the "Rong'ou+" strategy and overseeing their seamless implementation. The division conducts research and analysis on significant issues related to Chengdu's international capacity cooperation work and provides relevant policy recommendations. It also coordinates and supervises the support policies of districts and counties for international capacity cooperation and takes the lead in devising logistics solutions for international cooperation parks at home and abroad and organizing their implementation. In addition, the Chengdu Port and Logistics Office has established cooperation with major global logistics companies. On May 25, 2016, the logistics office signed a "China-Europe Logistics Channel Cooperation Memorandum" with DHL Global Forwarding. Both parties aimed to complement each other's strengths and extend the reach of the China-Europe Railway Express (Chengdu) to destinations including Turkey, Russia, and Southern Europe, thereby further enhancing bilateral trade between China and Europe. DHL is a well-known brand under Deutsche Post DHL Group, with a logistics service network spanning over 220 countries and regions globally, and it holds considerable influence in the industry. In the collaboration between DHL and Chengdu, the primary emphasis will be placed on harnessing the "Rong'ou Express" as the central transportation route. Concurrently, they will harness DHL's extensive global logistics network to enhance international operations through diverse multimodal transport modes, including "air-air intermodal," "air-rail intermodal," and "road-rail intermodal." This strategic expansion is designed to broaden the scope of the "Rong'ou Express," extending its coverage from Poland to encompass countries and regions such as Russia, Turkey, and Southern Europe.[4]

The logistics park forming the backbone of the "Rong'ou" initiative is in Qingbaijiang District. The district government is tasked with constructing the park's infrastructure and enhancing the logistics environment associated with the route. Aligning with the directives of the Chengdu Municipal Government's "13th Five-Year Plan," the district government has diligently pursued Chengdu's vision as an "International Logistics Center City," focusing notably on robust port development efforts. In terms of policies, the district government has established preferential policies to encourage freight forwarding companies and logistics

[4]Qianwei Li. "Chengdu Partners with DHL to Extend 'Rong'ou Express' to Countries Including Turkey," Xinhua Silk Road, May 26, 2016.

companies to set up operations within the Qingbaijiang Logistics Park. They have also implemented incentive policies for participation in the "Rong'ou." First, they have eased market access conditions by simplifying registration and capital requirements, eliminating capital verification reports, and simplifying residence registration conditions for logistics companies during the registration process. These measures are aimed at reducing market entry barriers, lowering the costs of starting businesses, and promoting the healthy development of logistics enterprises. Second, the district actively promotes foreign investment. When national open policies allow, restrictions on foreign involvement in logistics infrastructure development are eased. This initiative fosters collaborations between esteemed domestic and international logistics firms and the park. Cooperation encompasses diverse areas, including logistics technology, management strategies, service systems, information management, and talent development. Furthermore, they increase financial and tax support. For newly established logistics companies in the park, they provide support equal to 50% of the portion of their enterprise income tax received by the local government for the first three years from the date they reach the tax payment threshold, provided that their annual tax payment exceeds two million yuan ($27.3 million). If the annual cargo throughput of the Chengdu Railway Container Center Station increases by over 5% but less than 10% compared to the previous year, they reward the China United International Rail Containers Co., Ltd. Chengdu Branch with 100,000 yuan ($13,665) per year. For those achieving a growth rate exceeding 10%, an annual reward of 300,000 yuan ($40,996) will be granted. They encourage railway transport companies and road logistics companies to leverage their resource advantages to open "Five-fixed Trains," including fixed points, fixed routes, fixed time series, fixed schedules, fixed pricing. For operators of new domestic "Five-fixed Trains" with Chengdu Railway Container Center Station as the starting or ending point, a one-time reward of 300,000 yuan ($40,996) will be granted. The operator of a new "Five-fixed Trains" cross-border railway freight service, originating from or terminating at the Chengdu Railway Container Center Station, is eligible for a one-time reward of 500,000 yuan ($68,328). Freight forwarding companies based in the park, handling either 30,000 domestic containers annually or 2000 foreign trade containers per year, receive an annual reward of 50,000 yuan ($6833). These policies have yielded significant results. In less than half a year, Qingbaijiang has attracted 40 light-asset trade companies to settle in the Chengdu International Railway Port.

After the nationalization, there has been a significant increase in government investment. At the end of 2016, China Logistics Group Co., Ltd., a subsidiary of China Chengtong Holdings Group Ltd., invested two billion yuan ($2.7 billion) to build the China-Europe-Africa International Trade and Logistics Hub Center in Chengdu and Antwerp, Belgium. This project is in a part of the Qingbaijiang Industrial Park. It covers an area of 379 *mu* (about 25.3 hectares) and will have a total construction area of 250,000 square meters. This area will include international trade bonded warehouses, cold storage, new energy urban distribution warehouses, office buildings, a trading center, information center, exhibition grounds, and more. The project within the Port of Antwerp in Belgium will have a total construction area of approximately 600,000 square meters and is planned to include four main functional zones: The "International Commodity Trading and Exhibition Center," with a total construction area of about 150,000 square meters, aiming to create a global hub for commodity trading and exhibitions; the "International Euro standard A-grade Warehousing Center," with a total construction area of around 200,000 square meters, encompassing various functional areas such as customs-bonded and supervised warehouses, temperature-controlled and frozen storage, regular transit warehouses, and bonded and supervised yards; the "International Commodity Processing Center" with an area of 250,000 square meters, and the "International Distribution and Dispatch Center."[5] According to the head of the Qingbaijiang District Port Commission, this project aims to address the issue of insufficient cargo supply for the "Roug'ou" route and to reduce the operational costs. The person in charge of China Logistics Group Co., Ltd. mentioned that this project represents the next move in connecting China, Europe, and Africa in a grand strategy. The project will establish an international trade route for commodities linking China, Europe, and Africa, with a focus on creating a multifunctional logistics distribution center that integrates road, rail, and air transportation.

Thanks to the strategic alignment between the government and "Rong'ou" in constructing the transcontinental corridor spanning Central Asia and Europe, operational performance has significantly improved.

[5] "Investment of 20 Billion Yuan: Simultaneous Commencement of 'Rong'ou Express' Trade Hubs at Both Ends, China-Europe-Africa International Trade and Logistics Hub to Commence Construction in Chengdu and Antwerp, Belgium by Year-End," *Chengdu Daily*, June 30, 2016.

Under the operational management of Chengdu International Railway Service Co., Ltd. and government guidance, the number of train operations has increased, and routes have expanded to three, resulting in a higher cargo volume. The freight train's steady operation has enhanced its economic contributions. Initially, the route extended from Chengdu through Alashankou to Poland, serving as the primary central route. In September 2016, the south line was officially opened, connecting Chengdu to Istanbul, Turkey, with a travel time of approximately 15 days. This marked the first south line connecting China and Europe and extended the coverage to Central Asia, Western Asia, Southern Asia, and Southern Europe. The north line, connecting Chengdu to Moscow, Russia, had already been opened, and it further extended to cover other Eastern European countries. In terms of the number of operations, in 2016, the "Rong'ou" ran 409 trains, four times the number in 2015. The cargo volume also witnessed substantial growth. According to the Chengdu Port and Logistics Office, prior to 2015, the freight train had a cargo load factor of only 20%, but, by 2016, it had increased to 50%.

This chapter attempts to analyze the changes in the operation mechanism of the "Rong'ou" railway service from the perspective of the government's economic functions and its relationship with the market. Government economic functions involve government institutions acting as administrative authorities, taking an overall perspective on societal life, and engaging in comprehensive planning, coordination, service, and supervision of the national economy. These functions include implementing and executing macroeconomic control policies, guidelines, and measures established at the central level, as well as formulating regional economic and social development strategies and plans.[6] The relationship between the government and the market is a topic that scholars have frequently explored. In recent years, some academics have redefined the government's economic functions from the perspective of "systemic market failure." They argue that under market economy conditions the state should perform functions related to "selecting and adjusting long-term national development strategies" and "developing economic systems and models that are consistent with chosen development strategies."[7] Viewed

[6] Li Kang, Yuxia Yang, editors. "Local Government Management," Southwest Normal University Press, 2015, p. 143.

[7] Zhengfu Shi. "New Types of Market Failure and National Economic Functions," *Liberation Army Daily*, April 5, 2015.

in this light, the changes in the operating mechanism of the "Rong'ou" stem from the ongoing alignment of national strategies with Chengdu's economic development plans. In response to national development strategies, the Chengdu municipal government has periodically adapted the railway's role based on the evolving local circumstances and development objectives. This has led to the reacquisition of operational and managerial control over the railway by the government, with the intention of positioning the "Rong'ou" as a pivotal platform for driving social and economic development in Chengdu.

5.2 Chengdu's Early Positioning and the Evolution of "Rong'ou"

Chengdu, as an inland city, has relatively weaker geographical advantages compared to cities of a similar level in the eastern regions of China. Its degree of openness to the outside world is far less than that of its counterparts in the central and eastern coastal regions. To address this, the government, to accelerate Chengdu's socioeconomic development and harness its role in the economic development of the western region, has designated Chengdu as the "Central City in Western China." This initiative aims to vigorously develop the economy of the southwestern region with Chengdu at its core. In this context, the Chengdu municipal government outlined a specific plan during the "12th Five-Year Plan" to develop the city as the "Three Centers" in terms of commerce, logistics, finance, and technology. This initiative involves the development of headquarters-based economic activities and aims to enhance the city's ability to attract and radiate businesses and economic activities. The goal is to transform Chengdu into a powerful and functionally robust central city that drives coordinated development in the western region.[8]

Although the government has designated Chengdu as a western central city, the city's relatively weak geographical advantages have not manifested its international and open characteristics prominently. In terms of transportation planning and logistics system development, the Chengdu government has strengthened the construction of a railway passenger and freight hub system composed of Chengdu East Railway Station, Chengdu Railway Station, Dawan Station, Xinjin Station, and others. It aims to establish a half-hour transportation circle within the Chengdu Economic

[8] "Chengdu's 12th Five-Year Plan."

Zone, a transportation circle within the Chengdu-Chongqing Economic Zone, and transportation circles connecting Chengdu to neighboring provincial capital cities such as Guiyang, Lanzhou, Kunming, and Xi'an. These efforts are still oriented toward positioning Chengdu as the central city in the western region of China. In the era of the maritime economy, Chengdu faces challenges in breaking free from the constraints of inland city development. Its geographical disadvantage weakens the city's socio-economic development.

After BRI was launched, China's western inland provinces and cities have experienced notable economic transformations. Chengdu, situated as a central city in the west, has witnessed its transportation and economic advantages come to the forefront. In response to the BRI, the Chengdu municipal government strategically positioned Chengdu as a "bridge-head" to Western China, with "Rong'ou" serving as a crucial pathway to realize this objective. On March 26, 2013, the "Promotion and Signing Ceremony of the China Europe Railway Express (Chengdu)" took place at the Tianfu International Convention Center, jointly organized by the Chengdu Municipal People's Government, Sichuan Provincial Logistics Office, Sichuan Provincial Department of Commerce, Chengdu Municipal Logistics Office, Chengdu Municipal Bureau of Commerce, and the People's Government of Qingbaijiang District in Chengdu. The ceremony was attended by leaders from the provincial and municipal governments, relevant central government units in Chengdu, foreign trade associations, business organizations, Chengdu Chamber of Commerce, over 70 renowned domestic and international shipping companies, international freight forwarders, foreign trade enterprises, and more than 300 representatives from various media outlets. The gathering aimed to enhance the influence of the China Europe Railway Express (Chengdu) and make active preparations for its regular operation.

After the formation of the rail service, the Chengdu municipal government aimed to develop the rail service into a major freight corridor connecting Chengdu to the European continent. It would serve as a logistics platform for Chengdu's export production base to access European markets and become a trading hub for European products. This initiative fundamentally broke the traditional reliance on ports for the development of an export-oriented economy in western China, transforming the geographical disadvantage of being an inland area in the western region into an advantage for establishing a forefront position for exporting to Europe. However, the China-Europe Railway Express (Chengdu) is an international logistics corridor that requires high levels of coordination between the government and businesses, substantial operational costs, and a local industrial base suitable for railway transportation products. Regrettably, the local government lacked deep insights in this area. Research reveals that the initial operational approach was modeled after "Yuxin'ou," albeit with a more market-oriented orientation for "Rong'ou." In response to market demands, the operation of the train service was entrusted to the Sino-foreign joint venture, Chengdu Eurasia Rail Logistics Co., Ltd., which was tasked with providing end-to-end logistics services in a market-oriented manner. The joint venture company was formed voluntarily by pooling the resources and expertise of Poland's HATRANS Logistics Ltd., Jiangsu Feiliks International Logistics Co., Ltd., and Shenzhen YH Global Logistics Co., Ltd. It offered comprehensive services such as cargo sourcing, warehousing, and transportation. However, the operational approach deviated from the government's initial vision for the service. Due to the government's limited understanding of the train service, which simply entrusted its operation and management to the joint venture company, the market-oriented operation of the train service struggled to meet the economic planning requirements set by the Chengdu municipal government.

Firstly, the "Rong'ou" train service had relatively low frequency and a limited volume of return cargo. According to the head of the Chengdu Port and Logistics Office, as of November 15, 2015, Chengdu had dispatched approximately 237 trains with around 9710 carriages to Europe, and 125 return trains with around 4930 carriages, totaling 362 trains with roughly 14,650 carriages. From 2013 to 2014, only a few dozen trains were operated, and in 2015 there were just 103 trains in operation. The number of train services operated could not achieve economies of scale. From the perspective of return cargo volume, Chen Zhongwei, the director of Chengdu's Logistics Office, once told the media that Chengdu required companies to secure return cargo in the first quarter of 2014 to achieve a balanced budget for the "Rong'ou Express." However, it wasn't until July 31, 2014, that the route conducted its first test run with return cargo, which consisted of only three containers. One-way operations are a significant concern in the logistics industry, and the lack of return cargo can impact the sustainability of the train service. Moreover, due to the limited number of trains runs and the scarcity of return cargo, the train has struggled to drive economic development in Chengdu, let alone in the southwestern region or the broader Chinese economy. The economic benefits generated by the train service fall far short of the initial expectations and plans.

Furthermore, substantial government subsidies are a critical driver of the "Rong'ou"'s operation, as they are essential for ensuring a stable supply of cargo. Given the relatively high transportation costs, the Chengdu provides substantial subsidies to the companies involved. Based on research into the Chengdu International Railway Service Co., Ltd., the cost for transporting each container by the train is approximately $7000, while the fees charged to companies are in the range of $3000 to $3500 per container. This means that the government's subsidy per container amounts to $3500 to $4000. Therefore, it can be estimated that the government needs to provide subsidies of approximately $143,500 to $164,000 per train. The government subsidies are limited to the outbound journey, leaving no financial support for the return trips. Consequently, there is a significant surplus of empty containers during the return journeys. The "Rong'ou" only completed its inaugural return trip on July 17, 2015. According to data from the Chengdu Port and Logistics Office, the loading rate was a mere 20% in 2015. It is evident that the "Rong'ou" heavily relies on these subsidies to sustain its operations. Without these financial incentives, the train's continuity would face substantial challenges. In this context, most of the goods transported are negotiated directly by the Chengdu Port and Logistics Office with large-scale suppliers, commonly referred to as "direct customers." These direct customers include companies like TCL, GREE, Lenovo, Changhong, Dell, and others. The government coordinates the pricing of goods to ensure a stable supply. The future direction of the train operation in a post-subsidy era is indeed a significant challenge to address.

Furthermore, a lack of industrial support has resulted in insufficient momentum for the continued development of the "Rong'ou" route. Compared to maritime and air transport, railway freight offers both a time advantage and cost advantage. However, when considering the overall factors of time and cost, the goods suitable for "Rong'ou" are mainly electronics, electrical products, automobiles, and similar commodities. Under the government's subsidy policy, the time and cost advantages are more apparent for these product types. Considering the time factor, it's clear that shipping products from Chengdu to Europe via the Yangtze River via Luzhou Port takes a lengthy 55 days to reach Europe. This extended transit time is a concern for businesses seeking more efficient transportation routes to European markets. Taking Chengdu Qingtie Machinery

Equipment Co., Ltd. as an example, this company mainly exports clothing, electronic products, and machinery equipment. They have compared the transportation costs of using the "Rong'ou" with sea and air freight. Regarding transportation time, sea freight involves a 42-day journey, where goods are initially shipped to Shanghai before being further transported to Europe. In contrast, the "Rong'ou" covers the distance in just 12 days, with an additional 1 to 3 days for distribution to customers. This totals about one-third of the time required by sea freight. In terms of shipping costs, even though railway transport is more expensive than sea freight, when considering costs from both time and freight aspects, the total expenses are quite similar. The company's cost to transport one container from Chengdu to Europe is $5500, while the average total cost for one container on the "Rong'ou Express" is approximately $8500. Considering the total expenses involving both time and transportation costs, rail transport doesn't result in higher overall costs compared to sea freight. Their representative explained, "Even though it might seem like rail transportation costs $3,000 more per container than sea freight, the faster delivery time and quicker capital return compensate for it. With a typical cargo value of $200,000 per container, the capital investment can usually cover the transportation cost within a month."[9]

As per the information from the Chengdu Port and Logistics Office, Chengdu, as an inland city, often experiences a lag in government policies related to industries when compared to eastern regions. For instance, since 2009, the central and western regions have become important areas for the relocation of industries from the eastern regions. However, Chengdu has been somewhat slow in focusing on industrial relocation and has missed the opportunity to attract manufacturing and service industries on a large scale. Chengdu, however, has been relatively slow in shifting its focus toward industrial relocation, missing out on the opportunity to attract large-scale manufacturing and service industries. Compared to central cities in the eastern regions, Chengdu's manufacturing base is relatively weaker. Particularly in terms of manufacturing industries compatible with railway logistics channels, a significant gap exists. The absence of a corresponding industrial foundation after the establishment of the "Rong'ou" has forced increased reliance on freight forwarding companies

[9] "Companies Making Calculations Before Choosing Ron'ou Express," *Chengdu Daily*, January 19, 2015.

to consolidate goods from across the country. This reliance adds to costs and constrains the route's sustainable development."

The inception of Rong'ou reflects a government-led initiative, shaped by local administrations aligning with national strategies. The process, however, was rushed, lacking clear initial objectives. The market-oriented approach in its early stages overlooked Chengdu's potential as a central city in the western region. Essentially, the Chengdu government viewed Rong'ou primarily as a land transportation route, neglecting its broader potential in regional economic development and international trade. Furthermore, the key players in the train operation, including Chengdu Eurasia Rail Logistics Co., Ltd, and related logistics companies, often prioritize the operation of the train from a business profit perspective. They sometimes overlook the long-term benefits of the train and limit its stability. This hinders the development of the "Rong'ou" and falls short of the economic development requirements outlined in the new period for Sichuan Province. Rong'ou stands as a testament to the Chengdu municipal government's active economic role. Its inception was guided by the principles of market-oriented operation. While we recognize the efficiency of a market economy as a resource allocation system, like any system, it has its inherent flaws. The early operation n encountered various issues, which serves as evidence of this point. Therefore, with the introduction of Chengdu's "13th Five-Year Plan," which aims to establish the city as a national central city, the "Rong'ou" was incorporated into national strategies. Its operation was brought back under public ownership to better align with national strategies and promote regional economic development centered around Chengdu.

5.3 Forging a National Central City: Repositioning the China-Europe Railway Express (Chengdu)

In the context of the BRI, the Chengdu municipal government formulated and promulgated the "13th Five-Year Plan for National Economic and Social Development of Chengdu," in line with national strategies. This plan explicitly outlines the goal of establishing Chengdu as a "national gateway city and a national inland open highland." The change has led to a shift in the development focus of the "Rong'ou Express." The route has risen to a higher level in the government's strategic priorities and will become a crucial platform for contributing to the future economic development, foreign openness of Chengdu, Sichuan Province, and even China's economic growth.

When Chengdu embarked on the establishment of the route, its foremost objective was to align with national initiatives. This land route aimed to position Chengdu as a bridgehead in China's westward opening. In 2015, Chengdu commenced the development of the "13th Five-Year Plan for Economic and Social Development of Chengdu" and initiated the formulation of the "Chengdu-Chongqing Urban Agglomeration Development Plan," submitted for approval by the State Council. In this planning process, the urban positioning began to shift from being a "central city in the western region" to a "national central city." This transition was based on the five characteristics of a "national central city" outlined in the "Outline of the National Urban System Plan." These characteristics include being the central hub for organizing economic activities and resource allocation at the national level, a hub for comprehensive transportation and information networks, a center for national science, education, culture, and innovation, having international influence and competitiveness, and being the "leading city" with the strongest overall strength in the national urban system. Correspondingly, a national central city must possess five key functions: comprehensive service, industrial cluster, logistics hub, open highland, and cultural cohesion. It's evident that a national central city places a strong emphasis on the city's "centrality" and "internationality." In terms of its primary characteristics, a national central city represents the nation's participation in international division of labor, cooperation, and competition. It serves as the hub for organizing economic activities and resource allocation within the nation or a major economic region. The development of a national central city is not only imperative for solidifying and elevating its own stature but also intricately connected to regional harmonization. Moreover, it has far-reaching implications for the nation's holistic economic and social advancement, its international competitiveness, and global standing. As mentioned earlier, the changes in the operation mechanism are a result of the harmonization between national strategy and Chengdu municipal government's economic development plans. Therefore, based on the different economic development plans at various times, its positioning has evolved. Under the new phase of government policies, the "Rong'ou" has become an essential pathway for the Chengdu municipal government to build the national central city. Chengdu is utilizing the train to reconstruct its transportation network, nurture new markets, and establish itself as the center for China's production capacity transfer toward Europe and Central Asia. It's evident that Chengdu's urban positioning underwent a significant change in its "13th Five-Year Plan." The plan emphasizes Chengdu's "openness" and "internationalization," along with the measures taken to achieve these goals. Most of these measures are closely related to the "Rong'ou," including the construction of international railway ports, the positioning of the "Rong'ou+" strategy, and the encouragement of private capital to participate in the BRI.

The Sichuan Provincial Government has elevated the positioning of the "Rong'ou." The "13th Five-Year Plan" for Sichuan Province clearly states the intention to enhance the train's international transportation capacity and "to make the most of the local cooperation platform for the two river basins of China and Russia ('Yangtze-Volga mechanism'). It further emphasizes the implementation of the '251 Action Plan,' expanding cooperation with countries along the BRI in various fields, including energy resources, electronic information, equipment manufacturing, aerospace, and engineering construction."[10] From the perspective of the content, the "Rong'ou" is not only a logistics channel but a critical pathway to boost and drive economic development and foreign economic exchanges in Sichuan Province.

Chengdu's "13th Five-Year Plan" clearly defines the city's positioning as a "national gateway city" and a "national inland open highland." It also emphasizes Chengdu's role as a "strategic pivotal city" in the construction of the BRI and the Yangtze River Economic Belt initiatives. On December 17, 2015, Chengdu's municipal government, during a press conference, explicitly outlined the specific approach to achieve these objectives, which is to adhere to open development with the aim of addressing both internal and external linkages. Over the next five years, the government will vigorously implement the "comprehensive openness" strategy, focusing on institutional innovation, comprehensive integration into the BRI. This approach aims to achieve "two-way openness" internally and externally. This includes optimizing the open environment, expanding industrial openness, establishing an international inland comprehensive transportation hub, creating an international regional logistics center, and developing national-level China-Korean innovation and entrepreneurship parks,

[10] "Outline of Sichuan Province's Development Plan."

as well as key international industrial parks with Germany and France.[11] These measures will provide significant impetus to the development of the China Europe Railway Express (Chengdu).

Chengdu's "13th Five-Year Plan" aligns well with the BRI, and its development plan and positioning are clear. The plan places a strong emphasis on the role of railways in comprehensive transportation construction. It aims to "further consolidate and enhance Chengdu's status as the fifth-largest railway hub in the country. The plan involves constructing a railway transportation network with two circular lines and ten radial lines, organized in a clear hierarchy with complementary functions, seamless connections, and a comprehensive reach that covers both the north and south as well as the east and west. This network will ultimately extend to connect the regions from Sichuan Province to the sea, acting as a bridgehead that links Europe and Asia and serves as a critical railway gateway for China's westward opening-up." Within this framework, the plan specifically addresses the development of the "Rong'ou" and calls for the continuous improvement of its support system. It also emphasizes the opening of domestic interconnecting rail services and the stable and increased operation of Chengdu-bound "Five-fixed Trains" to Shenzhen, Xiamen, Ningbo, Wuhan, Liuzhou, Kunming, Pingxiang, and other destinations in both directions.

The plan not only underscores its self-development but also highlights the commitment to enhance interaction and collaboration with neighboring regional economies. Specifically, the "Rong'ou+" strategy focuses on fostering strategic partnerships with key regions and provinces in cooperation with Sichuan Province. The plan highlights the significance of capitalizing on opportunities arising from the BRI and the development of the Yangtze River Economic Belt. It relies on regional division of labor and collaboration, actively driving the construction of the "Diamond Economic Zone" encompassing Chengdu, Chongqing, Xi'an, Guiyang, and Kunming. The goal is to expedite the establishment of an efficient and mutually beneficial multilevel regional cooperation framework, with the objective of positioning Chengdu as a central driving force for development in China's central and western regions. The plan vigorously promotes the establishment of the "Diamond Economic Zone," with a focus on enhancing the framework for coordinated development and collectively establishing a strategic anchor for the BRI and the westward and

[11] "13th Five-Year Plan for the National Economic and Social Development of Chengdu."

southward expansion of the Yangtze River Economic Belt. This endeavor entails strengthening economic ties and collaboration among cities like Chengdu, Xi'an, and Chongqing, while expanding economic partnerships with urban centers including Kunming and Guiyang. The plan introduces innovative models for economic circle cooperation, giving due weight to a combination of government guidance and market-driven leadership. The objective is to foster comprehensive collaboration across various domains, encompassing infrastructure connectivity, the flow of resources, synergies in industry, linkages in innovation, major resource development, and environmental conservation.

To fully leverage the role of the "Rong'ou" in regional economic development and promote wider economic cooperation via the train, the Chengdu municipal government has implemented the "Rong'ou+" strategy and the "X Rong'ou" strategy. Driven by the logistics sector, the initiatives focus on the development of a three-dimensional international logistics hub utilizing the "Three Networks, Two Ports, and One Hub"[12] concept. The "Rong'ou+" strategy aims to further enhance international logistics channels, accelerate the establishment of a convenient, efficient, and fully functional international regional logistics system, and position Chengdu as a hub for international logistics, a regional international port city, and a national exemplar in the modern logistics sector. This strategy intends to facilitate Chengdu's transformation from a traditional inland city into an emerging port city, shifting from being a strategic rear area to a strategic forefront, and evolving from a regional center city into a national central city and an international regional central city. Its development goals encompass several key objectives. First, it aims to create a BRI grand corridor that connects Europe and Asia while also facilitating connectivity from Sichuan Province to the sea. In addition, the strategy seeks to expand both international and domestic logistics networks, with a specific emphasis on steadily increasing the frequency of "Rong'ou+" trains. Furthermore, it aims to extend the reach of the "Rong'ou Express" in Europe, fostering its presence in the European market. Another critical objective is the promotion of regular, high-frequency, and stable

[12] These networks are based on the dual utilization of Shuangliu International Airport and Tianfu International Airport, the Chengdu International Railway Port, and aim to establish Chengdu as a national gateway hub. This strategy envisions an "Air Passenger Network" with Chengdu as the hub, an "Air Cargo Network" to serve western regions, and a "Land-based Logistics Network" for intercontinental transshipment centered around Chengdu.

operation of the "Rong'ou Express" and the Central Asian trains on the "Double Golden Channel." These efforts are expected to enhance the efficiency and reliability of these rail services. Additionally, the strategy places a strong emphasis on strengthening cooperation mechanisms between the "Rong'ou Express" and other China Europe rail services. This collaboration is essential for establishing the "Rong'ou Express" as the most stable, fastest, and internationally competitive China Europe rail service. Furthermore, the plan aims to position Chengdu as a vital logistics hub that connects the country domestically and Europe and pan-Asian countries internationally. This will involve comprehensive expansion in various aspects, including hubs, nodes, hinterlands, and services. The goal is to coordinate and advance the development of the logistics industry, manufacturing industry, and service industry in a harmonious and integrated manner.

To better implement the "Rong'ou+" strategy, the Chengdu municipal government has initiated efforts in the construction of logistics system and international railway ports. In terms of logistics infrastructure, the plan focuses on establishing an international rail network with the "Rong'ou Express" as the main route. This network adopts the approach of "one main route, multiple branches, and direct connections to multiple destinations." The aim is to create a comprehensive logistics network spanning across Europe and Asia, linking the continents through the "Silk Road on Land."

In terms of railway port construction, the Chengdu municipal government has outlined plans to emphasize the development of both international and domestic markets. The goal is to facilitate the coexistence of manufacturing, logistics, and service industries, strengthen the four key pillars of "hubs, nodes, hinterlands, and services," and comprehensively transform it into the leading domestic "top international railway port" characterized by "multimodal integration, modern intelligence, and convenient services." Furthermore, they aim to successfully operate three international routes, which include the Northern route (Chengdu to Russia), the Central route (Chengdu to Poland), and the Southern route (Chengdu-Almaty-Turkey). These routes will comprehensively cover countries and regions within the BRI. The objective is to optimize the routes, reduce transit times, enhance operational quality and efficiency, extend the main lines to key European hub cities and regional centers, and accelerate the establishment of a freight network that spans across the entirety of Europe and pan-Asia. In 2016, the Chengdu initiated the "X

Rong'ou" strategy, which involves extending the "Rong'ou Express" rail service to multiple cities, including Chengdu to Xiamen, Chengdu to Ningbo, Chengdu to Shenzhen, and Chengdu to Kunming. These additional routes will radiate from regional node cities and connect regions such as Japan, South Korea, Hong Kong, Macao, and the ASEAN. The objective is to strengthen connectivity, leverage complementary advantages, and promote cooperative partnerships between coastal and inland cities, ultimately leading to mutual benefits for all stakeholders.

The "Rong'ou+" strategy aims to establish Chengdu as a bridgehead linking Europe and Pan-Asia. It also aims to align with the BRI and the Yangtze River Economic Belt, creating a strategic platform. This strategy involves building internal connections between domestic and provincial cities, as well as external links with European and Pan-Asian countries. It aspires to create a new land bridge that connects the Pacific Ocean to the Atlantic Ocean and the Pacific Ocean to the Indian Ocean. This strategy can be broadly divided into two parts: The first part focuses on the domestic aspect, with an emphasis on the comprehensive operation of the "Rong'ou+" railway freight services that connect Chengdu to eastern coastal free trade zones, key port cities, and central cities in the western region, including Shenzhen, Ningbo, Xiamen, Kunming, Wuhan, and Pingxiang. This expansion aims to extend the reach of the "Rong'ou Express" to cover cargo collection in Japan, South Korea, Hong Kong, Macao, Taiwan, and various ASEAN countries. The second part primarily concentrates on the European region by extending the reach into Europe, with the establishment of distribution centers in European cities such as Tilburg in the Netherlands, Nuremberg in Germany, and Hamburg. The goal is to create a network-based cargo collection system and foster cooperative relationships within the province, throughout the country, and across international markets, establishing a pattern of "one main line, two hubs, and multiple points."

It is apparent that the government's policy direction for "Rong'ou" has shifted, emphasizing capacity relocation as its new developmental focus in this phase. This shift aligns with current economic development plans in China. Addressing domestic overcapacity has become a pivotal challenge in economic development, and the China-Europe Railway Express presents a crucial avenue for diverting excess domestic capacity to international markets. Against this backdrop, the Chengdu Port and Logistics Office, leveraging the "Rong'ou," aims to establish Chengdu as a hub for relocating domestic capacity to European regions. Excess capacity from central and eastern regions can be redirected via Chengdu to Central Asia and Europe, providing Sichuan Province with an opportunity to continually refine its economic structure and drive regional economic development.

With the stable operation of the "Rong'ou," Chengdu's industrial agglomeration capacity has started to shine, attracting various industries such as automotive, materials, and information technology to congregate in the city. By the end of 2016, several companies, including TCL, Dell, Philips, and Lenovo, explicitly expressed their intentions to shift production capacity to Chengdu for the European market. Among these companies, TCL will move 1500 large containers from Huizhou to Europe via Chengdu this year, with plans to shift $1 billion worth of production capacity to Chengdu over the next three years. Dell has decided to transfer approximately one-third of its desktop computer production capacity, which amounts to three million units, from its factory in Łódź, Poland, to Chengdu, and it plans to transfer its laptop production capacity, except for air freight operations, from its Kunshan facility to Chengdu. Philips has entered cooperation on train services and customs clearance transfer with Chengdu. Companies like Lenovo are expected to finalize cooperation agreements for trade and production capacity transfer soon.[13] Shanghai Baowei Industrial Co., Ltd. steel deep processing and automobile parts production line project, with a total investment of 500 million yuan($68.3 million), including fixed asset investment not less than 350 million yuan ($47.8 million), mainly engaged in steel deep processing and automobile parts production. Gansu Cao Wenxia (Natural Person) annual production of 300,000 tons of copper-based new material production base project, with a total investment of 500 million yuan ($68.3 million), including fixed asset investment of 3.8 billion yuan ($0.5 billion), mainly focused on the production of copper-based new materials. China Jushi Co., Ltd. Chengdu branch annual production of 90,000 tons of alkali-free glass fiber pool kiln drawing production line project, with a total investment of 800 million yuan ($109 million), is expanding its production capacity further. Attestation of Global Compliance (Shenzhen) Co., Ltd. investment construction of testing laboratory project, with a total investment of 300 million yuan ($41 million), mainly for the construction of testing laboratories, includes investments in physical and chemical testing laboratories, Bluetooth and RF laboratories, EMC, and automotive electronic

[13] "Seizing Development Opportunities and Advancing the 'Rong'ou+' Strategy Comprehensively," *People's Daily*, August 23, 2016.

laboratories, among others. According to statistics, since 2016, Qingbaijiang District has successfully attracted 22 major projects with a total investment of 7.17 billion yuan ($0.97 billion) and 30 billion yuan ($4 billion) in industrial funds. Additionally, 40 light-asset trade-oriented companies have registered with the Chengdu International Railway Port. Currently, the Chengdu International Railway Port has successfully established three major functional zones: modern logistics, new trade, and near-port industries. It has attracted 25 *Fortune* Global 500 companies, including China Railway Group Limited, COSCO Shipping, and Yihai Kerry Arawana Holdings Co., Ltd., as well as more than 70 listed companies and industry leaders such as China Logistics, Yuan Cheng Logistics Co., Ltd., and Prologis. In addition, it is home to 45 internationally and domestically renowned logistics and trade companies, along with 263 large-scale industrial enterprises. In the first nine months of 2016, the "Rong'ou Express" operated a total of 287 trains, accelerating the relocation of production capacities to Chengdu by companies like GREE, Lenovo, Dell, and fostering international production and trade cooperation.[14]

In summary, Sichuan Province and Chengdu have made it clear in their plans that Chengdu's urban positioning and future development planning are well defined. The "Rong'ou Express" has clearly risen to a strategic level and become an important platform for Chengdu's economic development. The government is making full use of its central city status in the western region to vigorously develop trade between Sichuan Province and Europe using the route. This approach enhances Chengdu's industrial agglomeration capabilities, aligns with national strategies, and promotes its own economic development, making it a win-win situation.

5.4 Conclusion

"Rong'ou" are indeed a product of the BRI. National planning, as a top-level design, often precedes or supersedes local development realities. Looking at its establishment and operation, it becomes evident that the successful operation of such a train requires substantial local industrial support. Furthermore, these industries must align with the practical needs of railway transportation and China-Europe trade. In practice, many China-Europe express trains have faced a lack of corresponding industrial

[14] See *Chengdu Business Daily*, November 3, 2016.

support, leading to various issues. These include regions engaging in price wars to secure sources of goods, even at the expense of market principles.

The early operation was indeed an attempt at market-oriented development. However, it appears that the government's planning for the trains was overly "idealistic." The development of such trains has proven to be exceptionally challenging. As described by the head of the Chengdu Port and Logistics Office, "Getting the trains up and running has been extremely difficult." It can be said that the early market-oriented operation was unsuccessful. However, with the robust execution of the "Rong'ou+" strategy, the train's role underwent a significant transformation. It transitioned from being a mere freight transportation channel to becoming an investment environment, actively contributing to the economic development of Sichuan Province. Specifically, it enhances Chengdu's industrial clustering capacity and provides a vital conduit for Sichuan Province's foreign trade. After the change in its positioning, "Rong'ou"'s strategic importance was elevated. To better leverage its significant role in local development strategies, the government restructured its efforts, bringing the operation rights under state ownership. This move allowed the government to play a leading role and adopt a model of "government-led, state-owned enterprise operated." However, after the government has ensured that local industries can support its self-operation, they are reintroducing market-oriented operations. In the general trend, the "Rong'ou" is expected to go through a developmental process of "marketization-state ownership-marketization," which may also be a common development pattern for all the China-Europe Railway Express routes.

CHAPTER 6

China-Europe Railway Express (Zhengzhou): Operational Mechanism in the Context of National Strategy

Huihui Feng

6.1 Introduction

Since the official operation of the Chongqing-Xinjiang-Europe Freight Train or Yuxin'ou Railway in March 2011, numerous provinces and cities in China have successively opened various international railway transport services, including both container and full-load international rail transport services that run on fixed schedules, routes, frequencies, and full journey timetables, connecting directly to Europe and countries along the Belt and Road Initiative (BRI) route. These services are collectively referred to as the China Railway Express. The "Zhengzhou-Xinjiang-Europe" freight train services or Zhengxin'ou Railway was opened in July 2013. Compared to other China-Europe railway express services operated in various regions,

H. Feng (✉)
National Research Center on Strategic Development of High-Speed Railway,
Southwest Jiaotong University, Chengdu, China
e-mail: bai.gao@duke.edu

B. Gao, Z. Zhen (eds.), *The China-Europe Railway Express*, China and Globalization 2.0,
https://doi.org/10.1007/978-981-19-2882-6_6

the "Zhengxin'ou" stands out for two prominent characteristics. Firstly, it has gradually risen to prominence,[1] maintaining a leading position among all domestic China-Europe railway express services due to its advantageous location, excellent transportation infrastructure, extensive coverage, high freight volume, and frequent services; secondly, its development does not primarily focus on supporting local industries or industrial clusters. Instead, it aims to integrate transportation and trade through logistics development as its primary goal. The emphasis is on serving as a platform to fulfill the positioning of Zhengzhou as an international business hub.

The fundamental reasons behind the two prominent characteristics of the "Zhengxin'ou" lie in the ultimate "independent variable" of national strategy, which directly influences the development positioning of the Zhengzhou municipal government. This is mainly manifested in the following aspects: on the one hand, Zhengzhou municipal government, leveraging its geographical location and transportation advantages, has prioritized the modern logistics industry as a primary development strategy and pillar industry. Building upon the existing logistics infrastructure, it has actively supported the development of the "Zhengxin'ou" freight train. As a result, it has consistently maintained a leading position among the various China-Europe freight trains operating in the country; on the other hand, after the introduction of the BRI, Zhengzhou further reviewed its development strategy. It seized the opportunity presented by the Initiative to intensify its "westward opening" efforts. Building upon the existing logistics framework, it enhanced various means of logistics development, aiming to create an integrated platform for "transportation and trade integration." This platform is designed to realize Zhengzhou's positioning as an international business hub.

Therefore, this chapter focuses on the "Zhengxin'ou" in the context of national strategy. It begins by discussing the distinctive feature of the freight train coming from behind and later taking the lead. It then delves into the train's characteristic of establishing an integrated platform for "transportation and trade." Subsequently, it explores how Zhengzhou, leveraging its geographical location and transportation advantages, organized a business development model primarily focused on modern logistics in anticipation of the BRI. Finally, it discusses how Zhengzhou,

[1] Yaohua Li, (2015). The Current Operation and Development Strategies of China-Europe Express. *Foreign Economic Relations Trade*, No. 2, pp. 91–93.

under the framework of the BRI, organized modern logistics around the China-Europe freight train.

6.2 Zhengxin'ou's Surging Ahead

"Zhengxin'ou," inaugurated on July 18, 2013, has achieved remarkable growth in less than four years and has emerged as a leading player in China-Europe freight train services. This progress is evident in several aspects:

The freight train offers a competitive advantage with its long transportation route and short delivery time. It plays a pivotal role in Henan Province's integration with the BRI. Its primary route runs from Zhengzhou to Hamburg, Germany, via Xi'an, Lanzhou, Urumqi, and passes through the border crossings of Alashankou and Erenhot, traversing Kazakhstan (or Mongolia), Russia, Belarus, Poland, and Germany. The entire journey covers 10,214 kilometers (10,484 kilometers via Erenhot), involving two border crossings and two-gage changes, with a transit time of approximately 12 days. This significantly reduces the time compared to shipping by sea, saving 25–30 days, and is much more cost-effective, with an 80% cost reduction for heavy cargo compared to air freight and a 20% cost reduction for light cargo compared to air freight. This provides the train with a unique advantage of a long transportation route with short delivery times.

The "Zhengxin'ou" boasts a high frequency of trips, balanced round trips, high cargo value, heavy cargo weight, and excellent load rates, making it one of the leading services among China-Europe freight trains. The frequency of operations, total cargo value, and total cargo weight are major metrics used to measure the performance of China-Europe freight train services. The train's operational frequency has steadily increased since its inception (see Table 6.1). Starting with one departure per month in July 2013, it expanded to three departures per week in the latter half of 2016, consisting of three departures and three return journeys. The total number operated grew significantly from 100 services at the end of 2014, with a total cargo value of $475 million and a total cargo weight of 52,200 tons, to 251 services at the end of 2016 (137 departures and 114 arrivals). This represented a 151% increase in the number of services, with a total cargo value of $1.267 billion and a total cargo weight of 128,600 tons (see Table 6.2). As of June 30, 2017, "Zhengxin'ou" has achieved the normalization of five departures and five return journeys per week. This

Table 6.1 "Zhengxin'ou" train service frequency

Time period	*Train services*
July–October 2013	One departure per month (outbound)
November 2013–August 2014	One departure per week (outbound)
September–December 2014	Two departures per week (outbound), two departures per month (return)
January–June 2015	Two departures per week (outbound), one departure per week (return)
July–August 2016	Two departures per week (outbound), two departures per week (return)
September–June 2016	Three departures per week (outbound), two departures per week (return)
July–December 2016	Three departures per week (outbound), three departures per week (return)

Source: *Advantages of Regular and High-Frequency Operations*, Official Website of Zhengzhou International Hub Development and Construction Co., Ltd, http://www.zzgu-ugang.com/zhengou-banlie/banlieyoushi/2016/0708/31.html, Last accessed July 7, 2017

Table 6.2 Accumulated freight information for Zhengxin'ou

	Cumulative classes (classes)	*Total value of goods (billions of US dollars)*	*Total freight (ten thousand tons)*
End of 2014	100	5.22	4.75
End of 2015	256	11.5	11.96
End of 2016	251	12.67	12.86

Source: *Advantages of Regular and High-Frequency Operations*, Official Website of Zhengzhou International Hub Development and Construction Co., Ltd., Available at: http://www.zzgu-ugang.com/zhengoubanlie/banlieyoushi/2016/0708/31.html, Last Accessed July 7, 2017

well-balanced and high-frequency round trip structure has led to an annual reduction of approximately 20% in the overall operating costs of this train service.

The "Zhengxin'ou" freight train network has emerged as a leader in the realm of China-Europe train services, showcasing an extensive domestic and international collection and distribution network. Anchored by key hubs in Zhengzhou and Hamburg, this network has strategically built a multi-hub system for efficient cargo collection and distribution, both domestically and internationally. The practice of multiple point loading and unloading has become a standard procedure within this network. With 52 offices strategically positioned nationwide, this network revolves around Zhengzhou, forming a well-connected and centralized system. The system has a cargo collection radius of over 1500 kilometers, a distribution radius of 2000 kilometers, covering three-quarters of China's provinces. Additionally, it extends eastward to regions like Japan and South Korea through transshipment. Internationally, Hamburg serves as the main hub, and secondary collection and distribution centers are in cities such as Paris, Milan, Prague, Warsaw, Malaszewicze, Brest, Moscow, Almaty, and Zamin Uud, covering 24 countries and 121 cities across the European Union, Russia, and Central Asia.[2] This dual-hub and multi-point collection and distribution system helps consolidate cargo for the trains, ensuring a stable source of goods for the service. Currently, the composition of the cargo sources for the freight train network includes 75% of shipments from outside Henan Province, with international cargo sources accounting for 20% of the total.[3] The network is currently operating multiple entry and exit points on both the western route (via Alashankou) and the northern route (via Erenhot) and is in the process of establishing a southern route through Turkey/Bulgaria to Southern Europe, making it the only train service with multiple entry points, multiple routes, and a dual-channel operation.[4]

6.3 Transportation and Trade Integration with a Platform-Centric Approach

Currently, China-Europe freight trains operate under three distinct modes: "industry-driven," "establishing public platforms and expanding markets," and "government image projects." In contrast to other cities

[2] *Advantages of Dual Hubs at Home and Abroad and Multiple Collection and Distribution Points*, Official Website of Zhengzhou International Hub Development and Construction Co., Ltd. http://www.zz-guojilugang.com/zhengoubanlie/banlieyoushi/2016/0708/29.html. Last accessed: July 4, 2017.

[3] "Why Chengdu, Wuhan, and Zhengzhou Are So Impressive?" Sohu Web. http://www.sohu.com/a/128786415_330850. Last accessed: March 14, 2017.

[4] "Advantages of Multiple Port and Multiple Route Entry and Exit," Official Website of Zhengzhou International Hub Development and Construction Co., Ltd. http://zzguojilugang.com/zhengoubanlieshi/2016/0708/30.html. Last accessed: July 10, 2016.

operating China-Europe freight trains, such as Chongqing, which has laid a foundation for investment promotion through the development of "Yuxin'ou," and Wuhan, leveraging its manufacturing sector to export local electronic products and automobiles to Europe using the "Hanxin'ou" (Wuhan-Xinjiang-Europe) freight train, Zhengzhou has strategically positioned its development model as "primarily focused on establishing public platforms and expanding markets." It does not emphasize supporting local industries or industrial clustering but treats the "Zhengxin'ou" as an industry, aiming to use it to promote logistics development and achieve the goal of transportation and trade integration. During the research process, the person in charge of Zhengzhou International Hub Development and Construction Co., Ltd. (hereinafter referred to as the Hub Company), which operates the "Zhengxin'ou," explained:

> The success of "Zhengxin'ou" hinges on fostering robust trade activities. While a logistics-focused approach allows us to provide comprehensive door-to-door services along the industrial chain, it falls short when it comes to stimulating diverse industries. Our experiences from 2013 and 2014 revealed that a logistics-only train route lacks profitability and fails to catalyze substantial industrial growth. Ultimately, it is trade that holds the key to driving comprehensive industrial development.

Zhengzhou, serving as a pivotal national hub and pivotal transfer point for goods, has been instrumental in seamlessly integrating transportation and trade. Capitalizing on its strategic location as a transportation nexus, Zhengzhou has rightfully earned the title of the "City of Commerce." Yet, as the national economy has advanced, the commercial landscape has also transformed, prompting an upgrade in the city's commercial endeavors. The train route is widely regarded as forging a modern-day "New Silk Road" between China and Europe, transforming the Central Plains into a fresh departure point for the Central Asia-Europe land bridge. Zhengzhou has become a major hub and transfer point for goods from central, northwestern, northern, and northeastern China. More "Made in China" products are continuously aggregated from all over the country to Zhengzhou and are then transported to countries along the BRI economic belt in Central Asia, East Asia, and Europe through the "Zhengxin'ou" route. This has created a convenient and vital transportation route for these countries and regions and has facilitated the integration of more domestic companies into the BRI.

Professional operating organizations play a key role in the comprehensive expansion of the transportation and trade integration platform. The Hub Company is fully responsible for the operation of the "Zhengxin'ou" train service. As a multimodal transport operator, Hub Company holds not only the qualification as a non-vessel operating common carrier (NVOCC) and the ability to issue multimodal transport bills of lading, but it has also obtained the "Certificated Sales Agent,"[5] allowing it to issue its own cargo transport main bills of lading and offer door-to-door full-service transport agency services. Moreover, Land Port Company has established effective collaborative relationships with domestic and foreign railway, road, shipping, and aviation transport companies, as well as strong partnerships with multiple freight forwarders and logistics companies. They possess a comprehensive multimodal transport logistics network that covers rail, road, sea, and air transport, providing services such as pickup, delivery, transportation, warehousing, distribution, customs clearance, and financial services to both domestic and international customers.[6] Since its establishment in June 2013, the company has experienced rapid development and continuous innovation. While consolidating its leading position in the "Zhengxin'ou" rail service, it has also laid a long-term vision and shifted from a single transport service model to a focus on both logistics and trade. In addition to operating full-container and general cargo services, the Hub Company has expanded its services to include transit

[5] The "Certificated Sales Agent" is a sales license issued by the China Air Transport Association (CATA) to air cargo agents. It is categorized into Class 1 and Class 2. The Class 1 allows agents to engage in air cargo services on routes to Hong Kong, Macao, Taiwan, and international destinations. The Class 2 permits agents to handle domestic air cargo services under the jurisdiction of the CATA.

[6] "Logistics finance" refers to financial services that are developed and generated based on the common needs of various parties involved in the logistics value chain, including suppliers, end-users, financial institutions, and logistics companies. In a broader sense, logistics finance involves effectively organizing and allocating the movement of monetary funds within the logistics field throughout the entire supply chain management process by applying and developing various financial products. This integration aims to achieve the organic unity of commodity flow, physical flow, capital flow, and information flow, enhancing the efficiency of supply chain operations and ultimately realizing the development of a state where the logistics industry and financial sector are integrated. In a narrower sense, logistics finance specifically involves activities within the supply chain management process where third-party logistics providers and financial institutions offer goods and money to customers, complete settlements, and facilitate financing activities, creating an economic model where all parties grow and prosper together. This chapter primarily discusses the narrower concept of logistics finance services.

shipments, multimodal transportation by rail, sea, air, and road, as well as business related to specialty ports such as automobile imports, cross-border e-commerce, international postal services, international trade, and cold chain logistics. In particular, the company leverages its extensive business networks in Europe, Central Asia, Japan, South Korea, and other regions to actively engage in cross-border e-commerce activities. Additionally, the Company capitalizes on its status as the first multimodal transportation customs supervision center in the central region of China to establish a distinctive cross-border e-commerce comprehensive service platform. This platform seamlessly integrates the transportation advantages of railways with the expeditious benefits of air transportation, providing a diverse range of cross-border e-commerce solutions to both domestic and international clients. With the operation of various online e-commerce platforms like Zheng'ou Mall, WeChat Mall for imported goods, and physical stores such as the Imported Goods Display and Experience Center, "Zhengxin'ou" rail services have been fully integrated into the transport and trade strategy. This expansion has brought more opportunities for direct procurement and purchase, facilitating the convergence of a variety of goods, including personal care products, cosmetics, food and beverages, baby products, toys, and nutritional supplements transported using refrigerated containers. These items, known as "Silk Road Merchandise," ride the rail services to gather in Zhengzhou, resulting in a rapid increase in cross-border trade volume. This dynamic has created a unique development advantage that combines "rail services + cross-border trade" and promotes both transportation and trade simultaneously. At the end of 2015, the integrated transport and trade strategy of the Zhengxin'ou rail services had been fully expanded. Various channels, including online, offline, and physical stores, were utilized for promotion. The "Zheng'ou E-commerce Platform" and "Zheng'ou WeChat Mall" achieved significant operational results. Imported goods were also selling well in various supermarkets and convenience stores in Zhengzhou.[7] In 2016, the online and offline sales of the "Zheng'ou E-commerce Platform"

[7] "Zheng'ou Freight Train Services Establishes Co-operation with More Than 300 Merchants Along the BRI," Xinhua News Network, Henan Channel. Website: http://www.haxinuanet.com/news/20170320/3681249.html, Last access on: March 20, 2017.

exceeded 10 million yuan ($1.4 million), showing a growth of 180% compared to 2015.[8]

6.4 Organizing Modern Logistics Around Location and Transportation Advantages

When examining successful logistics hubs globally, their rapid development and success are largely attributed to unique location advantages, well-established infrastructure, favorable industrial environments, high-quality logistics services, and robust government support.[9] Prior to the initiation of the BRI, Zhengzhou primarily capitalized on its comparative advantage in "location + transportation," making logistics one of the key supported and planned industries. This groundwork laid a strong foundation for the rapid development of "Zhengxin'ou," and the establishment of a modern business development model centered on advanced logistics.

Henan, known as "the center of China," boasts exceptional location and transportation advantages for developing the modern logistics industry. Situated at the heart of China, Henan lies between the Yangtze River Delta, Beijing-Tianjin-Hebei, Pearl River Delta, and Chengdu-Chongqing city clusters, serving as a gateway to the northwest. It connects the east and west, north, and south, making it the central hub for communication and collaboration among various economic regions nationwide. A network of main railway lines such as the Beijing-Guangzhou, Beijing-Kowloon, and Jiaozuo-Zhicheng railways crisscrosses the province, and the New Eurasian Land Bridge, running from China's coastal city of Lianyungang to Rotterdam in the Netherlands, traverses the entire province. Henan, with its extensive and well-connected transportation network, links to developed coastal regions in the east, including Shanghai, Guangzhou, and Taiwan, fostering cooperation and industrial transfer. To the west, it facilitates trade with countries like Kazakhstan and Uzbekistan via Urumqi, fostering a connection between eastern, central, and western regions, ensuring efficient resource allocation. Through participation in the BRI and free trade zones, it integrates the Asia-Pacific region with

[8] "How Has the 'Iron Camel Caravan' Made Its Mark on the New Silk Road? Insights into the Three Years of the Zheng'ou Freight Train," Sohu Finance Channel. Website: http://mt.sohu.com/20170220/n481175603.shtml, Last access on: February 20, 2017.

[9] Hongli Zhang (2015), Research on the Development Strategy of Zhengzhou's Logistics Industry with a Focus on the "Major Hub" Strategy, *Logistics Technology*, No. 8, pp. 54–56.

Central Europe.[10] Furthermore, Henan Province is situated in the transitional zone from the developed eastern coastal regions to the economically developing northwestern regions of China. It is conceivable that the development of the logistics industry in Henan Province will not only drive the local economic growth but also play a pivotal role in promoting the rise of central China, the extensive development of the western regions, and the future construction of logistics networks in the western regions. Moreover, it will contribute significantly to achieving strategic regional coordinated development by acting as a catalyst and connector.[11] Zhengzhou, located at the geographic center of China, serves as a crucial transportation and logistics hub in the country. It boasts an advanced comprehensive transportation network, acting as the central "double cross" for both the national regular railway and high-speed railway networks. A Chinese character for "米" (or rice) shaped high-speed rail network is taking shape, providing the capability to reach every corner of Henan within one hour, neighboring provincial capitals like Wuhan and Xi'an within two hours, and major domestic economic centers such as Beijing and Shanghai within three hours. Zhengzhou Xinzheng International Airport is one of China's eight regional hub airports. With a 1.5-hour flight range, it covers two-thirds of major cities across China, currently operating 185 passenger and cargo routes, including 34 cargo routes (28 international cargo routes). Henan boasts an extensive expressway network, with a total mileage of 6315 kilometers in 2015, ranking second in the nation.

Centered around its advantageous location and transportation infrastructure, Henan has vigorously developed modern logistics, thereby supporting the growth of the "Zhengxin'ou" route. In an era of economic globalization and rapid advancements in modern information technology, logistics has emerged as a vital industry with limitless potential and room for development on a global scale. It has become a key indicator for measuring regional economic development. Furthermore, the logistics economy is a unique economic form that hinges on the foundation of economic and policy considerations. The governments of Henan Province and the city of Zhengzhou have consistently recognized logistics as a pivotal

[10] Jiayuan Wang. (2015). New Opportunities for Henan under the BRI Regional Development Strategy, *Academic Theory*, No. 3, p. 111.

[11] Jinhua Li, (Dec. 2019). *Research on the Development of Henan's Logistics under the Conditions of Central China's Rise*, Master, Henan University of Science and Technology.

industry, leveraging their strategic location and transportation advantages. This steadfast commitment has established a robust groundwork for the rapid growth of "Zhengxin'ou." Since 2005, Zhengzhou formally incorporated the modern logistics industry into national economic and social development statistics, enabling continuous monitoring of its progress, timely support, and the implementation of standardized management practices. In October 2005, the Henan provincial government issued the "Development Plan for China Zhengzhou Modern Logistics Center," which explicitly called for the establishment of a modern logistics core zone centered around Zhengzhou within the Central Plains urban cluster. This approach aimed to promote regional coordinated development and the creation of a "tight circle" of modern logistics that extends throughout the province. These initiatives leveraged the critical role of regional logistics hubs in facilitating economic development. To foster logistics industry growth, since 2006, the government has extended substantial support to logistics construction projects. Enterprises exhibiting rapid growth and robust profitability were duly rewarded. Technical upgrades were secured by acquiring national debt funds through government channels in partnership with the local National Development and Reform Commission. In terms of logistics development financing, the government encouraged commercial banks to proactively provide loans and credit guarantees. They also aimed to diversify the sources of investment. Privately funded projects were subject to approval and filing, with relaxed policies to expedite capital injections and promote the rapid development of the logistics industry. In 2008, the "Master Plan of Zhengzhou City (2008–2020)" outlined Zhengzhou's future role as a "comprehensive transportation and communication hub" and "a modern logistics center of national importance." Zhengzhou City also plans to build an "International Logistics Center" over approximately 20 years, based on the existing plan. The city aims to complete the "Strategic Plan and Layout for Zhengzhou International Logistics Center" and transform Zhengzhou into a globally leading modern logistics center by the year. During the "12th Five-Year Plan," Henan Province placed a strong emphasis on the vigorous development of the modern logistics industry. In this context, the provincial government introduced the "Development Plan for the Modern Logistics Industry in Henan Province (2010–2015)." This strategic initiative encompassed a range of preferential policies tailored to the logistics sector. These policies fostered an enabling environment, particularly contributing to the flourishing growth of the Zhengzhou logistics industry cluster. This plan played a pivotal role in guiding and accelerating the rapid development of the industry.[12] In 2010, in the "12th Five-Year Plan for Zhengzhou's National Economic and Social Development (2010–2015)," the modern logistics industry was recognized as a strategic support industry. The plan articulated that the construction of the Zhengzhou International Logistics Center would lead the development of the entire modern logistics industry in the city. The focus will be on the construction of dry ports and the development of international logistics. Efforts will be accelerated to promote the collaboration between logistics, industries, and markets, establishing logistics distribution centers for warehousing, sorting, and distribution. Rapid development of express logistics and bonded logistics will be emphasized, aiming to construct a nationwide logistics network. In September 2011, the introduction of the State Council's "Guidance for Accelerating the Construction of the Central Plains Economic Zone" elevated the Central Plains Economic Zone to a national strategy. The document explicitly calls for building Zhengzhou into a "national logistics center." In 2011, the Development and Reform Commission of Henan Province formulated the "2011 Work Plan for Promoting the Development of the Logistics Industry," which set the target for Zhengzhou's logistics sector, achieving a value-added growth of 20% with the logistics industry reaching 23 billion yuan ($3.1 billion). According to the relevant planning, Zhengzhou aimed to construct the "Seven Major Logistics Projects" and "Five Regional Logistics Hubs." The 2013 government work report for Henan Province emphasized that efforts should be made to expedite the improvement of the transportation and logistics systems as well as various supporting facilities for industrial carriers. Additionally, there was a focus on the development of open platforms like comprehensive bonded zones, and the establishment of a "one-stop customs clearance" mechanism. The report highlighted the imperative to reinforce Zhengzhou's pivotal role as a logistics center, augment the logistics capabilities of key regional cities, and actively develop specialized logistics sectors including aviation, ports, bonded logistics, and cold chain logistics. Furthermore, the strategy underscored the importance of giving precedence to air cargo transportation, nurturing international e-commerce distribution centers, and enhancing seamless connectivity from the city's railway hub to eastern seaports and western routes reaching Central Asia

[12] Li Tian, (2015). Efficiency Evaluation of Henan Province's Logistics Industry Based on DEA Model, *Logistics Technology*, No. 1, pp. 161–164.

and Europe. This strategic vision aims to position Zhengzhou as a worldwide hub for streamlined and efficient goods collection and distribution. In conclusion, the logistics industry has made an increasingly significant contribution to the economic and social development of Zhengzhou, particularly after the completion of the "Rice" shaped high-speed railway network. Zhengzhou has proactively created a four-hour express logistics corridor that connects major economic regions across the country. Concurrently, it has pushed forward the construction of freight rail lines, eliminated bottlenecks in national road transport, upgraded congested sections of national highways, accelerated the construction of major waterways like the Huai River and Shaying River, and established an extensive freight transport network that connects in all directions. Moreover, in the context of economic liberalization and trade globalization, an increasing number of companies, motivated by cost and service considerations, are outsourcing most, if not all, of their logistics tasks to external providers. Taking regional conditions into account, Henan is fostering the growth of large logistics enterprises and actively promoting the development of third-party logistics services.[13]

Undoubtedly, Zhengzhou's exceptional geographical location, coupled with its convenient transportation infrastructure and the national emphasis on logistics development, along with supportive government policies, has created an advantageous policy environment for the modern logistics industry's growth. This has effectively propelled the rapid and robust development of the Zhengxin'ou railway route, making it the most widely covered rail line in terms of the source of goods. Its goods consolidation center already covers 121 cities in 24 countries in the EU, Russia, and Central Asia. Notably, domestic customers' goods originate from three-fourths of China's provinces, providing a stable foundation for goods sourced from key economic regions like the Pearl River Delta, Yangtze River Delta, and the Bohai Economic Rim.[14]

[13] Lixiao Li. (2010). Research on the Countermeasures for the Development of the Logistics Industry in Henan Province, *Modern Logistics*, No. 6, pp. 92–94.

[14] "Advantages of Dual Hubs Inside and Outside the Border and Multiple Points Along the Way," Official Website of Zhengzhou International Hub Development and Construction Co., Ltd., http://www.zz-guojilugang.com/zhengoubanlie/banlieyoushi/2016/0708/29.html, last accessed on July 4, 2017.

6.5 Organizing Modern Logistics Around the China-Europe Railway Express

The BRI stands as China's highest-level national strategic blueprint and a pivotal plan for comprehensive opening-up, poised to drive development both within China and abroad. Establishing efficient logistics channels between different countries is paramount within the BRI, facilitating international trade and connectivity on a global scale. Despite Zhengzhou's inland location, the development of the "Zhengxin'ou" rail service has provided a unique opportunity for the city to participate in global outreach and western expansion. This initiative has significantly expanded the scope and impact of land transportation. Since its introduction in September 2013, Zhengzhou has utilized its existing logistics infrastructure to strengthen various development methods, providing essential support for the growth of "Zhengxin'ou." With great determination, the goal is to ensure the success of the "Zhengxin'ou," using it as a gateway to further open up to the world and lay the foundation for becoming an "International Business Hub."

Zhengzhou's strategic positioning under the BRI. From a strategic perspective, only by placing Zhengzhou within the larger framework and strategic vision of China's development can the correct development direction be truly understood. Henan Province is situated at the intersection of the "Silk Road Economic Belt" extending west and south and connecting with the "Maritime Silk Road." To the east, it can achieve connectivity with the "Maritime Silk Road" by constructing a land port, developing rail-sea intermodal transport, and promoting land-sea connectivity. To the west, it can enhance the operational level of the "Zhengxin'ou," deeply integrating with the development of the "Silk Road Economic Belt." The "Eastward Connection and Westward Expansion" strategy aims to strengthen the position of Zhengzhou Airport Economy Zone as an international logistics center, linking it globally.[15] Based on this strategic geographical advantage, the development positioning and strategies of Henan Province and Zhengzhou City have undergone significant changes after the introduction of the BRI. In May 2014, during his inspection tour in Henan, President Xi Jinping expressed his desire to transform Zhengzhou into a logistics hub that connects domestic and international markets and

[15] "Zhengzhou's Vision under the BRI," People's Daily Online, http://news.zynews.cn/2015-04/30/content.10161574.htm. Last Accessed: April 30, 2015.

radiates in all directions, making a significant contribution to the construction of the "Silk Road Economic Belt." In March 2015, the State Council released the "Vision and Actions on Jointly Building Silk Road Economic Belt and 21st-Century Maritime Silk Road," which proposed: "The objective is to develop Zhengzhou into an inland open economy highland by supporting the construction of Zhengzhou Airport Economy Zone, the international land port, initiating cross-border trade e-commerce pilot projects, and enhancing the brand of the 'Zhengxin'ou' freight train services." In this context, in November 2015, Henan Province published the "Implementation Plan of Henan Province for Participating in the Building of the Silk Road Economic Belt and 21st-Century Maritime Silk Road," (hereinafter referred to as "Plan"), positioning Henan Province as an "important comprehensive transportation hub and trade logistics center for the BRI, a significant platform for regional interaction and cooperation in the New Eurasian Land Bridge Economic Corridor, and a highland for inland opening-up." As a crucial comprehensive transportation hub and logistics center in China, Zhengzhou leverages its geographical advantages and has adopted a new approach is to "move eastward, connect westward, establish a major hub, develop major logistics network, and nurture substantial industries" to support the BRI. The operation of the "Zhengxin'ou" freight train, connecting Asia and Europe, is a specific measure taken by Zhengzhou to actively participate in the Initiative.[16]

During the research, the person in charge of the Hub Company operating the "Zhengxin'ou" explained:

> Our initial focus was on a land port, and then we expanded it to a land port. What we aim to create is a hub through Zhengzhou, where quality domestic products can be exported, and excellent foreign products can enter through Zhengzhou. We are confident in turning Zhengzhou into a central hub for distribution. Henan Province has positioned Zhengzhou as an international business hub, so we need to work around this positioning.

Organizing modern logistics around the "Zhengxin'ou" freight trains. The regular operation of China-Europe freight trains has established a smooth trade route for the "New Silk Road," making it an important carrier and platform for connecting with the country's BRI and turning it

[16] "Zheng'ou Freight Trains Carrying the Dream of 'International Business Hub,'" NetEase News, http://news.163.com/15/1214/10/BAPPU2GP00014AEF.html. Last accessed on October 15, 2014.

into an open frontier.[17] The Initiative has bestowed upon the China-Europe freight trains a more significant and noble mission. An increasing number of provinces and cities have recognized the strategic value and role of these trains and are providing more support for their development and market cultivation.[18] However, the swift integration of China-Europe freight trains into the BRI is guided by local development objectives, industrial policies, and the influence of the national initiative. Local development goals and industrial policies are, to a certain extent, molded by national initiatives, constituting a continuous process of capitalizing on regional advantages. Under the umbrella of the BRI, the developmental focus of Henan Province and Zhengzhou municipal governments has shifted, particularly emphasizing the BRI's role in opening up the "westward direction" for Zhengzhou and providing a rare opportunity to expand land transport. As a result, both the provincial government and the municipal government have intensified their support for the development of the "Zhengxin'ou" freight trains. They have organized modern logistics around these trains, creating an integrated transportation and trade platform. With the high-frequency regular operation of these trains, Zhengzhou, as an important key city along the BRI and a crucial transportation hub in the Eurasian passage, has fully leveraged the advantages of multimodal transportation via road-rail, sea-rail, and air-rail connections. It has gradually established a global freight network connecting Asia and Europe, radiating into the Asia-Pacific region, and aims to develop into a modern comprehensive transportation hub that links China with the world.[19]

The government's macro-level guidance ensures the regular operation of the "Zhengxin'ou" freight train service. The governments of Henan Province and Zhengzhou City prioritize the operation of these trains. Following the principle of "provincial and municipal cooperation with the city taking the lead," and adopting a model of "government-led and enterprise-operated," they have established a two-tier leadership group for the promotion of the Zhengzhou International Railway Express, with

[17] Jiafeng Li. (2015). Optimization Strategies for China-Europe Trains under the BRI, *Railway Transport and Economy*, No. 5, pp. 41–45.

[18] Yingming Xu. (2015). Exploring the Path of Comprehensive Benefits of the China-Europe Railway from the Perspective of the BRI, *Frontiers*, No. 10, pp. 45–48.

[19] "Which Cities are China's National Central Cities: A List of the Latest Cities and Their Reasons, Fortune Power," http://wap927953.com/content.aspx?newsId=260149. Last Accessed: December 21, 2016.

participation from Zhengzhou City and the Economic and Technological Development Zone. In addition, to effectively manage the operation, a platform company called "Hub Company" was jointly established by the Zhengzhou Economic and Technological Development Zone and the Henan Provincial Materials Group. An official from Zhengzhou City expresses their commitment to collaborate with countries along the Silk Road Economic Belt, working together to develop economic cooperation demonstration zones in logistics, trade, e-commerce, and other sectors, aiming to create multiple mutually beneficial platforms and mechanisms for cooperation and development.

During the research, the person in charge of the Hub Company operating the "Zhengxin'ou" freight train explained:

> The unique advantages of Zhengzhou compared to other cities like Wuhan and Chengdu. Zhengzhou is strategically positioned as a key support point for the BRI, located within the Yangtze River Economic Belt. This geographic location offers numerous development opportunities. However, lacking coastal access or direct sea borders, Zhengzhou is compelled to invest its full efforts into ensuring the success of the China-Europe freight train route. Consequently, substantial support is provided by the provincial and municipal governments, along with the district government. Notably, in negotiations related to the "Zhengxin'ou" routes, the provincial governor and secretary lead the efforts, underscoring the province's significant commitment to this initiative and taking the lead in administrative endeavors.

Both the government documents of Henan Province and Zhengzhou City contain references to "Zhengxin'ou" (see Table 6.3). The policies related to route play a directive role in its operation.

Multiple measures have been implemented to ensure an adequate supply of cargo. The operation and launch of China-Europe freight trains are primarily driven by local governments. During the initial phase, known as the market cultivation period, government financial subsidies are the primary source of support. However, the goal for "Zhengxin'ou" is to transition toward market-driven operations within five years. As the number of train services increases, competition in the domestic market intensifies, sometimes leading to fierce competition, especially in areas related to domestic cargo sourcing and subsidies for train operation. In the initial phase of operation, Zhengzhou implemented a pricing model derived from maritime shipping prices to offer financial subsidies to train operators. These subsidies covered the entire cost of rail and road transportation

Table 6.3 Government-related policies for the planning of "Zhengxin'ou"

Title	*Date*	*Contents related to the "Zhengxin'ou" freight trains*
Henan Provincial 13th Five-Year Plan for National Economic and Social Development	May 2016	It aims to enhance the brand influence of the Zhengxin'ou freight train services. It emphasizes accelerating the development of Zhengxin'ou in terms of multiple outbound ports, multiple routes, multiple sources of goods, and multimodal transportation, while maintaining a leading position within the China-Europe rail logistics corridor. The plan focuses on expanding overseas collection and distribution networks, strengthening the organization of return shipments, and promoting the establishment of a number of overseas transshipment centers and distribution bases. This will lead to an expansion of the outbound cargo coverage area, facilitating high-level bidirectional transportation equilibrium and ensuring the regular operation of the railway with high density. Additionally, the plan encourages the construction of comprehensive logistics parks, bonded warehouses, and overseas e-commerce distribution centers in central cities along the railway, as well as the development of overseas transshipment operations.
The 13th Five-Year Plan for National Economic and Social Development in Zhengzhou	January, 2016	Its focus is on promoting open brands such as Zhengxin'ou and cultural brands. It aims to shape Zhengzhou's brand image as an international metropolis and a globally recognized historical and cultural city.
"Notice from the General Office of the People's Government of Henan Province on Issuing the Work Plan for Promoting the Integration of Transportation and Logistics in Henan Province" (The General Office of the Henan Provincial Government No. 〔2016〕 182)	January, 2016	(1) Air-rail Intermodal Transportation Project, promoting deep cooperation among entities like Hub Company. (2) Domestic and International "Dual Hub" Project, relying on the "Zhengxin'ou" to construct a logistics network framework with Zhengzhou as the central hub, Hamburg as the Western European hub, Warsaw as the Central European hub, and Prague as the Eastern European hub.

within a 1500-kilometer radius for domestic cargo destined for Zhengzhou. Currently, the subsidy model for the "Zhengxin'ou" freight trains is not solely based on the number of trains operated. Instead, it emphasizes two key factors. Firstly, subsidies are calculated based on the deficit generated from the difference between the number of trains operated each year and the expenditures incurred. Secondly, the Customs data for the load factor is proposed as a reference standard. This subsidy model, as compared to a simple calculation based on the number of trains, has the advantage of reducing subsidy costs by five to six times. Given that Zhengxin'ou's cargo collection radius extends beyond 1500 kilometers, covering approximately three-fourths of the provinces in China, Hub Company has established 52 specialized offices in eight domestic locations, including Tianjin, Shanghai, and Shenzhen. In addition, the company has set up branch offices in countries such as Germany and Poland, which are responsible for the distribution of outbound goods and organizing return journeys. These measures, to some extent, ensure an ample supply of cargo for the freight trains, establishing strong strategic partnerships to provide customers with a one-stop service. The strategic partnerships between the Hub Company and various freight forwarders and logistics companies facilitate the sharing of resources, such as information on cargo sources, facility equipment, and transportation capabilities, to ensure that customers receive a seamless, safe, punctual, and cost-effective one-stop service. Moreover, the "government-led, enterprise-operated" operational model also contributes to ensuring a sufficient supply of cargo. The local government establishes a platform company, with the Hub Company representing the local government and handling the operation of the "Zhengxin'ou" freight train. This includes the organization model and cooperation model of the train service. The railway department oversees transportation coordination. In the organizational framework, the Company takes charge and collaborates with large and medium-sized export enterprises domestically. It identifies the target customer base and enters into cooperation agreements. Presently, a fixed service price is in place, regardless of the customer's distance, with the Hub Company handling transportation responsibilities. Regarding the cooperation model, the first aspect involves international partners. The Hub Company entrusts foreign agencies to handle coordination for the overseas segment of the freight train service after it departs from China, as well as the organization of deliveries upon the train's arrival at its destination; the second aspect entails collaborating with railway authorities, customs, and inspection and quarantine departments. The Hub Company takes on the responsibility of coordinating with these entities and closely collaborating with the local railway bureau, Zhengzhou Customs, and the Inspection and Quarantine Bureau to manage relevant tasks; the third aspect involves multimodal transportation, with an agreement signed between Lu Gang Company and China Railway International Multimodal Transport Co., Ltd. (hereinafter referred to as CRIMT). CRIMT is responsible for handling outbound procedures, while the railway department oversees transportation coordination. To ensure the smooth operation of the train services, Zhengzhou Railway Bureau has established a dedicated leadership team. The team is led by the Deputy Director in charge of transportation, with the Director of Marketing Center serving as the deputy leader. Other team members include leaders from the transportation, freight, mechanical, vehicle, dispatching departments, China Railway Container Transport Corp., Zhengzhou Branch, Hub Company, and CRIMT's Zhengzhou Branch. This team is responsible for overall train service design, organization, and product promotion. In September 2013, Zhengzhou Railway Bureau issued a notice titled "Notice on the Interim Plan for the Organization of Zhengzhou-Europe International Container Trains," further specifying the responsibilities of Hub Company, relevant departments and sections of the railway bureau, China Railway Container Transport Corp., Zhengzhou Branch, and CRIMT's Zhengzhou Branch. It also clarified the timeframes for various stages, laying the foundation for the regular operation of the train service. Particularly, after China Railway adjusted the operating train number for "Zhengxin'ou" to 80001, it received a nationwide "green light" treatment, reducing the total travel time to approximately 63 hours, which was about one day less than before.

6.6 Conclusions and Discussions

In recent years, to stimulate regional economic development and promote external openness, the government has implemented a series of policies that favor Zhengzhou. Following the establishment of the Zhengzhou Comprehensive Experimental Zone for Airport-based Economy in 2013, Zhengzhou has seen the establishment of over ten national-level strategic initiatives, including the China (Henan) Pilot Free Trade Zone, the Central Plain city cluster, the China (Zhengzhou) Cross-Border E-Commerce Comprehensive Pilot Zone, the Zhengzhou-Luoyang-Xinxiang National Independent Innovation Demonstration Zone, the

National Comprehensive Transportation Hub Demonstration City, the National General Aviation Industry Comprehensive Demonstration Zone, and the Demonstration Base for Entrepreneurship and Innovation, among others. These initiatives underscore the government's dedication to fostering development and cooperation in Zhengzhou. Particularly with the recent official launch of the "13th Five-Year Plan for Promoting the Rise of the Central Region" by the National Development and Reform Commission, Zhengzhou has officially attained the status of a national central city. This progress centered around "Zhengxin'ou" is poised to reach new heights. In recent years, the governments of Henan Province and Zhengzhou have consistently utilized the advantages of their geographic location and transportation networks. They have intensified their efforts in external openness, actively aligned with national strategies, and embraced an international development direction. The overarching objective is to shape Zhengzhou into a global commercial hub city renowned for its seamless facilitation of factor exchange, robust support for modern industry growth, the preservation of urban harmony and stability, and its appeal as an ideal location for both residence and business activities. The operation signifies a significant milestone in Zhengzhou and Henan Province's openness to the global community. It enhances Henan's standing as a key logistics hub along the BRI, solidifying the province's pivotal role in China's engagement with this national initiative. With the rising frequency and enhanced efficiency of these rail services, economic and trade interactions between Henan and countries along the BRI are becoming notably vigorous. Consequently, there is a gradual diversification in the range of traded goods.[20] Some scholars argue that the introduction of the "Zhengxin'ou" brought about the establishment of Zhengzhou International Hub, which serves as a prominent symbol of the city's aspiration to become an "International Business Hub."

Based on the analysis presented above, this chapter explores the following questions.

In light of formidable competition from maritime shipping, China-Europe rail freight services must strategically decrease transportation costs to stay competitive. A crucial element in achieving cost reduction is

[20] "Zheng'ou Freight Trains Surpassing Others: Establishing Henan as a Strategic Node in the BRI", Sina Henan News, http://henan.sina.com.cn/news/z/2015-03-12/detail-icczmvun6677882.shtml, Last Accessed: March 12, 2015.

ensuring a substantial volume of return cargo.[21] However, since its inception, the service has grappled with a shortage of return cargo, resulting in an imbalance between outbound and return journeys.

Compared to other China-Europe rail freight services operating in diverse regions, "Zhengxin'ou" has established a standardized operating schedule featuring high-frequency outbound and return trips. As of the end of 2016, it had essentially realized a weekly schedule of three outbound trips and three return trips, becoming a regular part of its operation. In 2017, it further expanded its operation to include four outbound trips and four return trips per week, marking a continuous commitment to high-frequency and balanced services in both directions. However, emphasizing the sheer number of rail services is not valuable on its own because the actual data relies on customs statistics. The goal of China-Europe rail services is to become market-oriented and exit government subsidies. To make these services cost-effective, it's essential for them to have return cargo. This entails achieving a high-frequency, bidirectional operation for both outbound and return trips. At the present stage, achieving two-way operations for both trips necessitates self-owned containers. Firstly, by using self-owned containers for return cargo, it ensures that the container itself is returned along with the goods. Secondly, container ownership enables flexible circulation on a global scale, eliminating concerns related to added costs associated with container transfers. The Hub Company owns nearly 2000 self-owned containers, including specialized containers like refrigerated containers, garment containers, and open-top containers, which are regularly used in their operations. When it comes to return cargo, they primarily employ three modes, "freight forwarders, regular customers, and self-operation." "Zhengxin'ou" primarily relies on its staff members in 52 domestic local offices to handle cargo collection throughout the country, including sourcing cargo from abroad. In most cases, the organization of return cargo falls under the responsibility of the domestic team. This can be attributed to the absence of related supporting industries for the rail service development in Henan Province. To fulfill the cargo demands for the advancement of the "Zhengxin'ou" rail service, it is imperative to coordinate the cargo through a dedicated team. Presently, the primary types of return cargo comprise medical equipment from Germany and imported food, automobiles, and other products.

[21] Bai Gao. (2016)."Fully Grasping Chengdu's Position in National Strategy and Becoming the Vanguard in Implementing the "Belt and Road" Initiative, *Vanguard*, Issue 4, pp. 7–10.

The relationship between the Hub Company and China Railway follows the "government-led, enterprise-operated" operating model for the "Zhengxin'ou" rail service. In this arrangement, local governments establish platform companies, with the Hub Company acting on behalf of the local government and being accountable for the operation of "Zhengxin'ou." The railway department, which includes the China Railway and the China Railway Container Transport Co., Ltd. (abbreviated as CRCT), is responsible for transport coordination. Currently, while the China Railway has already lowered its prices, CRCT continues to operate in a monopolistic manner. This system determines that the domestic segment's costs cannot decrease. Although the China Railway reduced prices, it did not benefit the customers directly. Their point of contact was with CRCT, which acted as an intermediary, bundling volume and price, and thus, earning a portion of the profit. Therefore, in the operation of the "Zhengxin'ou," the relationship between the Hub Company and China Railway can be understood as follows: the Hub Company serves as a customer of the China Railway, which acts as the cargo owner. However, CRCT, acting as an intermediary, receives most of the profits.

The relationship between freight charges and costs. During the initial stages of launching China-Europe rail services in different regions, there is a tendency for high costs due to overlapping routes. However, for later entrants into the market, costs may vary. Competition within the industry significantly influences these costs. In standard market conditions, charges are somewhat proportional to the route's length. In the case of China-Europe rail services, the government adheres to market principles, allowing various regions to compete in launching these services. Consequently, all routes initially set high-cost prices. However, competition tends to shift from service quality to price comparison, leading to price wars.

The driving and spillover effects of the intermodal rail services and their relationship with open platforms. In the "12th Five-Year Plan Outline for the Economic and Social Development of Henan Province," modern logistics is designated as one of the pillar service industries. The plan emphasizes expediting the construction of the Zhengzhou International Logistics Center, expanding and enhancing the bonded logistics functions, vigorously developing international logistics, establishing an internationally aligned logistics service system, creating a "land port," and initially forming a modern logistics center rooted in the Central Plains, serving the entire nation and connecting with the world. Furthermore, the plan advocates for the coordinated growth of the logistics industry alongside manufacturing and modern agriculture. It emphasizes the creation of a public logistics information service platform, with the goal of gradually constructing a regional integrated logistics development framework. In this framework, Zhengzhou serves as the hub, supported by various logistics nodes.[22] It can be observed that during the "12th Five-Year Plan" period, Henan Province has significantly prioritized the development of the logistics industry as a pillar industry, but primarily within the domestic scope. The "13th Five-Year Plan Outline for the Economic and Social Development of Henan Province" sets forth the strategic orientation for Henan Province: to establish major hubs driving extensive logistics, substantial logistics propelling major industries, major industries propelling urban clusters, and urban clusters leading to the rise of the Central Plains, fostering a new phase of development for Henan's revitalization, prosperity, and strength for the people. The plan also aims to build an inland open platform, enhancing and upgrading the support platform for external openness.[23] In the "Strategic Plan Outline for the Development of Zhengzhou as an International Business Hub," the provincial committee and government have proposed the strategic concept of "Building Zhengzhou as an International Business Hub."[24] This concept was formulated through a comprehensive assessment of the city's fundamental advantages and development trends. Unlike focusing primarily on supporting local industries or industrial clustering, the development of the "Zhengxin'ou" rail service places its emphasis on integrating transportation and trade through logistics development. If we consider the Zhengxin'ou intermodal rail service as an independent component of logistics development, it can, at most, provide door-to-door services through the industrial chain. However, the development of trade involves multiple industries. Therefore, the primary aim of its development is to act

[22] "Notice of the People's Government of Henan Province on Printing and Distributing the Outline of the 12th Five-Year Plan for National Economic and Social Development of Henan Province" (The General Office of the Henan Provincial Government No. 〔2011〕 38), Henan Provincial People's Government Website. http://www.henan.gov.cn/zwgk/system/2011/04/29/010241505.shtml, Last accessed: April 29, 2011.

[23] "13th Five-Year Plan of Henan Province," Henan Daily Website. http://henan.people.com.cn/n2/2016/0518/c351638-28352742.html, Last accessed: May 18, 2016.

[24] "Outline of the Strategic Plan for the Development of Zhengzhou as an International Business Hub (Discussion Draft)," Sina News Center, Available at: http://news.sina.com.cn/o/2016-01-13/doc-ifxnuay7982068.shtml, Last accessed: January 13, 2016.

as a platform, facilitating the integration of transportation and trade to realize Zhengzhou's positioning as an international business hub.

Understanding of Customers and Sources of Goods. In terms of sourcing, Zhengzhou possesses distinct geographical and transportation advantages, but it lacks relevant industrial support, and its foreign trade sector requires further development. Therefore, in the initial stage of market cultivation to ensure a sufficient supply of goods, expand the radius for cargo acquisition, and adopt incentive mechanisms with financial subsidies, Zhengzhou follows a financial subsidy model like maritime shipping rates for intermodal rail companies. It provides full subsidies for the transportation costs of sourcing within a 1500-kilometer range to Zhengzhou via rail and road transport. This has allowed the "Zhengxin'ou" to become the route with the broadest coverage of goods sourcing. After reaching maturity in operations, the market's proactive role will be harnessed, and attempts will be made to phase out the subsidy mechanism. For "Zhengxin'ou," subsidies are currently provided based on the deficit formed by the difference between the annual operated trains and the associated expenditures. Additionally, it is proposed to use customs data on load factor as a reference standard. This model can significantly reduce subsidy costs and offers certain advantages. The Zhengxin'ou primarily focuses on major customers, stability being its main competitive advantage, while avoiding excessive reliance on a single dominant customer. As long as the container can accommodate the goods without exceeding length or width limits and the items being shipped are not prohibited by national regulations, both businesses and individuals can use land ports to transport their cargo. This is because land port shipping is more cost-effective than air freight and faster than sea freight. Since the successful launch, it has attracted an increasing number of customers and the participation of more countries. The China-Europe freight trains (Zhengzhou) do not strictly select their cargo sources due to various factors such as price competition, long-term stable cooperation with clients, and other subjective elements. In this scenario, it is the sources of cargo that opt for the "Zhengxin'ou" freight trains.

Hence, this chapter delves into the operational mechanism of the "Zhengxin'ou" route from the perspective of local development within the framework of the national strategy. It becomes evident that the evolution of "Zhengxin'ou" represents a process where the ultimate "independent variable" of the national initiative directly shapes the city's development trajectory. Zhengzhou and, by extension, the government of

Henan Province, continue to leverage their comparative advantages to establish competitive strengths. Prior to the proposal of the BRI in 2013, Zhengzhou capitalized on its geographical and transportation advantages, making logistics development a key strategic focus and placing significant emphasis on the development of "air + railway." However, this logistics development was limited to the domestic scope. In September and October 2013, following the successive proposals of the "Silk Road Economic Belt" and the "21st Century Maritime Silk Road," Zhengzhou capitalized on its designation as a key point along the "Silk Road Economic Belt" and "a logistics hub for the China-Europe Railway Express." Leveraging its existing logistics infrastructure, Zhengzhou transformed its comparative advantages into competitive advantages, wholeheartedly supporting the development of the China-Europe freight trains. This strategic focus on expanding and strengthening the logistics industry served as a window to enhance external engagement and laid the foundation for transforming Zhengzhou into an international commercial center.

CHAPTER 7

China-Europe Railway Express (Wuhan): Mechanism Exploration for Normalized Operations

Bin Wang

The China-Europe Railway Express serves as a transformative catalyst for the advancement of the "Belt and Road" Initiative. Beyond introducing a novel logistics organizational model for the exchange of goods between Asia and Europe, it establishes a fresh trade route for cross-border commerce between China and the countries along its path. Since 2010, various Chinese cities have been actively involved in exploring the localized operation of the China-Europe Railway Express. Among them, the China-Europe Railway Express (Wuhan), previously known as "Hanxin'ou" before the adoption of the unified name, stands out as a crucial and distinctive component of this initiative. In October 2016, the "Development Plan for the Construction of China-Europe Railway Express (2016–2020)"

B. Wang (✉)
China High-Speed Rail Development Strategy Research Center, Southwest Jiaotong University, Chengdu, China
e-mail: bai.gao@duke.edu

B. Gao, Z. Zhen (eds.), *The China-Europe Railway Express*, China and Globalization 2.0,
https://doi.org/10.1007/978-981-19-2882-6_7

issued by the National Development and Reform Commission designated Wuhan as one of the main inland cargo source nodes.[1]

Considering this, this chapter aims to conduct an academic analysis of the current operation of the China-Europe Railway Express (Wuhan) with the objective of elucidating its underlying mechanisms. The author identifies three main characteristics of the China-Europe Railway Express (Wuhan): (1) differentiation in phases: its operation can be divided into three phases: the trial run, suspension period, and normalization; (2) control of traffic: unlike other railway express routes that focus on increasing traffic, the China-Europe Railway Express (Wuhan) exhibits a trend of controlling traffic; (3) platform dilemma: the operation faces a dilemma concerning whether to establish an open platform or a monopolized one. These characteristics are closely related to the policies established by the Wuhan municipal government. Therefore, the author also aims to analyze the unique operational mechanisms of the China-Europe Railway Express (Wuhan) from the perspective of local government as an analytical unit, focusing on the "institutional" aspect. The chapter argues that: the Belt and Road Initiative (BRI) proposed by the central government was a key factor in Wuhan's decision to open to the West, making the China-Europe Railway Express (Wuhan), even during its suspension period, a carrier for implementing this initiative; the interaction between profit-oriented railway operation platform companies and government departments with a "performance-oriented" approach plays a crucial role in shaping the "traffic" control model. The diverse objectives of different departments concerning the development of the China-Europe Railway Express (Wuhan) platform are shaped by structural differences and departmental interests within the government, resulting in what can be termed as the "platform dilemma." This chapter aims to offer theoretical explanations for the formation of these characteristics, examining them through the lenses of central-local relations, government-enterprise relations, and interdepartmental relationships.

[1] According to the "Development Plan for the Construction of China-Europe Railway Express (2016–2020)," an inland major cargo source node refers to a city that has stable cargo sources, operates two or more point-to-point direct trains per week, has the capability to organize return trains, and serves as a hub for the direct delivery of cargo for the China-Europe Railway Express. These nodes include Chongqing, Chengdu, Zhengzhou, Wuhan, Suzhou, Yiwu, Changsha, Hefei, Shenyang, Dongguan, Xi'an, and Lanzhou.

7.1 Three Distinctive Features of China-Europe Railway Express (Wuhan)

As mentioned earlier, the China-Europe Railway Express (Wuhan) has three distinctive features that set it apart from other freight routes originating in different cities. Firstly, the route went through a phased transition from trial operation to suspension and then to regular operation. This, in fact, reflects the dynamic adjustments made by the local government regarding the development model of this rail service. In particular, during the trial operation phase, the China-Europe Railway Express (Wuhan) faced challenges due to the absence of essential institutional support from the local government, leading to a lack of sustainability and eventual service suspension. With the advent of the BRI, the local government took initiatives to integrate local resources, reposition the railway, and offer targeted services and incentives. The institutional framework established by the local government emerged as the primary driving force behind the railway's consistent operation. Secondly, after entering regular operations, unlike other cities with China-Europe freight trains that sought to expand their "flow," the China-Europe freight train (Wuhan) aimed to maximize the value of each standard container while controlling "flow." Thirdly, in contrast to the landscape in other cities, China-Europe Railway Express (Wuhan) has now entered a stage of "platform dilemma." Presently, the state-owned enterprise managing this train service grapples with two divergent directives. One faction advocates for its development as a monopolistic platform, encompassing logistics, trade, park management, and other businesses. In contrast, the opposing viewpoint insists on the establishment of a service platform open to other small and medium-sized enterprises. This ongoing tension has consistently pushed the train service in conflicting directions, posing challenges in attaining a clear and defined positioning. The following offers a concise overview of these two conflicting perspectives.

7.1.1 From the Trial "Shutdown" to Regular and Stable Operation

The China-Europe Railway Express (Wuhan) began its trial operation on October 24, 2012. The first departure was fully funded by the Wuhan municipal government, providing support of 2 million yuan ($0.3 million). China Railway International Multimodal Transport Co.,

Ltd. (CRIMT) was authorized as the full-service carrier, which started its journey in Wuhan and transported approximately $5 million worth of electronic products to Pardubice, Czech Republic, passing through Alashankou. The successful trial operation marked the establishment of a major land transportation route from Wuhan to Europe. Consequently, Wuhan became the second inland city, following Chongqing, to operate international railway freight services to Europe. Regrettably, following a single trial, the China-Europe Railway Express (Wuhan) encountered an extended hiatus, lasting nearly a year and a half. Throughout the trial operation, the train operated on just one route, heavily dependent on government-led initiatives for cargo consolidation. Lacking an autonomous cargo transportation platform, it predominantly transported electronic equipment. During this period, the route selection and cargo structure seemed notably constrained.

Since September 2013, the BRI has become a conceptual framework for China's participation in global governance. The introduction of the "Silk Road Economic Belt" concept highlighted the significant importance of "opening up to the West" for inland cities. The China-Europe Railway Express thus became a crucial link to connect with this initiative, and trains from various cities started to expand rapidly.[2] The Wuhan municipal government adjusted its logistics planning, established a dedicated logistics company for the China-Europe Railway Express, and introduced relevant freight subsidy systems to attract more cargo sources. On April 23, 2014, the China-Europe Railway Express (Wuhan) was given the green light for a "restart." Commentators on the *Chinese Railway Network* highly praised this re-launch, referring to it as the "Restart of 'Hanxin'ou' Boosting the Economic Takeoff of the Silk Road."[3] The first train to restart was a dedicated service from Wuhan to Lodz, Poland, reducing the total travel time for the 10,000-kilometer journey to just 13 days and five hours. On May 5 of the same year, the second train was launched, marking the formal beginning of regular operations. As the transition to regular operations took place, the China-Europe Railway Express (Wuhan)

[2] According to the "Development Plan for the Construction of China-Europe Railway Express (2016–2020)" data, as of the end of June 2016, there were 16 domestic cities from which the China-Europe Railway Express initiated its journeys, and it reached 12 cities in foreign countries, with a total of 39 operating routes.

[3] Hui Hu, "Restart of 'Hanxin'ou' Boosts the Economic Takeoff of the Silk Road," China Railway Network, http://www.chnrailway.com/html/20140504/370047.shtml, May 4, 2014.

witnessed rapid growth. The value and diversity of goods entering and departing from the city continued to rise, and the frequency of train services steadily increased.

In the transition from the trial operation in 2012 to regular operations, the China-Europe Railway Express (Wuhan) underwent significant changes and breakthroughs in both route development and the structure of goods transported. On the one hand, concerning route development, the train adopted both the Western and Eastern routes of the China-Europe Railway Express. It initiated its journeys from Wujiashan Railway Station of Wuhan, exiting through Alashankou and Manzhouli. This development included establishing 11 round-trip international railway routes, which are as follows: Wuhan to Pardubice (Czech Republic), Wuhan to Gorzów Wielkopolski (Poland), Wuhan to Moscow (Russia), Wuhan to Minsk (Belarus), Wuhan to Tashkent (Uzbekistan), Wuhan to Hamburg, Wuhan to Duisburg, Hamburg to Wuhan, Duisburg to Wuhan, "Russian-Manzhouli-Wuhan" raw materials return journey route, and Wuhan to France (Lyon). The train travels through seven countries, including Kazakhstan, Russia, Belarus, Poland, Czech Republic, Germany, and France, effectively covering the entire European continent. The "13th Five-Year Plan" of Wuhan emphasizes further extending international railway freight routes, with a specific focus on opening new routes toward Iran in Western Asia, and France in Western Europe, underlining the continued expansion of international railway freight services.

Conversely, looking at the structure of the sources of goods, in alignment with Wuhan's "Industrial Double Increase Plan"[4] and the ongoing optimization of the city and regional industrial structure, the China-Europe Railway Express (Wuhan) has strategically directed its services primarily toward industrial manufacturing hubs like Germany and France, as

[4] In early 2011, the Communist Party of Wuhan Municipal Committee and the People's Government of Wuhan issued a document titled "Several Opinions on Implementing the 'Double Increase Plan' for Industrial Development to Accelerate the Promotion of New Industrialization." This document outlined the significance of the industrial sector in Wuhan's economic growth, emphasizing its role as a crucial pillar of the economy, a source of fiscal revenue, a significant job provider, and a key driver for urbanization and the development of modern services. As such, the industrial policy orientation for Wuhan was established to leverage its geographical advantages and industrial strengths, maintaining a robust growth momentum in the industrial sector. The goal was to further enhance the role of industry in supporting and driving the economic development of Wuhan. This strategy aimed to lay a solid foundation for transforming Wuhan into a central city in the central region of China and a nationally important advanced manufacturing center.

well as resource-rich nations such as Russia and Belarus. This targeted approach in selecting destination cities has consequently shaped the product composition of both exported and imported goods transported by the China-Europe Railway Express (Wuhan). For exported goods, they encompass a wide range of products, including light industrial goods, clothing, electronic products, industrial items, and automotive components. For imported goods, the focus is primarily on items like timber, industrial machinery, electrical products, automotive components, electronic products, and light industrial goods. (As of September 2016, its specific product structure can be found in Table 7.1.) Furthermore, with the continuous improvement of the qualifications of various ports in Wuhan and the establishment of related foreign trade companies, everyday consumer goods for residents will account for an increasingly higher proportion of imported goods.

7.1.2 The "Flow Control" of the China-Europe Railway Express (Wuhan)

At a time when competition among cities to operate train services has intensified, China-Europe Railway Express (Wuhan) has taken a different approach by not aggressively pursuing "volume" (i.e., increasing the volume of train services). Since the launch of the China-Europe Railway Express (Chongqing) in 2011, various cities have rapidly expanded their train services in just five years. However, overall, different cities' services not only differ in terms of route selection, cargo composition, and

Table 7.1 Product structure of the China-Europe Railway Express (Wuhan) for imports and exports

Destination	*Product categories* *Trade*					
	Light industrial products	*Clothing*	*Electronic products*	*Industrial goods*	*Automotive parts*	*Others*
Exports	31.3%	19.5%	15.7%	11.29%	9%	13.21%
Imports	16%	—	15%	37%	18%	14%

Source: Internal statistical data from WAE-Logistics

destinations but also vary in logistics strategic planning, leadership organization, and subsidy program development.

Particularly noteworthy is the gradual escalation in transport volume and rapid development of the route after achieving regular operations, evident in the data. In 2014, the China-Europe Railway Express (Wuhan) operated just 26 trains (without return trips), a number that surged to 164 trains (98 outbound and 66 return trips) in 2015. By October 27, 2016, the service had operated 205 trains, comprising 100 outbound and 105 return trips.[5] Concurrently, internal data from Wuhan Asia Europe Logistics Co., Ltd (Wae-Logistics) indicates a substantial increase in the volume of goods transported by this service from 2014 to September 2016, with a notable surge in return journey cargo (refer to Fig. 7.1). However, it appears that pursuing increased traffic volume is not the primary strategic focus of the China-Europe Railway Express (Wuhan).

Throughout the research, the leader of Wae-Logistics, the entity managing the China-Europe Railway Express (Wuhan), clarified that the company's chief goal is not solely to maximize the quantity of train services. Rather, the developmental trajectory of the China-Europe Railway Express (Wuhan) adheres to a strategy of "choosing the best" options.

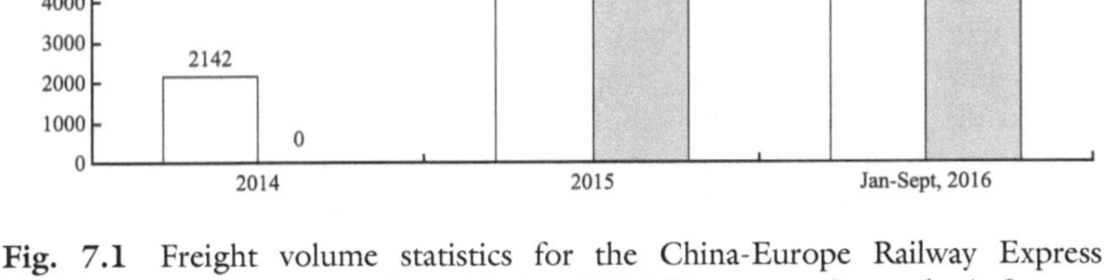

Fig. 7.1 Freight volume statistics for the China-Europe Railway Express (Wuhan) in both directions from 2014 to 2016 (January to September). Source: Internal documents provided by Wae-Logistics

[5]The data is sourced from internal documents provided by Wae-Logistics in November 2016.

> This year, we are controlling the number of our train services. We are not running them daily, nor are we making bold claims like Chengdu, announcing the operation of 1,000 trains. Taking it easy. This year, we are keeping it within the range of 250 to 260 trains. Then, we filter and optimize our customer base, gradually providing better capacity and more optimal timings for valuable customers who genuinely want to use our service.

Especially in the context of the growing number of cities participating in China-Europe Railway services and the escalating competition, the unique strategy of the China-Europe Railway Express (Wuhan) not to vie for "volume" and even to control it becomes more distinct. Many regions are entering into price wars with the backing of government subsidies, all striving to fortify their China-Europe Railway logistics platforms by aiming to secure higher "volume." For instance, Chengdu's "Rong'ou+" strategy sets ambitious targets for the China-Europe Railway Express (Chengdu) at 1000 trains by 2017 and 3000 by 2020.[6] In contrast, the China-Europe Railway Express (Wuhan) has a more modest plan, aiming to operate 200 trains in 2017.[7] Therefore, understanding the rationale behind the China-Europe Railway Express (Wuhan)'s approach of controlling "volume" becomes a pivotal question for exploration.

7.1.3 *The China-Europe Railway Express (Wuhan) Platform Development Dispute: Openness or Monopoly*

The question of how to develop the regular operation of the China-Europe Railway Express (Wuhan) has been an ongoing issue. During its trial operation, there was no dedicated logistics company tasked with overseeing transportation services. The initiation of Wae-Logistics represented the initial step by the municipal government to support ongoing operations. For instance, in the "Implementation Plan for the Normalized Operation of International Rail Freight Transport for 'Hanxin'ou'" released in March 2014, the Wuhan municipal government emphasized the importance of "building a logistics platform" as a key task to promote regular operations. Specifically, this pivotal document emphasized the necessity of addressing challenges posed by dispersed foreign trade

[6] Fangjie Lai, "Chengdu to Run 1000 Rong'ou Express Railway in 2017", *Huaxi Metropolis Daily*, 18 January 2017.

[7] Refer to "In 2016, the China-Europe Railway Express (Wuhan) Successfully Concluded with A Total of 122 Trips," *Hubei Daily*, December 30, 2016.

enterprises, intricate rail freight routes traversing multiple countries, and complex operational structures. It underscored the immediate need to establish a platform company responsible for organizing cargo sources, declaring transportation plans, and coordinating transportation practices.[8] Hence, WAE-Logistics, as a state-owned enterprise owned by the city, has been positioned as a "public platform for providing international logistics transportation services to the whole society on behalf of the Wuhan Municipal People's Government" since its establishment.

However, there have been differences of opinion within the local government regarding how the platform should be developed. Departments under the purview of the Wuhan Municipal Commission of Transport advocate for the transformation of WAE-Logistics into a comprehensive platform, integrating logistics, industrial park development, and foreign trade operations. This approach would establish a scenario wherein the state-owned platform company holds a monopoly.

On the other hand, departments like the Wuhan Municipal Bureau of Commerce argue that Wae-Logistics is more suitable as a public logistics platform and, therefore, should be open to other relevant enterprises in the upstream and downstream sectors. A leader from the Bureau of Commerce expressed this view in an interview:

> We believe that Wae-Logistics should focus on being a logistics platform and concentrate on its transportation services, while other companies can handle the logistics park operations. We have everything here—both the logistics park and its supporting facilities. Whoever should oversee what they're best at, should be in charge. For Wae-Logistics, its primary role should be maintaining its logistics platform. Furthermore, Wae-Logistics does receive financial support, but this support is intended for its logistics transport activities and not for engaging in operational activities.

Comparing the models of the China-Europe Railway Express in Wuhan and Zhengzhou reveals a significant distinction. The latter has already established an "integrated transport and trade" structure, while the former is still in the phase of platform development. Notably, the frequent operations of the China-Europe Railway Express in Zhengzhou led to the launch of the Zhengzhou-Europe Commercial City cross-border trade e-commerce platform at the end of 2015. This initiative enabled a

[8] Refer to the "Implementation Plan for the Normalized Operation of International Rail Freight Transport for 'Hanxin'ou'" (Wuhan Government Document No. 33, 2014).

comprehensive implementation of the "transport promoting trade, trade boosting transport" strategy. It's worth pondering over what factors led to the hesitance in the platform strategy choice for the China-Europe Railway Express (Wuhan), and what structural elements are involved in the essence of this platform dilemma.

Superficially, the characteristics of phase differentiation, "volume" control, and platform development in the operation of the China-Europe Railway Express (Wuhan) may appear unrelated. However, fundamentally, these features represent concrete manifestations of the localized operating model, shaped by the actions of multiple stakeholders. These stakeholder actions are not devoid of logic; on the contrary, they influence one another within a specific institutional "field." The following will attempt to construct a theoretical framework related to institutions to elucidate the principles behind the emergence of these characteristics in the operation of the China-Europe Railway Express (Wuhan).

7.2 Analytical Framework: Local Government Behavior from an Institutional Perspective

Usually, our research on the China-Europe Railway Express is approached from a predominantly economic perspective, focusing on concepts like cost and benefit. However, the operation of the China-Europe Railway Express is fundamentally a sociological issue, profoundly shaped by social institutions. For instance, some scholars have argued that the resurgence of regular operations after a year and a half of stagnation was primarily a result of government-led reforms in the operational framework, streamlining customs procedures, and resolving issues related to the supply of goods and freight rates.[9] This perspective underscores the significant role of institutions in shaping the railway's operation. This explanation focuses on the role of institutional development in the railway's operation, but its scattered arguments do not directly address the core issue. Therefore, this chapter will employ a perspective from the field of new economic

[9] Refer to Rong Chen, "SWOT Analysis of China-Europe Railway Express (Wuhan) in the Integration of China-Europe Railway Express", *Comprehensive Transportation*, No. 1, 2016; Li Zhenzhen et al., "Discussion on the Construction of 'China-Europe Railway Express (Wuhan)' as an International Freight Corridor," *Silk Road*, No. 22, 2014; Wang Jiapu and Wang Yiling, "'China-Europe Railway Express (Wuhan)' Should Contribute to the Expansion of Hubei's Opening Up," *Policy*, No. 6, 2015.

sociology to reevaluate the concept of "institutions." Historically, new economic sociology emerged in the 1980s. The core theoretical propositions of this branch of sociology, as articulated by its prominent figure Mark Granovetter, can be summarized in three propositions: (1) Economic actions are a specific type of social action, (2) Economic actions have a social position, and (3) Economic institutions are a form of social construction.[10] Therefore, the central research area of new economic sociology revolves around the mechanisms through which different types of economic institutions are created, maintained, and changed. Essentially, the China-Europe Railway Express, driven by local governments, is also a form of economic institution. Its specific arrangement directly determines the railway's phase transitions and its current characteristics. Therefore, we need to construct an analytical framework from the "institutional" perspective to understand the operation of the China-Europe Railway Express (Wuhan).

The theoretical framework is composed of two aspects: why and how system influences the operation of the China-Europe Railway Express (Wuhan). On one hand, we need to theoretically clarify how system impacts the operation of the train within the broader context of China's social structure. From the perspective of new economic sociology, the strategic choices made by economic actors engaged in economic interactions are constrained by specific political, ideological, and existing policy factors. Economic exchanges in the market are influenced by the distribution of power under the influence of institutions more than they are guided solely by price mechanisms.[11] In other words, both macro and microeconomic phenomena are regulated by the system. In China's context as a "strong state," where the government holds significant social and economic resources, its role in guiding and shaping economic activities becomes even more crucial.

However, the makers are not limited to the central government. In the context of China's "fiscal decentralization," the role played by local governments in setting up system in regional economic growth is particularly significant. Huang Zongzhi once regarded local governments as the

[10] Zhihong Zhen, "From Network Embeddedness to Institutional Embeddedness: The Frontier of Institutional Research in New Economic Sociology," *Jiangsu Social Sciences*, No.3, 2006.

[11] Zhihong Zhen, "Networks, Institutions, and Culture: Three Fundamental Perspectives in Economic Sociology," *Jianghai Academic Journal*, No. 4, 2009.

"engine" of China's economic miracles.[12] Zhou Li'an also pointed out, "Many significant reforms in China were initiated, promoted, and directly participated in by local governments, making them one of the most striking features of the reform process in China."[13] In fact, the China-Europe Railway Express is fundamentally an innovative product of local governments in exploring industrial systems. For example, Chongqing Municipal Government, as the pioneer in launching the China-Europe Railway Express, aimed to overcome its geographical disadvantage as a deep inland city. It did so by introducing a series of policies and systems to vigorously create this new form of international rail freight transport across Eurasia, thereby expanding its role as an inland "gateway to Europe." Furthermore, the diverse operating models and characteristics of China-Europe Railway Express in different regions are fundamentally a result of the varying strategies and policies introduced by local governments. Especially in the current situation where there is a lack of substantial financial support from the central government for China-Europe Railway Express, local governments are undoubtedly the main actors shaping the institutional environment through practical services and incentives.

On the other hand, we also need to clarify at a structural level how the policies enacted by local governments institutionalize and influence the operation of the China-Europe Railway Express. Before delving into this query, it is imperative to precisely define the notion of a local government. In China, a local government is established by the central government and wields certain national powers to administer a designated region or specific social affairs within that region.[14] For example, some scholars have pointed out that local government competition includes three dimensions: "competition within the local government," "competition between different local governments," and "competition outside of the government."[15] This essentially highlights the multidimensionality of local governments. Based on this analysis, it is suggested that the ways in which local governments institutionally influence the China-Europe Railway Express should

[12] Zongzhi Huang, Shengfeng Yu, "Rediscovering Political Space: The Local-National System in Reform," *Cultural Horizons*, No. 6, 2009.

[13] Li'an Zhou, *Local Governments in Transition: Official Incentives and Governance*, Shanghai People's Publishing House, 2008, p. 2.

[14] Ping Zhou, *Local Governments in Contemporary China*, People's Publishing House, 2007, p. 5.

[15] Yaping Liu, *Inter-Governmental Competition in Contemporary China*, Social Sciences Academic Press, 2007, p. 6.

encompass the institutional dynamics of local governments in their relationship with the central government (central-local relations), the internal institutional structures of various departments within local governments (departmental relationships), and the institutional arrangements between local governments and enterprises (government-enterprise relationships).

Elaborating further, within the framework of central-local relations, the emergence of the China-Europe Railway Express is an inexorable result of shifts in policy paradigms. Despite local governments maintaining control over the planning and distribution of most products, the central government retains the ability to steer local governments toward the implementation of nationwide macroeconomic strategies or regulations through "promotion incentives."[16] In this mechanism, the central government's policy guidance can be promptly accepted by local governments. Furthermore, local governments may adapt central policies to suit their specific circumstances, developing new regional plans or readjusting and upgrading existing ones. From this perspective, the central government's strategic deployment effectively provides legitimate "policy paradigms" for local governments. These paradigms influence local governments' prioritization of current government work through cognitive structures, strengthening central control over the results of local work.[17] In the present context, the BRI, particularly the development plan for the "Silk Road Economic Belt," has prompted local governments nationwide to adopt the policy paradigm of "opening up to the West." As a result, several large and medium-sized cities have begun to develop plans for the operation of the China-Europe Railway Express, actively aligning their policies with those of the central government. The fundamental reason for the transition of the China-Europe Railway Express (Wuhan) from trial operation to stable and regular operation, after its initial suspension, lies in the strategic shift of local governments. In alignment with the BRI, they redirected their logistics emphasis from "river-sea combined transport service" to international rail freight penetrating deep into the inland Western regions. Therefore, the central government's adjustment of local governments' work priorities through policy paradigms is a key perspective for

[16] Li'an Zhou, *Local Governments in Transition: Official Incentives and Governance*, Shanghai People's Publishing House, 2008, p. 12.

[17] Bai Gao, "China's Economic Development Model Transformation and the Economic Sociology Institutional School," *Sociological Research*, No. 4., 2008.

understanding the phased development of the China-Europe Railway Express (Wuhan).

Secondly, the government-enterprise relationship is also a key variable in shaping the operational mode of the China-Europe Railway Express. In the early days of the People's Republic of China, state-owned enterprises were not purely economic organizations but undertook various political, social, educational, and other functions assigned by the government. With the establishment of China's socialist market economy, the market-oriented reform of state-owned enterprises has accelerated, primarily manifested in four aspects: the transformation of the state-owned asset management system from administrative to market-oriented, the shift of state-owned enterprise property rights from singular to market-oriented, the transformation of the operational behavior of state-owned enterprises from government-oriented to market-oriented, and the formation of mechanisms for the market exit of generally competitive state-owned enterprises.[18] These transformations have directly led to two key outcomes. Firstly, state-owned enterprises have adopted a market-oriented "profit-driven focus." In other words, these enterprises have obtained operational autonomy, with their fundamental guiding principles centered on prioritizing profit generation, as well as the preservation and appreciation of state-owned assets. During this phase, state-owned enterprises do not obediently follow administrative directives from local governments but rather engage in "negotiations" to safeguard the enterprise's interests and comply with market regulations. On the other hand, while local governments no longer directly intervene in market operations, they can still use a variety of organized methods to embed themselves in state-owned enterprises, thereby guiding and influencing their market actions. For instance, as highlighted by Li Hanlin, managers of government and state-owned enterprises engage in formalized and organized appointment mechanisms, facilitating mutual communication and interchange. This dynamic has profound and far-reaching effects on government-enterprise relationships and their interactions.[19] Regarding the specific situation, Wae-Logistics, as a municipally owned state enterprise, must ensure the train service's prof-

[18] Jun Ren, "The Path of Market-Oriented Transformation for State-Owned Enterprises," *People's Forum*, No. 21, 2009.

[19] Hanlin Li, Qingong Wei, "The Subject and Structure in the Embedding Process: A Social Analysis of Changes in Government-Enterprise Relations," *Social Science Management and Review*, No. 4, 2013.

itability within certain policy constraints and meet the expectations of provincial and municipal leaders regarding the route's competitiveness. Due to the quantitative government subsidies, Wae-Logistics has reduced the number of outbound shipments to maintain profitability, fundamentally embodying the characteristic of not actively pursuing "volume." Emphasizing the increased value of each standard container's cargo serves as a response to the government's pressure to showcase "political achievements." Hence, the fundamental decision not to actively pursue "volume" is an enterprise's rational choice to balance market and government relations within the context of specific government-enterprise relationships.

Thirdly, from the dimension of interdepartmental relationships within the government, departmental structure can also impact the operation of the express. Scholars like John L. Campbell et al. suggest that the state is both an actor and a type of structure. The term "actor" refers to the distinctive position of the state in contrast to the market and society. The term "structure" refers to the specific organizational systems of the government that may trigger struggles among interest groups within, and these competitions can easily lead to unexpected outcomes in economic governance.[20] Even in a country such as the United States, characterized by a "limited government," the state's impact on the economy cannot be disregarded. In China, where the government wields considerable power, its influence on economic phenomena is even more significant. This theory helps explain the phenomenon in China. Local governments in China are an integral part of the national power structure, encompassing various departments. The cooperation and competition between these departments inevitably determine the operational mode of the China-Europe Railway Express. This complexity is further magnified when it comes to the China-Europe Railway Express, which is a cross-border rail logistics service, involving various government departments and administrative relationships. At the local level, the China-Europe Railway Express interfaces with multiple departments, including transportation, commerce (port offices), finance, industry and commerce, foreign affairs, development zones, and management committees. Furthermore, some scholars have highlighted that as government departmental interests become more entrenched, the competition among departments for these interests has

[20] Leon N. Lindberg, John L. Campbell, "The State and the Organization of Economic Activity", in John L. Campbell et al., *The Organization of American Economic Governance*, Shanghai People's Publishing House, 2009, p. 332.

emerged as the primary force shaping market behavior.[21] Therefore, the various government departments undoubtedly have a significant influence on the operation of the railway express, and these interests directly contribute to shaping the mode of the China-Europe Railway Express. When we specifically examine the China-Europe Railway Express (Wuhan), the municipal government has established relevant leadership groups to promote the regular development of the express. This has resulted in a complex structure involving multiple departments and intricate distribution of departmental interests in shaping the operation of the China-Europe Railway Express (Wuhan). The Wuhan Municipal Commission of Transport supports the idea of creating a monopolistic platform for the operating company with the goal of "expanding logistics." On the contrary, the Wuhan Municipal Bureau of Commerce advocates for an open platform centered on logistics, with the goal of attracting substantial commercial capital for investment in Wuhan. Thus, the dispute over platform construction in the operation of the China-Europe Railway Express (Wuhan) reflects the assertions and negotiations of interests among various departments of the local government. In the subsequent discussion, the article will employ an institutional perspective to analyze the internal mechanisms that give rise to the characteristics of the China-Europe Railway Express (Wuhan).

7.3 The Phased Operation of the China-Europe Railway Express (Wuhan) and Its Causes

In October 2012, the first China-Europe Railway Express (Wuhan) was launched. According to a leader from the Wuhan Municipal Bureau of Commerce, this train was "an experiment" and aimed to keep pace with Chongqing's freight trains.[22] However, afterwards, this train came to a halt, and some have attributed the suspension to factors such as

[21] Zhihui Tong, "Departmental Interests and Local Politics", *Cultural Horizons*, No. 6, 2009.

[22] During the survey and interviews participated in, a representative from the Wuhan Municipal Bureau of Commerce's Port Office mentioned that in 2012, after witnessing the success of the China-Europe freight train service in Chongqing, the municipal government decided to invest its own resources. They organized companies like Foxconn to conduct trial runs, with the goal of assessing the time and costs involved in the process. This initial trial phase helped inform subsequent planning and actions.

inadequate local freight demand and high return trip costs.[23] So, what drove the Wuhan's local government to restart the freight train service in April 2014? As previously mentioned, under the current framework, local governments are obligated to actively respond to major strategic initiatives from the central government. The BRI, particularly the "Silk Road Economic Belt," prompted a shift in Wuhan's policy paradigm from its previous "Eastward development" strategy to a logistics plan aligned with "opening up to the West." Consequently, the resumption of the China-Europe freight train service was placed on the agenda.

7.3.1 *Trial Operation of the China-Europe Railway Express (Wuhan): An Attempt Under the New Port Strategy*

As economic globalization and the transformation of urban government functions in China continue, the logistics industry has become a key driver of urban development. The formulation of corresponding logistics strategies has also become an integral part of urban development planning, significantly enhancing a city's competitiveness. In this context, in May 2008, the Hubei Provincial Party Committee and the Provincial People's Government proposed the strategy of "Wuhan New Port," positioning it as a "river-sea combined transport service." This concept implies a mode of transportation where goods are transported from inland rivers to the open sea without transshipment, all within the same vessel. In many ways, the New Port strategy represents an institutional construction by the Wuhan municipal government to align with central government policies. As Zhang Lin, Director of the Wuhan New Port Management Committee, stated, the construction of New Port is seen as a crucial breakthrough "in building an important strategic support point to boost the rise of the central region and to drive the construction of the 'Two-Oriented' comprehensive reform experimental zone in the Wuhan city cluster."[24] During the trial phase, Wuhan was in a critical period of constructing the new port and attempting to realize the "city development driven by the port." As a result, the local government had little time to concentrate on the novel logistics model represented by the China-Europe Railway. Moreover, the New Port strategy received acknowledgment and endorsement from the

[23] Chuang Lei, "The Challenges of the 'Hanxin'ou' Halt", *Hubei Daily*, July 29, 2013.

[24] Lin Zhang, "Wuhan New Port: Building a New Engine for the Rise of the Central Region", *Policy*, Issue 4, 2012.

central government,[25] further downplaying the significance of the China-Europe Railway's "inland penetration" during that specific timeframe.

Since the official establishment of the Wuhan New Port strategy, "direct access to rivers and seas" has become the focal direction for Wuhan's comprehensive external transportation system and the development of the logistics industry. As a result, the integration of river and sea transport has increasingly become a vital mode of transportation for Wuhan's foreign trade, while the proportion of railway transport in this regard has steadily decreased.[26] Simultaneously, the New Port strategy has led to a concentration of resources in the construction of inland river ports. As Wuhan New Port, serving as a major gateway for international trade through maritime transportation, experienced rapid development during this phase. In contrast, the infrastructure for inland land ports, well-suited for rail freight, lagged, hindering the transition of the China-Europe Railway (Wuhan) from trial operations to a regular service. The lag in the construction of international railway freight facilities is evident in three aspects. Firstly, there is a deficiency in port qualifications. As per statements from officials at the Wuhan Municipal Bureau of Commerce, unlike other cities where China-Europe Railway services operate, the China-Europe Railway (Wuhan) adopts the approach of "developing ports gradually after the train is in operation." The Wujiashan Central Station, the starting point of the China-Europe Railway, is a provisional port that lacks the qualifications for handling full trains, food, meat, fruit, international parcels, cross-border e-commerce, and other railway import operations. This limitation has hindered the further development of the rail service. Another issue is the outdated port infrastructure. Due to the relatively small construction area of the Wujiashan Central Station (including the customs supervision

[25] In 2011, the State Council issued the "Opinions on Accelerating the Development of Water Transport on the Yangtze River," stating the goal of "Promoting the development of Wuhan as a shipping center in the middle reaches of the Yangtze River." The clear positioning of inland river shipping by the central government further elevated the strategic importance of the New Port.

[26] According to relevant statistics from the Hubei Provincial Bureau of Statistics, from 2010 to 2014, the proportion of railway freight volume to the total volume of transportation modes (rail, road, water, and air) in the province decreased from 10.46% in 2010 to 4.96%. Additionally, the proportion of cargo turnover to the total volume of transportation modes decreased from 33.93% in 2010 to 19.13%. See "Reasons for the Current Decline in Railway Freight and Suggestions for Development Countermeasures," Hubei Provincial Bureau of Statistics website, http://www.stats-hb.gov.cn/tjbs/qstjbsyxx/111953.htm, February 10, 2015.

area) and the lack of supporting logistics parks, once the cargo volume becomes substantial, the basic storage and supply services may struggle to keep pace.[27] Finally, there is an inadequate provision of supporting services for national inspection, customs, and multimodal transport supervision. The "last mile" of achieving seamless rail-water transport integration has remained unconnected, resulting in high transportation costs for intermodal transport.[28] Data indicates that the operating cost for the short 70-kilometer transit from the central station to Yangluo Port is as high as 1200 yuan ($168). In contrast, the cost for the direct river-sea combined transport service from Yangluo Port to Shanghai Port is only around 1200 yuan ($168).[29] As a result, the delayed government services create a systemic environment and the lagging infrastructure, hindering the sustained development of the China-Europe Railway Express (Wuhan) by failing to provide favorable conditions.

The extended suspension of the China-Europe Railway (Wuhan) for a year and a half can also be attributed to the lack of government incentive mechanisms. While the train significantly reduces the shipping time between Asia and Europe, its freight charges are considerably high. According to statistics, the market price for transporting a 40-foot container through waterways is approximately $4500. In contrast, the market price for transporting the same container via the China-Europe Railway (Wuhan) is around $120,000, making rail transport nearly twice as expensive as water transport.[30] Furthermore, the return journey often involves

[27] See "'Hanxin'ou' Public Train to Russia Inaugurated," *Hubei Daily*, October 25, 2015.

[28] The constraints on the rail-water transportation in Wuhan are also due to the relatively low aggregation of its ports. For example, the Wuhan railway marshaling yard is located at Shekou, Huangpi District, the container station is in Wujiashan, East and West Lake districts, while the starting point of the "river-sea combined transport service" is in Yangluo, Xinzhou. When a batch of container goods arrives from Europe by train to Wuhan and needs to transfer to water transport to Shanghai, they must first go to Shekou for marshaling, then distribute to Wujiashan, and finally, take trucks via the road to Yangluo port. This fragmented layout makes it challenging for the China-Europe Railway (Wuhan) to effectively utilize its intermodal advantages.

[29] Meijie Ke, Xun Liu, "Speeding up the Development of 'China-Europe Railway (Wuhan)' and 'Yixin'ou' Trains," *Changjiang Business Daily*, January 29, 2016.

[30] Mengxin Cui, Zuowu Lv, "Restart of 'Hanxin'ou' Railway to Create a 'New Silk Road' Connecting the Central Region with the European Continent," *Central Asia Information*, No. 4, 2014.

empty trains, further driving up transportation costs.[31] Without the financial subsidies provided by the government, it is challenging for the China-Europe Railway (Wuhan) to compete with water routes. During the trial operation, the Wuhan municipal government offered a subsidy of two million yuan ($28 million) for the first run. The lack of systematic subsidy incentives has impeded the full utilization of the stimulating and guiding functions of public finance. Market entities struggle to establish stable expectations for new logistics forms. In essence, during this phase, as the central government did not establish a comprehensive framework for "opening to the West," Wuhan continued to adhere to its eastward logistics plan of "river-sea combined transport service." Consequently, it failed to provide effective basic services and incentive measures, collectively resulting in the prolonged suspension of the China-Europe Railway (Wuhan) after just one run.

7.3.2 Normalization of the China-Europe Railway (Wuhan): A Transport Carrier Aligned with the "Belt and Road" Initiative

In late September 2013, an article titled "How Long Do We Have to Wait for the Restart of 'Hanxin'ou'?" was published in the *Economic Daily*, signaling that the Wuhan municipal government had proactively responded to the "Silk Road Economic Belt" construction initiative. Qin Zunwen, Vice President of the Hubei Provincial Academy of Social Sciences, pointed out, "From a macro perspective, the strategic plan for the country to construct the Silk Road Economic Belt provides an opportunity for the revival of 'Hanxin'ou.'"[32] Consequently, preparations for the reopening and normalization of the China-Europe Railway (Wuhan) have been in full swing since September 2013. This underscores that the "restart" is a result of the Wuhan municipal government aligning with the central BRI.

During the trial operation, the China-Europe Railway (Wuhan) was merely seen as an experimental logistics initiative aimed at expanding Wuhan's openness. Its significance was overshadowed by the concurrent "New Port Strategy" that was underway. However, with the introduction of the BRI, the framework of "opening to the West" gradually became

[31] Chuang Lei, "The Predicament of 'Hanxin'ou' Railway Suspension," *Hubei Daily*, July 29, 2013.

[32] Jiulong Cheng, "Wuhan Paves the Path for the Resumption and Normalization of 'Hanxin'ou'," *Economic Observer*, July 18, 2014.

clearer. As a novel international goods transportation mode, the China-Europe Railway has evolved into a crucial element and a driving force for the BRI. Particularly, with the concept of the "Silk Road Economic Belt," the anticipation is that railway freight transport will consistently generate economic benefits spanning the Asian and European continents. Inland Chinese cities aspire to proactively establish westward transportation channels, leveraging the China-Europe Railway to catalyze their ascent as "inland open economic hubs." Against this backdrop, on February 20, 2014, Tang Liangzhi, then Mayor of Wuhan, hosted the "Special Symposium on Accelerating the Normalized Operation of 'Hanxin'ou.'" The meeting concluded that the normal operation of the China-Europe Railway (Wuhan) was a mutually beneficial strategic logistics choice for the Wuhan region and should be promptly promoted.[33] On March 14, 2014, the "Implementation Plan for the Normalized Operation of International Rail Freight Transport for 'Hanxin'ou'" was officially released by the Wuhan municipal government, marking the comprehensive launch of preparatory work for the regular operation of the China-Europe Railway (Wuhan). At the same time, the governments at both the provincial level and the municipal level, along with various departments, incorporated the China-Europe Railway (Wuhan) into their "13th Five-Year Plan" (see Table 7.2). This decision confirmed the important strategic positioning of the railway and the priority in government resource allocation.

In fact, local governments, when aligning with national strategies, are not entirely blind to their specific circumstances. For instance, the Wuhan municipal government faced two significant realities: the growth in foreign trade volume and intensified competition among cities in the central and western regions. These factors collectively impelled Wuhan to use the China-Europe Railway (Wuhan) as a focal point and accelerate the reconfiguration of the city's logistics strategy. On the one hand, confronted with the industrial shift from the eastern coastal areas and the continuous development of an outward-oriented economy within the province, the rapid growth in foreign trade necessitated a completely new transport corridor to alleviate the immense freight pressure. The "2015 Statistical Communiqué on National Economic and Social Development of Wuhan" reveals that from 2011 to 2015, the total import and export volume of the

[33] Refer to "Comprehensive Launch of 'Hanxin'ou' International Freight Transportation Normalization," Wuhan Municipal Transportation Committee website, http://www.whjt.gov.cn/jtzx/zwdt/2014/03/21/51759.htm, March 21, 2014.

Table 7.2 Planning by governments at the provincial and the municipal levels for the China-Europe Railway (Wuhan)

Name	*Release date*	*Content related to the China-Europe Railway (Wuhan)*
Hubei Province's 13th Five-Year Plan for National Economic and Social Development	April, 2016	Promoting the regular two-way operation of the China-Europe Railway (Wuhan) for international freight transportation with the goal of establishing it as a national backbone railway for China-Europe transportation.
Hubei Province's 13th Five-Year Plan for National Economic and Social Development	April, 2016	Promoting the regular two-way operation of the China-Europe Railway (Wuhan) for international freight transportation with the goal of establishing it as a national backbone railway for China-Europe transportation.
Wuhan City's 13th Five-Year Plan for National Economic and Social Development	April, 2016	(1) Building the central consolidation and distribution center for the China-Europe Railway (Wuhan), enhancing its international transportation capabilities, and expanding train services to more cities in Europe, Central Asia, Southeast Asia, and other regions; (2) Striving to double the number and throughput of the China-Europe Railway (Wuhan) by 2020 compared to the end of the "12th Five-Year Plan."
Wuhan City's Modern Logistics Industry Development "13th Five-Year Plan"	November, 2016	By 2020, the China-Europe Railway (Wuhan) was expected to achieve regular two-way operations, doubling both the number and volume of services for the China-Europe Railway (Wuhan) and domestic cities' "scheduled trains."
Wuhan City's Transportation and Logistics Development "13th Five-Year Plan"	December, 2016	(1) Solidifying and enhancing the operational level of the China-Europe Railway (Wuhan) and leveraging its special driving role; (2) Constructing the central consolidation and distribution center for the China-Europe Railway (Wuhan), improving the "Hanxin'ou" s international transportation capabilities.

city increased at an average annual rate of 9.2%. Imports grew at an average annual rate of 6.8%, while exports saw a growth rate of 11.6%. It became evident that the "river-sea combined transport service" facilitated by Wuhan New Port alone could not entirely meet the demands of this rapidly expanding foreign trade situation. Therefore, the inherent need to develop new opportunities and routes for foreign trade also drove the

Wuhan government's efforts to normalize the operation of the China-Europe Railway. On the other hand, significant cities in the central and western regions, including Chongqing, Zhengzhou, and Chengdu, are consistently broadening their transcontinental logistics and trade across Eurasia by utilizing the China-Europe Railway Express. These cities are diligently working toward transforming themselves into novel open gateways for inland urban involvement in globalization. In the context of this "political championship," local governments are not only required to align "upward" with the central government's directives but find themselves in competition with peer cities due to the pressure for "promotion." In contrast to central and western cities that successfully initiated routes and achieved remarkable results, the China-Europe Railway (Wuhan) had an early trial run but underwent a prolonged period of suspension. This prompted the urgent requirement for the Wuhan government to "reclaim" the China-Europe Railway (Wuhan) and engage in a new phase of intercity competition. For the reasons outlined above, Wuhan's prior strategy of exclusively engaging in eastward opening through the "river-sea combined transport service" became increasingly misaligned with both central strategic directives and local socio-economic conditions. Consequently, Wuhan had to readjust its New Port strategy, integrating international railway freight transport into its logistics development planning. Therefore, the resurgence of the China-Europe Railway Express (Wuhan) after a one-and-a-half-year suspension is now more comprehensible.

Indeed, following Wuhan's realignment of its logistics strategy with the BRI, a suite of measures was imperative to guarantee the consistent operation of the railway service. These measures encompassed bolstering infrastructure and instituting incentive mechanisms. In the realm of infrastructure enhancement, elevating port qualifications emerged as the foremost concern for Wuhan's municipal government in advancing regular operations. In October 2013, the local government assisted in the completion and acceptance of the railway port at Wuhan Railway Center Station, enabling the local clearance of import and export goods. Concurrently, the Municipal Port Office spearheaded applications across various pertinent departments, including customs, with the objective of establishing a dedicated supervision area in East Lake and West Lake, endowed with functions equivalent to temporary railway ports. Following a year of meticulous preparation and application, Wuhan's railway temporary port secured official approval in early 2015. Leveraging the Wuhan Railway Port as a cornerstone, the Port Office actively pursued and advocated for the designation of Wujiashan Railway Center Port as the primary port for the import of complete vehicles, thereby optimizing the return cargo structure for the China-Europe Railway Express.

Throughout the trial operation, a critical factor impacting the train was the outdated infrastructure. The spatial arrangement of key functional nodes, including the container core port area, export-oriented industrial agglomeration areas, bonded areas, and the railway container center station, suffered from misalignment.[34] This misalignment resulted in disproportionately elevated transportation costs for intermodal transportation. Especially after the adjustment of Wuhan's strategic positioning, the importance of seamless multimodal transportation, including rail, water, and air transport, became increasingly prominent. Resolving the fragmentation of shipping and rail transport became a critical aspect of the government's service provision for the railway. Hubei Province's "13th Five-Year Plan" points out the need to construct the Wuhan New Port Jiangbei Railway and other essential port railway connections. The Jiangbei Railway is the "last mile" solution that ensures seamless connectivity between Yangluo Port, the Shekou Railway Freight Station, and Wujiashan Container Railway Center Station. Moreover, through concerted efforts at various government levels in their applications, the Wae-Logistics Container Rail-Water Intermodal Transportation was included in the first batch of 16 national demonstration projects for multimodal transport, as approved by the Ministry of Transport in May 2016.

It's worth mentioning that the Wuhan municipal government has taken an important measure by establishing a stable subsidy system to provide long-term incentives for logistics companies, thus promoting the China-Europe Railway. In contrast to the absence of a subsidy system during the trial operation, clear subsidy arrangements were established at the beginning of its regular operation. "Implementation Plan for the Normalized Operation of International Rail Freight Transport for 'Hanxin'ou'" stated: "The Wuhan Municipal Finance Bureau, in conjunction with the Wuhan Municipal Transport Commission, the Wuhan Municipal Commerce Bureau (Port Office), the Wuhan East Lake High-Tech Development Zone, and the Wuhan Economic and Technological Development Zone Management Committee, among other departments and units, will determine the subsidies for containers transported by the 'Hanxin'ou' logistics

[34] Sha Chen, Bo Quan, Feng Ye, "Transportation Development Strategies for Building Wuhan as a National Central City," *Urban Transportation*, No. 3, 2014.

companies based on the difference between the Wuhan-to-Europe international container railway and waterway transportation, following the subsidy standards not lower than Chongqing, Zhengzhou, Xi'an, and other places ... The subsidy policy, once approved, will remain unchanged for five years, with specific subsidy amounts fixed on an annual basis until it achieves full market-oriented operation ..." The local government's subsidy for the China-Europe Railway Express (Wuhan) through public finances not only enables the operating company to construct and improve a new logistics route but also helps businesses in need of China-Europe Railway services to establish stable expectations. The combination of these factors eventually made it possible for the China-Europe Railway (Wuhan) to transition from a period of suspension to regular operation.

7.4 Characteristics and Analysis of the Regular Operation of the China-Europe Railway (Wuhan)

As previously mentioned, "traffic control" and "platform dilemma" are two major characteristics of the regular operation of the China-Europe Railway (Wuhan). These characteristics are the result of institutional arrangements within various departments of the local government and the relationships between the local government and the enterprises. The following offers a detailed analysis of the cause-and-effect mechanisms in these two aspects.

7.4.1 "Traffic Control" Amid Changes in Government-Enterprise Relations

At the institutional level, government-enterprise relations can be understood as the interactions and evolution of these interactions between enterprises and governments as actors within the institutional domain, as well as the resulting societal consequences.[35] Once government-business relations become structured, they profoundly influence the behavior of enterprises and the decisions of governments. Currently, most of the operating China-Europe freight train services follow a model of "government support + enterprise operation." Additionally, the "Development Plan for the Construction of China-Europe Railway Express (2016–2020)"

[35] Tian Zhang, Tao Sun, "Political-Business Relations in Transforming China, A Multidisciplinary Perspective Analysis", *Economic and Management Research*, No. 4, 2015.

explicitly outlines the basic principles of "market operation and government guidance." For a significant period, government-business relations will have a significant impact on China-Europe freight train services. In a situation where various enterprises operating the train services are competing for starting points, nodes, and "traffic" under government promotion, why has Wae-Logistics made the unconventional choice to control "traffic"? This article argues that the main reason is the guidance of enterprise behavior by the government's subsidy system. In other words, the subsidy system established by the government for China-Europe freight trains (Wuhan) ultimately creates an inherent tension between the total amount of subsidies and the total volume of transportation. This is the fundamental reason why Wae-Logistics has chosen to control "traffic."

Specifically, subsidies, as a form of guidance by local governments to nurture new logistics routes, serve as an institutional incentive to market participants. Although, since the inception of the China-Europe freight trains, the high subsidies provided by local governments have become one of the criticized phenomena by the academic community. Some media outlets have even criticized that local government subsidies have led to a frenzied competition for limited Silk Road cargo across regions, resulting in a vicious cycle of "loss-making but clamorous" competition that is bound to disrupt the normal operation of China-Europe freight trains.[36] However, it must be acknowledged that government subsidies have played a crucial role in ensuring the smooth operation of China-Europe freight trains. As stated by the head of the Wuhan Municipal Transportation Commission, the freight trains' development in Wuhan relies on both market-driven dynamics and proactive government nurturing and support. It's a collaborative effort that requires "both approaches" to pave the way for a "New Silk Road."[37] Furthermore, during an interview, leaders from the municipal commerce bureau emphasized that the China-Europe Railway (Wuhan), as a novel initiative in China-Europe cargo transportation, would be challenging for state-owned enterprises and nearly impossible for private enterprises to undertake without subsidies and guidance. In light of this situation, the current government support

[36] Rui Zhang, "China-Europe Freight Trains: Losing Money to Promote 'Silk Road' Trade," Hexun.com, January 27, 2015. http://www.newshexun.com/2015-01-27/172785775.html.

[37] Mingqiao Zheng, "How Long Will It Take to Restart China-Europe Freight Trains (Wuhan)," *Economic Daily*, September 26, 2013.

and nurturing are still deemed necessary. According to the "Wuhan Municipal Special Fund Usage Plan for Logistics Industry Development in 2015," Wuhan's municipal finance allocated a direct subsidy of 30 million yuan ($4.2 million) to the China-Europe Railway Express (Wuhan) in 2015.[38] Additionally, the "Management Measures for Special Subsidy Funds for Wuhan Container Rail-Water Intermodal Transportation" established a specific subsidy fund to provide three years of financial support for containers transported through the Wuhan Railway Container Yard and the Yangluo Port Rail-Water Transshipment.[39]

Unlike other cities, Wuhan adopted a "dual quota" approach for subsidies, which means that the subsidy amount per standard container is fixed, and the total amount allocated per year is also fixed. Before 2016, due to the relatively small volume of the China-Europe freight train (Wuhan), the government's subsidy amount could generally cover the transportation costs of logistics companies. Therefore, the primary focus for enterprises was on maximizing "traffic" or the number of containers transported. However, as the freight train's logistics system and volume continued to grow, the "dual quota" subsidy approach gradually led to subsidies becoming insufficient to cover logistics costs. A representative from Wae-Logistics pointed out:

> The early stages of the China-Europe Railway Express (Wuhan) operation were not yet fully market-oriented and still heavily reliant on government subsidies. The budget for subsidies has its limitations, and if we operate more trains than budgeted, we would end up operating at a loss. Originally, our plan was to operate around 260 trains this year. However, due to the government's inability to keep up with subsidies, we can only run 240 trains or even fewer.

Therefore, companies relying on subsidies for survival have adopted the rational business strategy of controlling "traffic" by reducing the number of train services. However, local governments are all keen on expanding

[38] See "Wuhan Municipal Special Fund Usage Plan for Logistics Industry Development in 2015," Wuhan Municipal Transportation Commission website, http://www.whjt.gov.cn/ztzl/sjczjtzxj/2016/07/21/78117.html, July 21, 2016.

[39] See "Notice of the Municipal People's Government on Issuing the 'Wuhan Container Rail-Water Intermodal Subsidy Funds Management Measures (Trial)'," Wuhan Municipal Government Portal, http://www.wuhan.gov.cn/hbgovinfo_47/szfggxxml/zcfg/gfxwj/201611/t20161110_93481.html. June 3, 2013.

the China-Europe freight train and aiming to leverage it as a regional achievement in conjunction with the BRI. Wae-Logistics' approach to controlling "traffic" certainly seems unconventional and has raised inquiries from relevant departments within the Wuhan municipal government. Hence, how to legitimize the practice of controlling "traffic" becomes a creative strategy for companies when dealing with government pressure. For example, the head of Wae-Logistics explains the concept of "selective picking" to address the pressure from local governments. The essence of "selective picking" is to improve overall transport efficiency, which means increasing the value of each standard container's cargo. According to statistics, the average value of goods carried by China-Europe freight trains from various cities ranges from over 12 million yuan ($1.68 million) to over 50.09 million yuan ($7 million) per train, while the China-Europe Railway Express (Wuhan) carries goods with an average value of over 40 million yuan ($5.6 million) per train, making it one of the most efficient services in terms of overall transport efficiency in China compared to other cities.[40]

From this, we can observe that the government's subsidy system influences corporate behavior, while companies, as active entities, also impact government practices. The "dual quota" subsidy system, in its current form, encourages companies to enhance the value of their cargo. However, it has also posed certain challenges for companies in terms of logistics platform and system development. Under this subsidy system, Wae-Logistics aims to legitimize its control over "traffic" by focusing on increasing the value of its cargo. Simultaneously, the company engages in written negotiations with the government to adjust the subsidy method, relieving operational pressures. Wae-Logistics believes that the current subsidy amount and the single subsidy mechanism are insufficient to adequately support the development pace of the China-Europe freight train. Therefore, they advocate for a reform in city-level financial subsidies, based on principles of "precision, efficiency, standardization, and transparency." Their proposal involves shifting from a fixed quota per container to the government injecting a certain amount of capital annually. Additionally, it suggests establishing a corresponding performance evaluation system, fully utilizing the leverage of government capital.[41] This proposition

[40] Rong Chen, "SWOT Analysis of 'Hanxin'ou' in the Integration of China-Europe Railway Express", *Comprehensive Transportation*, No. 1, 2016.

[41] Refer to internal reports provided by Wae-Logistics.

ultimately represents the enterprise's desire for the government to increase subsidies. However, whether this request can influence the Wuhan municipal government's subsidy system, which is subject to annual adjustments, remains to be seen. Regardless, the impact of government subsidies on the relationship between government and enterprises has now become an essential factor in the routine operation of the China-Europe Railway Express (Wuhan).

7.4.2 "Platform Dilemma" and Departmental Interests

After the setbacks of trial operations, the Wuhan municipal government realized that the key to the regular operation of the China-Europe freight train was to establish a logistics company and build an operating platform. However, as the train gradually entered its regular operational phase, differing opinions emerged within the government regarding the direction of platform. The Bureau of Commerce advocated for Wae-Logistics to serve as the exclusive logistics platform for international railway transportation, open to various enterprises. On the other hand, the Transportation Committee emphasized that platform should move toward comprehensive development in logistics, industrial parks, and foreign trade, creating a monopolistic platform under state-owned enterprise management. Essentially, the "platform dilemma" is a struggle between different departments within the local government, and the leadership group established by the government to promote the regular operation of the China-Europe freight train in Wuhan has intensified this interdepartmental conflict over interests.

The establishment of the leadership group is the first major task outlined in the "Implementation Plan for the Normalized Operation of International Rail Freight Transport for 'Hanxin'ou.'" Headed by the Deputy Mayor of Wuhan Municipal Government, the group oversees over ten relevant government departments and units, including the Office for Supervision and Coordination of Government Key Projects, the Development and Reform Commission, the Transportation Commission, the Economic and Information Commission, and the Bureau of Commerce. Additionally, it is specified that the "leadership group will set up an office, located in the office of the Municipal Transportation Commission, with working members seconded from member units. They will operate independently from their original units, practicing centralized office work."[42] The establishment of the group essentially aims to create a coordinated mechanism among various departments to provide specific coordination, organization, and linking services for the China-Europe freight train. In the early stages, it indeed facilitated the operations of the China-Europe Railway Express (Wuhan). For instance, during the trial run, the train had to pass through Zhengzhou for transit to reach Alashankou, resulting in a significant delay along the way. However, after negotiations between the leadership group and the railway department, the route was adjusted in July 2014 to run from Wuhan Central Station to Xiangyang North, Xinfeng Town in Xi'an, Lanzhou, and Urumqi. This adjustment significantly reduced the travel time. Nevertheless, as the regular operation was achieved and development goals became uncertain, conflicts of interest among the various departments under the leadership group began to emerge. In particular, there was a fundamental disagreement and a stalemate between the Transport Commission and the Bureau of Commerce regarding how the operation platform should be developed.

For the Transport Commission, it is in their interest if Wae-Logistics can expand and strengthen the China-Europe freight train in Wuhan within a feasible framework. Developing new logistics routes aligns with the intrinsic responsibilities of the Transport Commission. That's why the "13th Five-Year Plan for Transport Development in Wuhan" includes "Accelerating the Promotion of Regular Bilateral Transport of China-Europe Railway Express (Wuhan)" as a significant freight enhancement task. In fact, the idea of developing the railway into a comprehensive platform is both the opinion of the Transportation Commission and an active exploration by Wae-Logistics under the "dual-quota" subsidy system. With the continuous improvement of the logistics system and the increasing volume of the China-Europe Railway Express (Wuhan), the limitations of the "dual-quota" system in subsidizing actual logistics costs have become evident. This has prompted operating companies to proactively explore new business growth opportunities.

The head of Wae-Logistics explained that the subsidies now are no longer sufficient to support the increasingly frequent operation of the train services. To provide more momentum to the railway, the enterprises are actively expanding their foreign trade and park development businesses, forming an integrated international supply chain management

[42] See "Implementation Plan for the Normalized Operation of International Rail Freight Transport for 'Hanxin'ou'".

service (as detailed in Fig. 7.2). This aims to generate new profit sources to support the logistics system required by the train services. From this, it's evident that diversifying the business and establishing a comprehensive platform that integrates trade and logistics is a market-oriented strategy for Wae-Logistics to generate profits. This approach contributes to increasing the frequency of China-Europe Railway train services, thereby promoting the growth of cross-border railway logistics. It aligns with the interests of the Wuhan Municipal Transportation Commission and, as a result, receives its strong support.

The Wuhan Municipal Bureau of Commerce holds a distinct perspective on the platform development of the China-Europe Railway Express (Wuhan). Their focus lies in investment promotion, with the attraction of investments from industrial giants serving as a crucial element of their department's objectives. The rationale behind the Bureau of Commerce's support for confining Wae-Logistics to the construction of a single logistics platform is rooted in their apprehension that the company's diversification into other domains could potentially impede the efficiency of their investment promotion endeavors. For instance, the Bureau of Commerce

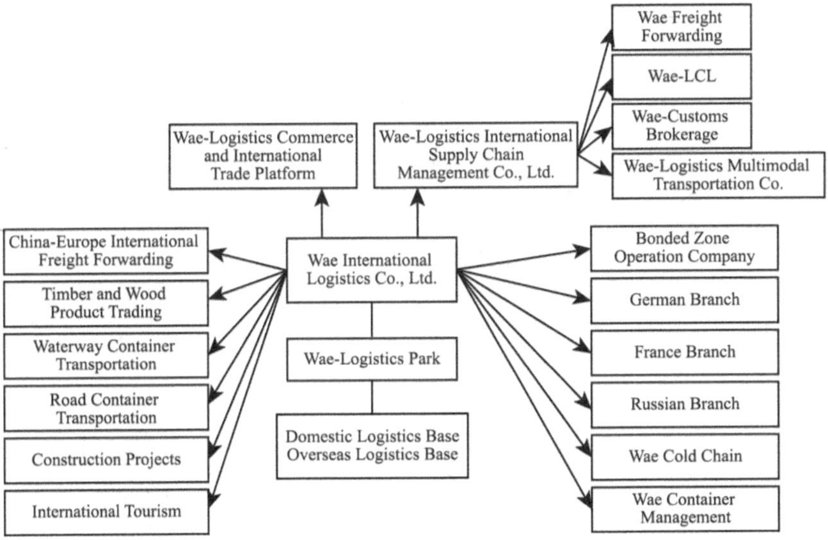

Fig. 7.2 Wae-Logistics development plan. Source: Compiled from internal reports provided by Wae-Logistics

has proper plans for the construction of logistics parks within the East-West-Lake Free Trade Zones, and Wae-Logistics' attempt to build new logistics parks for the railway express significantly disrupts the progress of the Bureau of Commerce's work plans. The "13th Five-Year Plan for Wuhan Business Development" clearly states that it should focus on four main areas, "Big Guanggu," "Big Chedu," "Big Linkong," and "Big Lingang." These are the key sectors for attracting investment and promoting economic development in the city. In the field of logistics, they particularly emphasize the need to "focus on the coastal area, vigorously attract large logistics enterprises to settle in, strengthen the collaborative development between the port and the logistics park in the coastal area, fostering an industrial cluster with more distinctive characteristics and more pronounced economies of scale and industrial agglomeration effects." Looking at the current operation of the China-Europe Railway Express (Wuhan), it's evident that the trade and industrial aggregation it can currently stimulate is quite limited. If Wae-Logistics significantly expands into other areas, it might encroach upon the Wuhan Municipal Bureau of Commerce's efforts to attract investments, especially from industry giants. This is the fundamental reason why the Bureau opposes its involvement in operations outside logistics and transportation. During interviews with the Bureau, their officials consistently stressed that Wae-Logistics should maintain its primary role as a public platform and refrain from getting involved in operational activities that deviate from this fundamental principle. In summary, the "platform dilemma" highlights the conflicting interests among various local government departments. Especially in the absence of a clear comprehensive plan for the future of the China-Europe Railway Express (Wuhan) by the Wuhan municipal government, different departments are naturally inclined to seek out potential paths where the train aligns with their interests, resulting in inevitable conflicts between these departments.

7.5 Conclusion and Discussion

At present, a convergence of major national strategies, including the BRI, the development of the Yangtze River Economic Belt, the planning of the Yangtze River midstream city cluster, the establishment of pilot financial reform zone for scientific and technological innovation in the Yangtze River Delta region, and the development of China (Hubei) Pilot Free Trade Zone Wuhan Area, has occurred in Wuhan. With the recent formal release of the "13th Five-Year Plan for Promoting the Rise of the Central Region" by the NDRC, Wuhan has officially attained the status of a national central city. This, coupled with the development of the China-Europe Railway Express (Wuhan), is anticipated to usher in a new pinnacle in Wuhan's development. Indeed, the China-Europe Railway Express (Wuhan), as a crucial route within the China-Europe Railway brand, serves multiple strategic purposes. On the one hand, it seamlessly connects the "Silk Road Economic Belt" and the "Yangtze River Economic Belt," two pivotal strategic spaces. On the other hand, it disrupts the traditional foreign trade pattern that predominantly focused on eastern coastal cities post-China's reform and opening-up. This acceleration has propelled Wuhan toward the realization of an international logistics corridor and hub, fostering the urban network construction process. Additionally, it has effectively established a bridge for economic ties and cultural exchanges between the central region and the regions along the BRI. In 2015, Wuhan's total foreign trade volume was $28.072 billion, with a cargo volume of 9.877 million tons. In contrast, the total cargo value of the China-Europe Railway Express (Wuhan) was only $500 million, with a cargo volume of 92,500 tons, indicating it still holds significant growth potential. Therefore, how to effectively open up the export routes of Hubei and the entire central region to the west through the construction of the China-Europe Railway, and drive the efficient development of multimodal transportation, becomes the key for Wuhan to successfully embark on the "Belt and Road" initiative. Understanding the reasons behind its phase differentiation and the characteristics of its regular operation is essential for optimizing institutional frameworks and promoting the development of the railway.

Building upon this perspective, the article considers local governments as crucial actors from the viewpoint of new economic sociology. The analysis of the China-Europe Railway Express (Wuhan) development encompasses three dimensions: the relationship between the central government and local government, interactions between local government and enterprises, and dynamics within the local government. Conducted from an institutional standpoint, this analysis seeks to uncover the mechanisms underlying the phased operation and normalized functioning of the China-Europe Railway Express (Wuhan). In essence, the shift of the railway from "suspension" to "resumption" is an unavoidable consequence of local governments aligning with central government strategies. Guided by the policy paradigm of the BRI, the Wuhan municipal government had to adjust its logistics planning to prioritize the China-Europe Railway Express (Wuhan) in line with central planning. As early as 2008, Wuhan initiated the New Port strategy, focusing on developing the Yangtze River waterway. During this period, its logistics planning, and industrial policies were primarily centered around this initiative, with international railway freight not being a primary focus. It was only in 2013, with the BRI becoming a top-level national proposal, that the Wuhan municipal government started developing various infrastructures, leading to the resumption of the China-Europe Railway Express (Wuhan).

Moreover, the features of "traffic control" and the "platform dilemma" in regular operations result from the interplay between local government and enterprises and the conflicting interests among government departments. "Traffic control" is a strategic decision made by railway operating companies within the framework of the "dual quota" subsidy system. Simultaneously, the "platform dilemma" emerges from divergent views on the development plan for the China-Europe Railway (Wuhan) between the Bureau of Commerce and the Transportation Commission, influenced by their respective responsibilities and interests. However, the combination of these two creates a paradox: on the one hand, the adoption of the "dual quota" subsidy system compels operating companies to broaden their scope, venturing beyond logistics into trade and logistics parks to diversify their sources of profit and facilitate the logistics system's development. However, on the other hand, due to conflicting departmental interests, the Bureau of Commerce maintains that operating companies should solely function as transportation platforms, posing a challenge to the further advancement of the comprehensive platform construction of the China-Europe Railway.

Indeed, local governments play an indispensable role in advancing the routine operations of the China-Europe Railway. Therefore, at the current operational stage, the China-Europe Railway (Wuhan) necessitates the government to re-establish new guidelines to clarify the relationships among various entities. In concrete terms, despite the Wuhan municipal government having introduced relevant policies and facilitated the significant development of the route, there still exists a lack of systematic planning for its subsequent development. This situation has resulted in a dilemma where, once the railway achieves regular and stable operation, it encounters a loss of focus regarding its positioning. Conflicts of interest between various departments inevitably emerge in this process. In the long term, Wuhan aspires to establish itself as a logistics hub for servicing the industrial chains in central China and connecting the transfer of goods between regions. The China-Europe Railway is a crucial avenue for realizing this goal. Unfortunately, at the present stage where the railway has entered a phase of regular operation, Wuhan lacks a clear top-level design for this westbound rail freight "gateway" to Europe. Compared to the strategies such as Chongqing's "Yuxin'ou+" and Chengdu's "Rong'ou+," Wuhan's municipal government has yet to introduce a dedicated strategic deployment for the China-Europe Railway. Currently, the Wuhan municipal government urgently needs to reevaluate and reposition the China-Europe Railway (Wuhan) based on the practical issues faced by the rail service. This reassessment aims to clarify its goals, identify problems to be addressed, and determine the support required after achieving regular operations, ensuring its sustainable development.

CHAPTER 8

Construction of the New International Land-Sea Trade Corridor and Cooperation Situation with Local Governments Along the Route

Dongkun Li and Xinyue Luo

8.1 Background and Significance of the Construction of the New International Land-Sea Trade Corridor

8.1.1 At the Policy Level

Since the inception of the Western Development Strategy, China's western regions have made significant strides in economic and social development. However, compared to their eastern counterparts, they still grapple with

D. Li (✉) • X. Luo
School of Public Administration, Southwest Jiaotong University, Chengdu, China
e-mail: bai.gao@duke.edu

B. Gao, Z. Zhen (eds.), *The China-Europe Railway Express*, China and Globalization 2.0,
https://doi.org/10.1007/978-981-19-2882-6_8

substantial developmental challenges, stemming from their distance from seaports and underdeveloped infrastructure networks. Consequently, these regions must now redouble their efforts to overcome such regional disparities and explore new avenues for development. In 2017, provinces and autonomous regions in the west, like Chongqing and Guangxi, embarked on initiatives such as the China-Singapore Connectivity Southern Transport Corridor (later rebranded as the New International Land-Sea Trade Corridor), aimed at bolstering economic and trade ties with Southeast Asian nations like Singapore. The successful implementation of these initiatives has seen a surge in participation from western provinces, amplifying its regional influence. In 2017, provinces and autonomous regions in the western part of China, including Chongqing and Guangxi, started exploring and promoting the China-Singapore land-sea trade corridor (later renamed the New International Land-Sea Trade Corridor) to strengthen economic and trade cooperation with Southeast Asian countries such as Singapore. This corridor's construction has yielded positive results, with an increasing number of western provinces participating, thereby expanding its influence. In August 2019, the National Development and Reform Commission formally designated this corridor as the "New International Land-Sea Trade Corridor" and released the "Master Plan for the New International Land-Sea Trade Corridor." This blueprint outlines the construction of three primary corridors (east, central, and west) and transportation hubs, aiming to streamline logistical challenges in the western regions and foster a coordinated pattern of regional development and openness. Subsequently, a series of significant policies and guidelines were successively issued, further affirming the strategic position and development requirements of the New International Land-Sea Trade Corridor as a major national southward transportation corridor. These include the "National Comprehensive Three-Dimensional Transportation Network Planning Outline" (2021), the "Guiding Opinions of the Central Committee of the CPC and the State Council on Promoting the Development of the Western Regions and Forging a New Pattern in the New Era" (2021), the "14th Five-Year Plan to Promote High-Quality Construction of the New International Land-Sea Trade Corridor" (2021), and the "14th Five-Year Plan for the Modern Comprehensive Transport System Construction of the New International Land-Sea Trade Corridor" (2022). The Regional Comprehensive Economic Partnership (RCEP) entered into force in January 2022, presenting significant opportunities for the development of the Corridor. It also emerged as a pivotal driver for western regions to advance a "dual circulation" development model, prioritizing the domestic economic cycle while extending and supplementing through the international economic cycle, thereby fostering a new paradigm of openness and development.

Under the impetus of national strategic planning and policies, enthusiasm among provinces and cities in the western region to participate in the Corridor has further intensified. In October 2019, within the framework of the "Master Plan for the New International Land-Sea Trade Corridor," 12 western provinces and autonomous regions, along with Hainan Province and Zhanjiang City in Guangdong Province, signed the "Framework Agreement for Cooperative Construction of the New International Land-Sea Trade Corridor" in Chongqing. Thus, a "13+1" cooperative pattern was established. Subsequently, its network of partners expanded further, enhancing both the linkage between the central and western regions and the connectivity between the eastern and western regions. Transport infrastructure and hub construction remain one of the important tasks in the current stage. Provinces and cities along the New International Land-Sea Trade Corridor have incorporated corresponding tasks into their provincial-level key special plans such as the "14th Five-Year Plan." They have also provided clear objectives, implementation milestones, and policy support in various aspects. Chongqing, as the pioneering city and core node of the Corridor, explicitly stated in its "Comprehensive Transportation Development Plan of Chongqing Municipality for the 14th Five-Year Plan (2021–2025)" the imperative to expedite the establishment of a modern, high-caliber comprehensive three-dimensional transportation network and to establish an economically efficient modern logistics system. The objective is to position Chongqing as a strategic hub for the advancement of the New International Land-Sea Trade Corridor. Additionally, nine districts within the city, including Fuling, Jiangjin, Jiulongpo, Qianjiang, Yubei, Bana, Tongliang, Wulong, and Nanchuan, have devised transportation-oriented schemes to bolster the Corridor's development. Sichuan Province has sequentially unveiled the "Sichuan Province Comprehensive Transportation Development Plan for the 14th Five-Year Plan" and the "Modern Logistics Development Plan for the 14th Five-Year Plan." These initiatives aim to expedite the construction of key routes and pivotal hubs along the Corridor. Additionally, there is a concerted effort to collaborate in establishing the New International Land-Sea Trade Corridor and the logistics hub of the Yangtze River Economic Belt. Chengdu, Dazhou, Luzhou,

Neijiang, and Yibin are slated to emerge as crucial cities along the Corridor, collectively bolstering its development. Guangxi Zhuang Autonomous Region has successively released the "Implementation Plan for the Operation Enhancement of the Main Line of Sea-Rail Intermodal Transport in the New International Land-Sea Trade Corridor (2019–2020)" and the "Three-Year Action Plan for Enhancing the Construction of the New International Land-Sea Trade Corridor in Guangxi Zhuang Autonomous Region (2021–2023)." These plans are geared toward significantly enhancing the infrastructure development of the corridor, bolstering the comprehensive service capabilities of Beibu Gulf Port, optimizing corridor logistics operations, improving customs efficiency, and enhancing the corridor's role in propelling local economic and industrial growth by 2023. Yunnan Province, as an important logistics hub in the southwest region, issued the "Outline of the 14th Five-Year Plan for Yunnan Province" and the "Outline of the Comprehensive Three-dimensional Transportation Network Plan for Yunnan Province," proposing to achieve the goal of building a strong transportation province and forming a modern comprehensive three-dimensional transportation network by 2035, which is of great significance for promoting the construction of the New International Land-Sea Trade Corridor in Yunnan Province. Guizhou Province views the construction of the Corridor as a pivotal task in its transportation development agenda. The "14th Five-Year Plan for Transportation Development in Guizhou Province (Draft for Soliciting Opinions)" unambiguously positions Guizhou as a key player and vital node in the Corridor. Leveraging this strategic advantage, the province is poised to expedite its integration into the Chengdu-Chongqing Economic Circle and establish seamless connectivity with prominent economic zones like the Beibu Gulf urban agglomeration. Consequently, cities such as Guiyang, Anshun, Bijie, and Liupanshui have rolled out comprehensive transportation development plans, actively engaging in the construction and advancement of the Corridor.

8.1.2 The "Corridor Economy" Created by the New International Land-Sea Trade Corridor

One significant illustration of how transportation affects economic development in regional areas is the "Corridor Economy," which was developed by the New International Land-Sea Trade Corridor. The understanding of this concept, which originated from China's regional economic development practices, has advanced significantly in recent academic research. In the 1990s, some scholars proposed the spatial development strategy of "Four Along" (namely "along the coast, along the river, along the border, along the line") based on China's regional economic development practices (Shi et al. 2012).

The theoretical underpinning of the corridor economy draws from several seminal theories, including Francois Perroux's Growth Poles Theory, Werner Sombart's Growth Axis Theory, and John Friedman's Core-Periphery Theory. Numerous scholars, such as Yongmin Long (2005), have contributed definitions for the corridor economy. In essence, the corridor economy refers to the collaborative development of economic regions along transportation corridors. It relies on these corridors as foundational infrastructure, leveraging economic openness and cooperation to foster economic agglomeration, industrial transfer, and regional economic collaboration through the mobility of factors and industrial clustering. Corridor economy emerges based on transportation corridors, and due to the different nature of transportation corridors, it can be classified into several types. For instance, there is the "Corridor Economy" generated by road and bridge infrastructure (Li 1999), the "Along-the-river Economy" relying on water transportation corridors (Jiang 2016), and even the "Network Economy" relying on modern transportation networks (Qin and Wang 2021).

The corridor serves as the fundamental carrier for the formation of the corridor economy. Transportation corridors are platforms for the circulation and distribution of factor resources. They are the prerequisite for the formation and development of the corridor economy, the precondition for industrial activities and layout, and the direct determinant of the level of development of the corridor economy. The formation of the corridor economy is the result of the coordinated development of transportation and the economy. Regarding the relationship between the corridor economy and transportation, Qixian Zhu (2010) analyzes the connection between corridor economy and infrastructure from three aspects: the basic form and functional positioning of transportation corridors, the evolution and development of transportation corridors, and the relationship between transportation and regional economic activities. Hongxia Gao (2021) believes that the development of transportation corridors drives the expansion of regional economic activities, and economic development simultaneously further improves transportation infrastructure. Hui Yue (2020) introduces the concept of the "diamond economy circle," arguing that comprehensive transportation corridors are critical in forming a regional economic network characterized by interconnectivity, efficiency, and environmental sustainability, thereby serving as a new engine for China's economic growth.

In terms of research on the attributes and mechanisms of the corridor economy, Qixian Zhu (2009) examines the historical origins of the corridor economy and concludes that it has progressed through five stages: land corridor economy, sea corridor economy, transportation corridor economy, industrial (transfer) corridor economy, and institutional corridor economy. Yongmin Long (2005) summarizes the characteristics of the corridor economy as scientific economic decision-making, diversified economic subjects, and diversified economic structures. Zhengfang Shi (2012) believes that the essence of the corridor economy lies in relying on the construction of transportation corridors to promote regional economic and integration development. Peng Yang (2012) analyzes the mechanism of the corridor economy from the perspective of production factors, stating that the accessibility of areas along the corridor can be changed by the connectivity of multidimensional corridor networks, and transportation corridors will further facilitate the free flow of factors such as labor and materials. Meichao Shi (2011) examines the mechanism of the corridor economy using the Guangxi to ASEAN corridor as an example. They contend that the improved transportation infrastructure along the corridor raises regional accessibility and lowers transportation costs, boosting the region's overall competitiveness. The presence of scale effects and agglomeration effects will help upgrade industries within the region, ultimately raising the overall level of regional economy.

Overall, corridors are seen as the "arteries" of material, energy, and information circulation and exchange within and outside economic-geographical systems, as well as the "bridges" for outward expansion and movement.

The New International Land-Sea Trade Corridor has developed into more than just a straightforward logistics route thanks to the combined efforts of the provinces, cities, and districts along its path. It is now a vital part of the western economy. Four years ahead of the China Railway Express routes, the Chongqing Sea-Rail Intermodal Block Train of the Corridor reached a train count of over 10,000 in 2020. It traversed 92 stations in 47 cities across 13 provinces in China by the end of 2021, with over 20,000 trains running along the corridor, including 12 inland ports. The corridor has improved trade by increasing logistics, which in turn promotes industrial prosperity and economic expansion. The economic and regional benefits of the corridor economy will become more apparent as the construction of the corridor moves forward, propelling the growth of the provinces along its path and bolstering the general prosperity of China's logistics industry. This is not only important practically, but it also emphasizes how important it is to investigate the viability of doing more research on corridor economy-related issues.

8.2 Development Status of the New International Land-Sea Trade Corridor and Its Hubs

8.2.1 Construction Status of the New International Land-Sea Trade Corridor

The New International Land-Sea Trade Corridor refers to the improvement of transportation infrastructure in the western region to meet the opening requirements of the Belt and Road Initiative (BRI), to construct a new pattern of western development, and to promote the formation of a larger, broader, and deeper level of opening-up pattern for China. The Corridor requires the basic connectivity of three railway transportation routes from Chongqing and Chengdu respectively to Beibu Gulf Ports (Qinzhou Port, Beihai Port, Port of Fangchenggang) through Guiyang, Huaihua, and Baise, forming a rational division of labor and complementary railway transportation network among the eastern, central, and western routes.

The eastern route departs from Chongqing, passes through Huaihua and Liuzhou, and reaches the mouth of Beibu Gulf; the central route also starts from Chongqing, passes through Guiyang, and Nanning to reach the mouth of Beibu Gulf; while the western route starts from Chengdu, passes through Luzhou and Baise, and finally reaches the mouth of Beibu Gulf. The three parts of the corridor involve a total of 11 railway lines as shown in Table 8.1 below.

Since the proposal to construct the Corridor's eastern, central, and western railway lines in 2019, specific railway construction has made corresponding progress: (1) The Eastern Corridor primarily focuses on improving existing functions, with most of the lines undergoing relatively comprehensive construction. For example, the Chongqing-Huaihua Railway and the Jiaozuo-Liuzhou Railway had completed electrification upgrades by early 2022, providing ample assurance for the smooth operation of the lines. The renovation and upgrading of the Hunan-Guangxi Railway have also been put on the agenda. (2) The Central Corridor focuses on increasing capacity and upgrading existing main lines to improve transportation efficiency. The Chongqing-Guiyang Railway, for example, was built early and to a low standard. Natural disasters have had a significant impact on its operations, as have numerous traffic accidents.

Table 8.1 Railway route list for the eastern, western, and central corridors

Corridor	*Railway*	*Section*	*Distance/ km*	*Track condition*
Eastern, corridor	Chongqing-Huaihua Railway	Chongqing—Huaihua	562	Double track, speed limit 120 km/h
	Jiaozuo-Liuzhou Railway	Huaihua—Liuzhou	613	Single track, speed limit 120 km/h
	Hunan-Guangxi Railway	Liuzhou—Shajiang	446	Double track, speed limit 120 km/h
Central corridor	Chongqing-Guiyang Railway	Chongqing—Guiyang	533	Single track, speed limit 120 km/h
	Guizhou-Guangxi Railway	Guiyang—Luoman	542	Single track, speed limit 120 km/h
		Luoman—Liuzhou	40	Double track, speed limit 120 km/h
	Hunan-Guangxi Railway	Liuzhou—Shajiang	169	Double track, speed limit 120 km/h
	Luzhou-Zunyi Railway	Luzhou—Zunyi	236	
Western, corridor	Chengdu-Chongqing Railway	Chengdu—Longchang	276	Single track, speed limit 120 km/h
	Neijiang-Liupanshui Railway	Neijiang—Liupanshui	503	Single track, speed limit 120 km/h
	Liupanshui-Hongguo Railway	Liupanshui—Hongguo	158	Single track, speed limit 120 km/h
	Weishe-Hongguo	Hongguo—Weishe	68	Single track, speed limit 120 km/h
	Nanning-Kunming Railway	Kunming—Weishe	291	Single track, speed limit 120 km/h
		Weishe—Baise	289	Single track, speed limit 120 km/h
		Baise—Nanning	234	Double track, speed limit 120 km/h

Source: Compiled by the authors

The construction of double tracks for the Chongqing-Guiyang Railway is complete, but capacity expansion has yet to begin. After the completion of the Guizhou-Guangxi Railway in 2009, it underwent a capacity expansion. To promote the construction of the Corridor, a project to convert it into a double-track railway is underway. On January 27, 2021, China Railway Group officially issued the "Guizhou-Guangxi Railway Double-Track Renovation Survey and Design Project Tender Announcement," proposing to renovate the Guizhou-Guangxi Railway from Guiyang to Liuzhou into a double-track line. The construction pace of the Luzhou-Zunyi Railway continues to accelerate. In November 2019, the governments of Luzhou and Zunyi signed the "Framework Agreement on Deepening Regional Cooperation between the People's Government of Luzhou City, Sichuan Province, and the People's Government of Zunyi City, Guizhou Province," clarifying joint efforts to promote the Luzhou-Zunyi Railway. In February 2021, the Development and Reform Commission of Guizhou Province issued the "List of Major Projects and Key Projects in Guizhou Province for 2021," listing the "Zunyi to Luzhou Railway Project" as one of the 65 preliminary projects for infrastructure. (3) The Western Corridor focuses on ensuring smooth transportation and supplementing the construction of missing sections to facilitate the western maritime route. Among them, the Huangtong-Baise Railway has been incorporated into the national "Medium and Long-Term Railway Network Plan" and marketed as a key project of the New International Land-Sea Trade Corridor. Plans include operating double-decker container trains. The Huangtong-Baise Railway project is an essential component of the Western Corridor of the New International Land-Sea Trade Corridor. Together with the Longchang-Huangtong Railway, it functions as the southern extension of the latter and provides the primary route for the export of goods from Guizhou, Sichuan, and the southwest region. In addition to improving overall transportation conditions in northwest Guangxi and southwest Guizhou, this will increase the capacity for cargo transportation in the hinterland behind the Beibu Gulf ports. It will also have a major impact on local economic development, encourage the development of territorial resources along the route, and hasten the reduction of poverty and advancement of prosperity in the region.[1] The "Outline of the 14th Five-Year Plan (2021-2025) for National Economic and Social

[1] The Development and Reform Commission of Guangxi Zhuang Autonomous Region organized and held a meeting to promote the preliminary work of the Huangtong-Baise

Development and Vision 2035 of Sichuan Province" includes the Chengdu-Chongqing Railway (from Chengdu to Longchang) as one of its key rail transportation projects. It will not only form an important route for southward external communication together with the Longchang-Huangtong Railway but also serve as an essential part of the comprehensive transportation development plan for the Chengdu-Chongqing urban agglomeration. Currently, the Chengdu to Longchang section of the Chengdu-Chongqing Railway has completed the bidding phase for survey and design and is about to enter the feasibility analysis stage. The railway from Liuzhou through Wuzhou to Guangzhou is an important component of the proposed Liuzhou-Guangzhou Railway. This route holds significant strategic importance as it not only enhances the railway network in the southwestern region but also facilitates the reduction of spatial and temporal distances between the southwestern region and the Pearl River Delta and the Greater Bay Area, thereby opening up a southern gateway for external communication. The Guangxi Department of Transportation approved the preliminary design of the Liuzhou to Wuzhou section of the recently constructed Liuzhou to Guangzhou Railway on September 6, 2021. The project is expected to be completed by the end of 2024, with a 48-month construction period. The second phase of the Nanning-Kunming Railway project from Nanning to Baise was put into operation in 2017. The feasibility study for the section from Baise to Weishe has been completed, and as of April 29, 2021, all contact wire lines for the Baise to Weishe section have been replaced.[2]

8.2.2 Construction Status of Hub Along the New International Land-Sea Trade Corridor

At the 2019 State Council executive meeting, it was proposed to develop a modern logistics system of "corridors + hubs + networks" through a variety of measures, including selecting cities with favorable locations, industrial conditions, and strong radiation capacities as carriers, as well as planning and building a number of key logistics hubs. At the national

Railway project. This information was shared on the official website of the Development and Reform Commission of Guangxi Zhuang Autonomous Region. www.gxzf.gov.cn.

[2] *The Entire Contact Wire of the Baise to Weishe Section of the Nanning-Kunming Railway has been Completely Replaced* – Company News – China Railway Electrification Bureau Group Co., Ltd. (eeb.cn) [EB/OL].[2021-05-01].http://www.eeb.cn/tabid/372/InfoID/20870/frtid/83/Default.aspx.

level, the construction of logistics hubs has reached new heights. The construction of logistics hubs is being pushed forward as basic transportation infrastructure improves. As vital nodes in the transportation network, logistics hubs play a crucial role in connecting all directions. Therefore, in the construction of the Corridor, the transportation hub stations along the route in various provinces play a pivotal role.

In the "Master Plan for the New International Land-Sea Trade Corridor," it is proposed to vigorously develop integrated comprehensive transportation hubs, enhance facility operation efficiency, and leverage the radiation function of transportation hubs. It aims to improve transportation station facilities, strengthen the construction of railway freight yards, and construct and expand a batch of railway freight bases with container handling capabilities, thereby enhancing the capability of railway trains to directly reach their destinations and consolidate cargo through transit. Moreover, it emphasizes the enhancement of highway transportation stations and supporting facilities to bolster the guaranteed capacity for cargo flow distribution. Additionally, it seeks to improve and upgrade the cargo transportation functions of ports, optimize yard layouts, advance port equipment upgrading and renovation, and enhance operational efficiency.

Currently, the significant logistics hubs along the Corridor are concentrated in the southwestern region. Among them, Chongqing and Chengdu serve as the logistics distribution centers in the southwestern region, undertaking the logistics distribution functions. Yunnan Province and Guangxi Zhuang Autonomous Region serve as cross-border transportation hubs, contributing significantly to the growth of international freight transport.

8.2.2.1 Chongqing Tuanjie Village Container Center Station and Chongqing Yuzui Railway Freight Station

In the entire Chongqing, including Wanzhou, Jiangjin, and the Liangjiang New Area, many counties have joined the construction of the New International Land-Sea Trade Corridor. In terms of the Corridor, Chongqing has established a cargo main artery in the shape of a "well" in Chinese in the main urban area and positioned Chongqing (including Jiangjin) as the main hub, with Wanzhou and Fuling as auxiliary hubs, and with Qianjiang, Changshou, Hechuan, and Qijiang as important nodes in the "One Main, Two Auxiliaries, Multiple Nodes" hub system. Currently, the Corridor has access to 106 countries and 304 ports worldwide. In the first half of this year, the rail-sea intermodal trains (originating from

Chongqing) operated 952 trains, transporting 47,880 standard containers, a year-on-year increase of 147%; the transport value amounted to 6.05 billion yuan (including 3.54 billion yuan in foreign trade value), a year-on-year increase of 128%. Cross-border road transportation (Chongqing to ASEAN) operated 1666 trips, transporting 3749 standard containers, a year-on-year increase of 70%; the transport value amounted to 997 million yuan, a year-on-year increase of 107%. China-Vietnam international freight train (Chongqing to Vietnam) transported 1006 standard containers, a year-on-year increase of 56%, with a transport value of approximately 1.7 billion yuan.

The Tuanjie Village Railway Container Center Station in Chongqing serves as the starting point for the Chongqing-Xinjiang-Europe Railway (Yuxin'ou Railway), benefiting from Chongqing's robust railway system. Currently, within the boundaries of Chongqing Municipality, there are five electrified mainline railways, including the Chengdu-Chongqing Railway, Chongqing-Guizhou Railway, Xiangyang-Chongqing Railway, Chongqing-Huaihua Railway, and Suining-Chongqing Railway, as well as two branch line railways, namely the Dazhou-Wanzhou Railway and Sanjiang-Nanchuan Railway. Under construction are the Lanzhou-Chongqing Railway, Chongqing-Lichuan Railway, Suining-Chongqing Railway Second Line, Chongqing-Huaihua Railway Second Line (Chongqing-Fuling section), Chengdu-Chongqing Passenger Dedicated Line, Nanchuan-Fuling Railway, Chongqing-Wanzhou Passenger Dedicated Line, and Chongqing-Guizhou Railway (Cui Qiushuang and Dong Qin 2018). The geographical location advantage of the Chongqing Yuzui Railway Freight Station is very prominent. The Yuzui Railway Freight Station, as an important logistics hub in the Liangjiang New Area of Chongqing Municipality and a demonstration base for multimodal transport in the China-Singapore (Chongqing) Demonstration Initiative on Strategic Connectivity, is also a key railway logistics hub highlighted in the "Master Plan for the New International Land-Sea Trade Corridor." It serves as a crucial support for the seamless transportation and shipping of goods along the New International Land-Sea Trade Corridor, China-Europe Railway Express (Chongqing), and the Yangtze River Golden Waterway, three major international logistics channels. Currently, it is integrated with the Guoyuan Port to become a significant multimodal transport hub in the Chengdu-Chongqing region. Located adjacent to the Yangtze River Golden Waterway, it seamlessly connects to the Guoyuan Port through a dedicated line spanning 3.7 kilometers. It is conveniently linked to major highways such as the Chongqing Ring Expressway and the Chongqing-Shanghai Expressway and is 15 kilometers away from the Jiangbei International Airport. As the only railway node of the Guoyuan Port, it plays a vital role in the national logistics network in the western region. Guoyuan Port, as the largest domestic and foreign trade river port in the upper reaches of the Yangtze River, serves as a vital national logistics hub within the Chengdu-Chongqing Economic Circle.

8.2.2.2 Chengdu Tianfu International Airport Air-Rail Cargo Station

Chengdu Tianfu International Airport is located approximately 50 kilometers north of the Chengdu city center, 50 kilometers northwest of Chengdu Shuangliu International Airport, and about 14.5 kilometers northeast of the downtown area of Jianyang City. It is classified as a 4F-grade international airport and serves as a key international aviation hub and one of the highest-grade aviation ports along the Silk Road Economic Belt. It is also the main hub of the Chengdu International Aviation Hub.

To accelerate the transformation of Tianfu International Airport into a central airport, the Tianfu International Airport-rail Freight Station utilizes advanced management methods and intelligent operational approaches to create an advanced air transportation network and an infrastructure transport platform relying on railway intermodal transportation. Chengdu Tianfu International Airport was officially opened on June 27, 2021, making it China's third city with two airports, after Beijing and Shanghai. The construction of "two airports in one city" will accelerate Chengdu's development and propel the Chengdu-Chongqing economic circle to new heights.

8.2.2.3 Qinzhou Port East Station Railway Container Handling Station in Guangxi Zhuang Autonomous Region

On March 19, 2011, the Guangxi Zhuang Autonomous Region People's Government approved the use of the unified name "Guangxi Port of Beibu Gulf Port" for the coastal ports of Fangchenggang, Qinzhou, and Beihai. Regional integration has become increasingly important, and the region has begun to promote the process internally, resulting in the integrated development of Qinzhou, Beihai, and Fangchenggang. During the "12th Five-Year Plan" period, Qinzhou, Beihai, and Fangchenggang began new port ventures with the support of the local government. During the "13th Five-Year Plan," the Guangxi government and the other three local governments began to actively promote the integration of Qinzhou, Beihai, and Fangchenggang. There are currently three ports in the Port of Beibu Gulf area: Beihai, Qinzhou, and Fangchenggang. Due to its advantageous location, the Beibu Gulf serves as both the "landing point" for trade from ASEAN enterprises entering China's inland markets and the "starting point" for exports from Chinese inland enterprises. With its natural geographic advantages, it is among the areas nearest to ASEAN nations and served as one of the starting points of the ancient Maritime Silk Road (Chen and Gong 2021). In 2021, the "National Comprehensive Three-Dimensional Transportation Network Plan Outline" was issued, clearly listing the Beibu Gulf ports as international transportation hubs, and aiming to build them into transportation fortresses, further driving the development of the Beibu Gulf ports. Internationally, during the "Diamond Decade" of "all-round, cross-domain, multi-level, and deep-level" new development between China and ASEAN countries, the next ten years will be a golden period for the development of the Beibu Gulf region, providing new momentum for the emerging development of the Beibu Gulf region and driving the vigorous development of the Guangxi region (Tang 2021). As of June 2018, the Beibu Gulf had 79 productive berths, 61 of which were over 10,000 tons, 24 were over 100,000 tons, and two were over 200,000 tons. The annual throughput was 240 million tons, with a container throughput capacity of 4.68 million TEUs. The port formed a "One axis, Two wings" pattern. In recent years, container business has opened 43 domestic and foreign trade routes, including 17 internal routes and 26 external routes, accounting for 60% of the routes. Most of them have achieved full coverage of the eastern ports. At the same time, 17 internal routes have basically covered major ports nationwide. In 2017, the cargo throughput reached 156.5 million tons, a year-on-year increase of 12.1% (Yu and Li 2021). In addition, the economic development level in the region has significantly improved. From 2006 to 2018, the per capita regional GDP increased from 9612 yuan ($1337) to 53,928 yuan ($7501), a 4.6-fold increase. Local fiscal revenue increased from 5.09 billion yuan ($700 million) to 45.6 billion yuan ($6.3 billion), an increase of eight times. The total import and export volume increased from $1.76 billion to $19.18 billion, an increase of 9.9 times, and its share in the entire region increased from 26.4% to 30.9%.

There are notable distinctions between the three ports in the Beibu Gulf region. Although Beihai Port has a thriving tourism sector, it is the port with the lowest cargo throughput and growth rate in the entire Beibu Gulf region. Being a natural harbor, Qinzhou Port has distinct geographic advantages and leads the region in port throughput. Its port throughput made up 46.25% of the region's total in the first half of 2021. Fangchenggang Port, an important seaport in southwestern China and a port hub connecting other parts of Asia, has enormous growth potential. The coordinated development of these three ports will significantly improve their status as transportation hubs along the "New International Land-Sea Trade Corridor."

The pandemic's effects notwithstanding, the ports in the Beibu Gulf region have seen a sharp increase in container throughput. The overall throughput of containers in the ports in this region increased fourfold between 2013 and 2020, from one million TEUs to over five million TEUs. In 2020, the total container transportation volume of the ports in the Beibu Gulf region reached 5.05 million TEUs, a 32% increase over 2019, entering the ranks of the top ten coastal ports in China. Although there is still a gap compared to international mega-ports, it demonstrates significant development potential (see Table 8.2).

8.2.2.4 Kunming South Asia International Land Port Logistics Road-Rail Intermodal Transportation in Yunnan Province

Yunnan Province shares borders with or is adjacent to 17 countries in Southeast Asia and South Asia, giving it the advantageous geographical position described as "connecting to coastal areas in the east through Guizhou and Guangxi, passing through Sichuan and Chongqing to enter the Central Plains in the north, extending to Vietnam, Laos, Thailand, and Cambodia in the south, and bordering Myanmar, India, and Pakistan in the west." Yunnan Province's economy has continued to grow at a moderate to rapid pace, and its modern industrial structure is constantly improving. As the demand for transportation and logistics rises in tandem with economic and industrial growth, Yunnan Province's development prospects become increasingly promising. Overall, the total volume of goods transported and turnover in Yunnan's logistics industry are increasing.

Situated in the mostly hilly southeast of Anning City's main urban area, Yunnan Province is home to the Kunming South Asia International Land Port. The logistics park stretches south to the Nanrao Railway and includes the KISC Railway branch line to the south. The town of Haikou is adjacent to the logistics area's southern boundary, and the Wujiazhuang area

Table 8.2 Beibu Gulf's Port traffic, January–June 2021

Region	*Jan–July Port total throughput (10,000 tons)*	*Ranking in the region*	*Cumulative year-on-year growth (%)*	*Ranking in the region*
Beibu Gulf	17,318.98		24.10%	
Beihai Port	1888.15	3	7.60%	3
Fangchenggang Port	7421.12	2	28.60%	1
Qinzhou Port	8009.71	1	24.60%	2

is bordered by its northern boundary. With the Anning-Chuxiong Expressway, Anning-Jinning Expressway, and Anning-Haikou Expressway encircling it, the logistics park's transportation system is well developed and comparatively complete. The Kunming-Yuxi branch line and the proposed Dushupu to Caopu dedicated line, along with the surrounding road network, form the framework for the "One port, Three parks" layout. The Daotaohua Freight Center serves as the focal point of the Kunming South Asia International Land Port Center. It is divided into seven functional areas that offer a wide range of services: the modern logistics industrial zone, the Daotaohua Railway Freight Port area, the multimodal transportation area, the comprehensive service operation center, the exhibition and trade zone, the bonded zone, and the road-port area.

8.3 Cooperation Among Provincial Governments Along the New International Land-Sea Trade Corridor

In February 2017, the China-Singapore Joint Coordinating Council for the China-Singapore (Chongqing) Demonstration Initiative on Strategic Connectivity held its first meeting, giving rise to the New International Land-Sea Trade Corridor concept. During the meeting, both sides discussed the creation of a land-sea trade route that connects the Beibu Gulf, Singapore, and Chongqing and integrates with the twenty-first Century Maritime Silk Road. On November 12, 2018, China and Singapore officially signed the "Memorandum of Understanding on Cooperation in the Construction of the 'New International Land-Sea Trade Corridor' as part of the China-Singapore (Chongqing) Demonstration Initiative on Strategic Connectivity." The "Southern Corridor" was officially renamed the "New International Land-Sea Trade Corridor," abbreviated ILSTC. The ILSTC was formally established by the cooperation agreement. China has taken advantage of opportunities like the Lancang-Mekong Cooperation, China-ASEAN Economic and Trade Cooperation, and Shanghai Cooperation Organization to advance the construction of the ILSTC. The Corridor has rapidly developed as a result of China's proposed shared construction, use, and sharing of the infrastructure. Simultaneously, its development heavily relies on domestic intergovernmental coordination and cooperation. Domestic government cooperation in its construction not only demonstrates friendly relations between governments but also strategically enhances the capabilities of local governments. It facilitates win-win outcomes, promotes balanced and coordinated regional development, and collectively addresses external challenges arising from opening to the outside world. Moreover, its construction facilitates the coordination of economic interests among local regions, improves the macro-system of intergovernmental cooperation among regional governments, establishes a rational cooperation mechanism, and ensures the efficient and high-quality construction of the corridor.

Against this backdrop, on May 16, 2019, the Second Western China International Fair for Investment and Trade was held. The governments of Chongqing, Guangxi, Guizhou, Gansu, Qinghai, Xinjiang, Yunnan, Ningxia, and Shaanxi jointly signed a cooperation agreement to build the "New International Land-Sea Trade Corridor." Shaanxi officially joined the existing cooperation mechanism of the "New International Land-Sea Trade Corridor," broadening its scope to include the nine western provinces and autonomous regions. The Inter-Provincial Joint Conference on the Construction of the New International Land-Sea Trade Corridor convened for the first time in December 2019, during which the conference's operating guidelines and the primary tasks for the Corridor's 2020 construction were reviewed. One of the primary duties of the inter-ministerial and inter-provincial joint conference was to lay the policy foundation for the construction of the Corridor's operation center. This included "guiding the inter-provincial consultation and cooperation, channel logistics, and the establishment of the operation center led by Chongqing for the New International Land-Sea Trade Corridor." In November 2020, the first meeting of the Inter-Provincial Consultation and Cooperation Joint Conference on the Construction was held, which principally approved important work plans for the construction of the New International Land-Sea Trade Corridor. The provinces, autonomous regions, and municipalities participating in the "13+1" initiative jointly signed the "Cooperation Agreement on the Construction of the International Trade 'Single Window' New International Land-Sea Trade Platform," reaching consensus on cooperation. Through the signing of the cooperation agreement, the scope of collaborative construction and sharing of the Corridor was further expanded. On May 12, 2021, the Inter-Provincial Joint Conference on the Construction of the New International Land-Sea Trade Corridor was held, providing development directions for the provinces and autonomous regions participated. The conference emphasized the importance of fully utilizing the joint conference mechanism and achieving better results in corridor construction, which would further promote cooperation among the provinces and autonomous regions involved in accordance with the signed agreements.

This study employs social network analysis to precisely depict the state of government cooperation and evaluate the network effects along the corridor. It aims to construct a comprehensive government cooperation network for the Corridor, facilitating an analysis of the temporal and spatial evolution of government cooperation processes from 2016 to 2021 within this region. Furthermore, it conducts an in-depth analysis of changes in various sub-regions and the roles played by key provincial and municipal nodes.

8.3.1 Research Methodology and Data Description

This study employs social network analysis to quantitatively investigate the cooperation network among local governments along the New International Land-Sea Trade Corridor. Social network analysis method analyzes the overall network effect based on the positions of each node and the degree of interaction between nodes, enabling a clear demonstration of the different statuses of each node and their impact on the network. Therefore, this study takes the frequency of cooperation among the "13+1" provincial and municipal governments within the scope of the Corridor from 2016 to 2021 as the variable. By comparing before and after the implementation of the "Master Plan for New International Land-Sea Trade Corridor," the changes in the overall network of government cooperation and the density of cooperation, as well as the changes in subgroups within the region, are demonstrated.

In the data collection process, cooperation areas and contents explicitly mentioned in policies, as well as agreements, intergovernmental meetings, official visits, roundtable meetings, joint statements, jointly organized government events, and symposiums found on official websites, are considered as government cooperation. By utilizing Python for search and manually removing irrelevant and duplicate information, a total of 3902 valid samples of government cooperation were obtained, forming a 14×14 government cooperation matrix from 2016 to 2021. The data in this study are sourced from the official websites of 14 provincial and municipal governments.

8.3.2 The Network Structure Characteristics of Local Government Cooperation Along the New International Land-Sea Trade Corridor

This study utilizes Ucinet to generate the topological map of the cooperation network among the "13+1" provincial and municipal governments along the New International Land-Sea Trade Corridor from 2016 to 2021. In the topological map, the connecting lines represent government cooperation between two provincial and municipal governments. The closer a node is to the center of the topological map, the more connecting lines it has with other nodes. The size of the nodes is determined by the degree assigned to each node, where the degree represents the number of connections with other nodes. Thicker connecting lines between nodes indicate closer cooperation between the two governments.

As depicted in Fig. 8.1, from 2016 to 2018, the network density of government cooperation shows a slow growth trend with fluctuations. During this period, there was a lack of a unified platform among the 14 provincial and municipal governments, and government cooperation was mainly based on partial cooperation in certain areas driven by geographical proximity. There was a lack of a comprehensive cooperation platform covering a larger scope and cross-regional cooperation within the region. 2019 marked an important turning point, with the release of the "Master Plan for New International Land-Sea Trade Corridor." The entire western region and Zhanjiang City, Guangdong Province, joined the planning and construction. Cooperation among the 14 provincial and municipal governments became increasingly frequent, and the overall cooperation network density increased significantly from 3.527 to 5.473, with a growth rate of 55.17%. In 2020, due to the impact of the pandemic, the density of government cooperation between provinces and cities decreased slightly. After the normalization of pandemic management in 2021, there was a rapid increase, reaching 6.220.

The network topology shows that the cooperation network density among local governments along the Corridor increased significantly between 2016 and 2021, and the scope of cooperation has continued to expand. In 2016, the pattern of cooperation among the "13+1" provincial and municipal governments was primarily localized, but by 2021, it had shifted to comprehensive.

Specifically, from 2016 to 2018, before the release of the Master Plan, cooperation among the governments along the route was primarily based on administrative proximity. During this period, there was a trend of "strengthened localized cooperation, but overall cooperation remained relatively scattered" (see Fig. 8.2).

In 2016, Sichuan, Guizhou, and Yunnan were primarily the focal points of cooperation in the southwestern region, with Guizhou and Yunnan cooperating closely with Guangxi. This was due to the three provinces establishing a cooperation platform and signing numerous related cooperation agreements. Other provincial-level cooperation was relatively dispersed, particularly in Zhanjiang, which only collaborated with Guangxi and Hainan on issues concerning the Qiongzhou Strait, putting it on the periphery of the network. Looking at the northwestern region, a pattern of government cooperation emerged, centered on Shaanxi, and radiating to the northwest. However, government cooperation between other provinces was infrequent, and some northwest provinces did not cooperate at

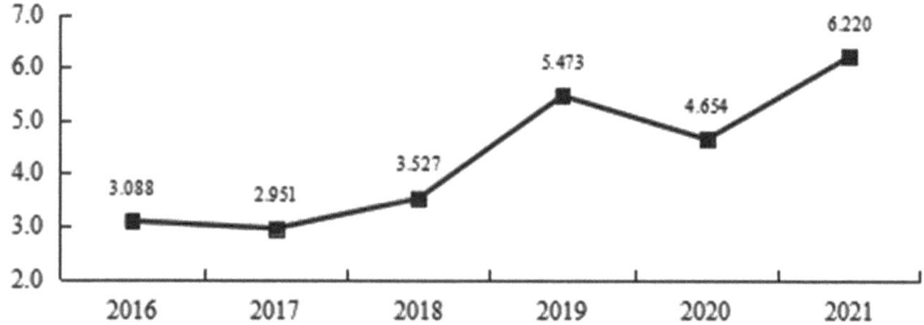

Fig. 8.1 The average density of government cooperation network from 2016 to 2021 (Since the original matrix has not undergone binarization, the interaction frequency between governments needs to be considered, so the network density is not less than 1)

all. Furthermore, cooperation between the southwestern and northwestern regions was minimal and low-intensity, with Shaanxi primarily assisting Tibet.

In 2017, at the first meeting of the China-Singapore Joint Coordinating Council for the China-Singapore (Chongqing) Demonstration Initiative on Strategic Connectivity, it was proposed to build a southward channel to strengthen connections with ASEAN countries, gradually forming relatively close government cooperation between Guizhou, Guangxi, Chongqing, Sichuan, and Yunnan, but cooperation with other provinces and cities was relatively loose. In terms of degree centrality, Hainan experienced significant changes. In 2017, the Hainan Provincial Government visited Chongqing, Sichuan, and other locations to promote tourism and strengthen collaboration among tourism departments in the southwestern region. In 2018, the cooperation between the governments of various provinces and cities in the southwestern region further strengthened. For example, in June 2018, Chongqing and Sichuan signed the "Action Plan for Deepening Cooperation between Sichuan and Chongqing to Further Promote the Development of the Yangtze River Economic Belt (2018–2022)," and Guangxi and Hainan signed the "2018–2019 Cooperation Focus on Promoting the Implementation of the 'North Bay

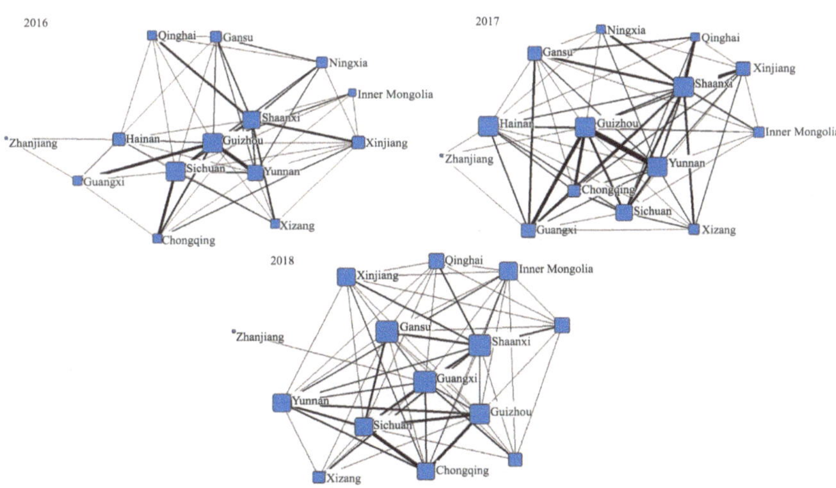

Fig. 8.2 The topological map of government cooperation network along the New International Land-Sea Corridor from 2016 to 2018

Urban Agglomeration Development Plan'" agreement. Cooperation between the southwestern and northwestern regions also significantly improved. For example, in September 2018, a Sichuan government delegation attended the third Silk Road (Dunhuang) International Cultural Expo, and Gansu and Sichuan provinces signed four specific cooperation action plans. Due to the continuous signing of inter-provincial government cooperation agreements, the density of inter-regional government cooperation increased rapidly in 2018.

The provinces and cities along the corridor gained a unified and higher-level cooperation platform in 2019, when the "Master Plan for New International Land-Sea Trade Corridor" was promulgated and elevated to a national strategy. Local government cooperation increased, sustaining a generally significant growth trend. Since 2019, the network topology map shows that all "13+1" provinces and cities have connection lines, indicating that cooperative relationships between provinces and cities are gradually being established. Among them, cooperation in the southwestern region has become increasingly close, and the central position of Chongqing has become more prominent (see Fig. 8.3).

In particular, compared to 2016, there were significant changes in the topology of the local government cooperation network along the Corridor in 2019. Overall, all "13+1" provinces and cities established cooperative relationships, and the frequency of cooperation increased, as evidenced by denser and bolder lines on the network topology map. The northwest region gradually evolved from a single center to several centers, with Gansu and Ningxia emerging as sub-centers. Northwest provinces grew closer to one another in 2019 as a result of multiple symposiums on environmental issues and poverty alleviation hosted by the provinces of Shaanxi, Gansu, and Ningxia. The northwest and southwest provinces gradually increased their cooperation as well. The cooperation between Shaanxi and Guangxi was particularly noteworthy. Guangxi Zhuang Autonomous Region's government sent a delegation to the 26th China Yangling Agricultural High-tech Achievements Fair in 2019, Guangxi's first time attending as the main guest of the fair. Deeper industrial exchanges between the southwest and northwest were achieved through the mutual engagement in in-depth discussions on smart agriculture and agricultural equipment. This progressed cooperation beyond poverty alleviation. In 2019, the "Master Plan for New International Land-Sea Trade Corridor" was released. In December of the same year, the first meeting of the inter-ministerial and inter-provincial joint conference on the

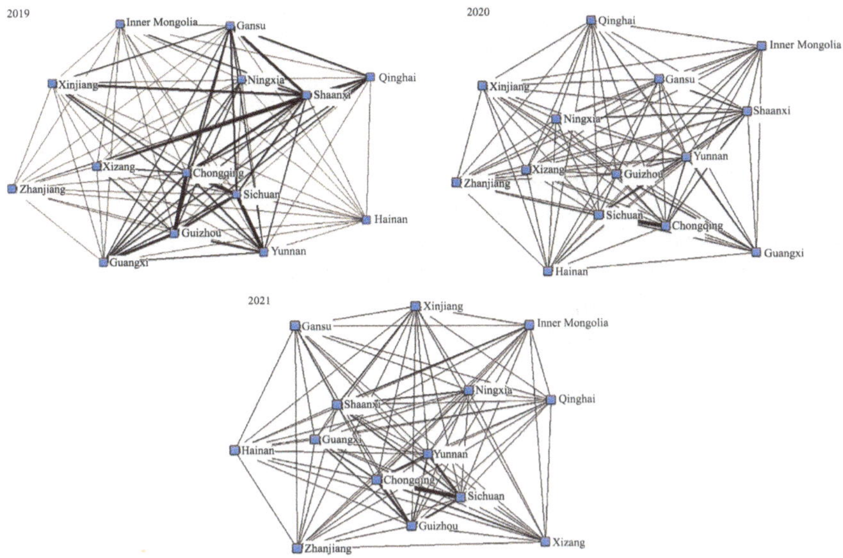

Fig. 8.3 The topological map of government cooperation network along the New International Land-Sea Corridor from 2019 to 2021

construction of the Corridor was convened, marking the formal commencement of cooperation among local governments along the corridor. During this meeting, the "Working Rules of the Inter-ministerial and Inter-provincial Joint Conference on the Construction of the New International Land-Sea Trade Corridor" and the "Key Tasks for the Construction of the New International Land-Sea Trade Corridor in 2020" were reviewed and approved, ensuring the smooth progress of subsequent cooperation among local governments along the corridor. Overall, 2019 marked a watershed moment for cooperation among local governments along the Corridor, shifting from primarily local and one-on-one cooperation to formal cooperation among the "13+1" provinces and cities. This represents the second significant development cooperation opportunity for the western region after the implementation of the Western Development Strategy in 2000.

In 2020, both the overall cooperation density and the network topology of local governments along the corridor showed a decrease in cooperation intensity. This could be attributed to the fact that previous forms of cooperation among local governments along the corridor were primarily informal, such as symposiums and reciprocal visits by officials, which were heavily influenced by factors such as the pandemic. However, with regional cooperation among local governments gradually transitioning to formal cooperation and the pandemic being managed as part of the new normal, the density of local government cooperation has once again increased. On November 17, 2020, the first meeting of the provincial inter-provincial consultation and cooperation joint meeting on the construction of the Corridor was held in Chongqing. The meeting discussed major policies regarding the construction during the "14th Five-Year Plan" period, laying the foundation for the development of the corridor during this period. In 2021, local governments along the Corridor held two joint meetings and one symposium, which collectively advanced the construction of the corridor. The southwest region's provinces and cities developed a particularly noticeable level of cooperation as the density of cooperation among local governments increased. Gradually, a pentagram-shaped pattern of cooperation took shape, with Yunnan, Guizhou, Guangxi, and Sichuan at the center, and other provinces and cities radiating outward from them.

8.3.3 Changes in Sub-Cooperation Among Local Governments Along the New International Land-Sea Trade Corridor

To examine changes in subsets of local government cooperation along the New International Land-Sea Trade Corridor, this study imported and analyzed local government cooperation matrices from 2016 to 2021 in the Ucinet software using Lambda sets. Lambda sets can reflect the network's hierarchical clustering relationship, which is primarily determined by the degree of association (K value) among nodes. The network nodes are classified into different sets, with higher K values indicating stronger node association and a more stable relationship structure.

Specifically, in the 2016 Lambda set of local government cooperation along the Corridor, the K values ranged from a minimum of 2 to a maximum of 78, showing significant differences. All subsets included nodes 11 (Guizhou Province) and 5 (Shaanxi Province), indicating that Guizhou and Shaanxi are the core of the network of local government cooperation along the corridor, with Guizhou being the core of the southwest region and Shaanxi being the core of the northwest region. The subset with a K value of 2 only included Zhanjiang City, indicating that its connections with other provinces and cities were not sufficiently close. The subset with a K value of 32, representing closer connections, mainly included seven provinces and cities: Guangxi, Xinjiang, Chongqing, Sichuan, Yunnan, Guizhou, and Shaanxi. Among them, five provinces and cities are in the southwest region, again indicating that in 2016, compared to the southwest region, the northwest region had lower levels of local government cooperation intensity and exhibited a certain degree of single-center pattern (see Fig. 8.4).

In 2017, the minimum and maximum values of Lambda rose from 2 and 78 in 2016 to 14 and 96, respectively. A higher minimum value of Lambda indicates a more stable network structure. The core provinces in the network remained Shaanxi Province and Guizhou Province, but Guangxi Zhuang Autonomous Region saw an increase in its position within the network. Guangxi Zhuang Autonomous Region strengthened its cooperation with southwestern provinces and municipalities as well as Shaanxi Province. In particular, in 2017, Shaanxi and Guangxi signed the "Strategic Cooperation Framework Agreement to Promote Agricultural Product Circulation," further enhancing cooperation in agriculture. Agriculture has always been a characteristic and advantageous industry in Guangxi, while Shaanxi ranks first in the country in terms of total special agricultural products. Based on the mutual benefits of their respective advantageous industries, cooperation between the two provinces has promoted further stable development of the cooperation network along the Corridor (see Fig. 8.5).

In 2018, the minimum value of Lambda rose from 14 to 18, while the maximum value slightly decreased. The core provinces of the network shifted from Guizhou Province and Shaanxi Province to Shaanxi Province and Sichuan Province. However, overall, the density of local government cooperation further increased. In particular, the connectivity density between Ningxia Hui Autonomous Region and Inner Mongolia Autonomous Region in the northwest region showed a slight increase, and Gansu Province entered the interval of closer connectivity represented by K values. In recent years, Gansu Province has made significant progress in developing the traditional Chinese medicine industry. In 2018, it signed four agreements with Sichuan Province, which also promoted closer ties between the northwest and southwest regions along the New International Land-Sea Trade Corridor, leading to an increase in clustering hierarchy (see Fig. 8.6).

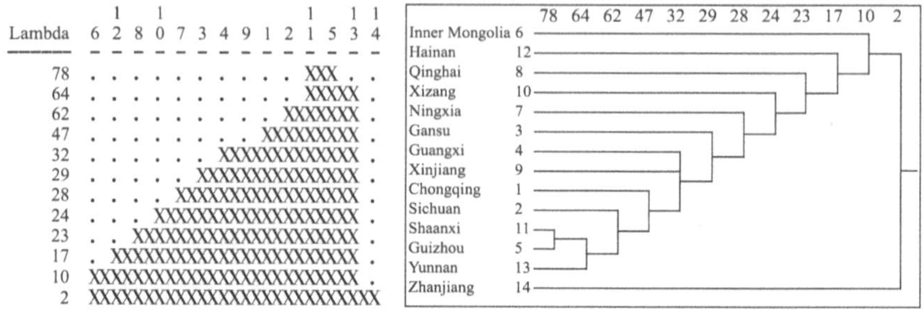

Fig. 8.4 Analysis of lambda set for local governments along the New International Land-Sea Trade Corridor in 2016

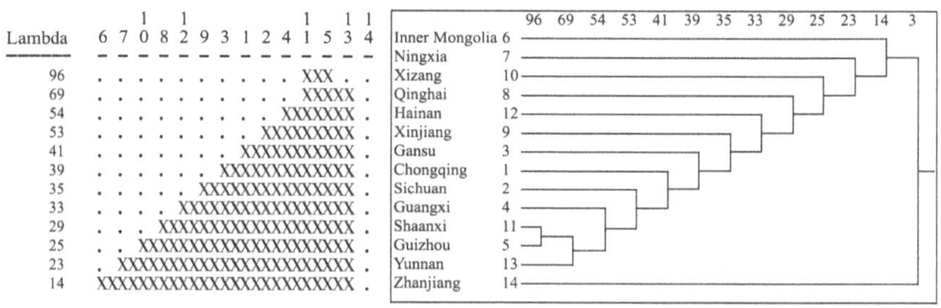

Fig. 8.5 Analysis of lambda set for local governments along the New International Land-Sea Trade Corridor in 2017

In 2019, following the introduction of the "Master Plan for the New International Land-Sea Trade Corridor," there was a notable increase in both the minimum and maximum values of Lambda, reaching 27 and 122, respectively. Chongqing Municipality and Shaanxi Province emerged as the core provinces and cities within the cooperative network. Chongqing, leveraging its status as a direct-controlled municipality and serving as the starting point for two of the Corridor's three main arteries, enjoyed a distinct advantage in local government cooperation. Consequently, it ascended from the second or third echelon in the years 2016–2018 to a core position. Meanwhile, Shaanxi Province and Gansu Province continued to serve as the nexus of cooperation among provinces and cities in the northwest region, maintaining relatively close ties with other provinces and cities (see Fig. 8.7).

In 2020, the maximum value of Lambda increased by approximately 20% compared to 2019, indicating a further enhancement in the connectivity of cooperation. The core provinces and cities in the cooperative network shifted to Chongqing Municipality and Sichuan Province. Cooperation in the Chongqing-Sichuan region made significant progress due to the development of the Chengdu-Chongqing Economic Circle, a major national regional strategy, leading to a substantial increase in the number of agreements signed and the intensity of cooperation. However, in 2020, there was a significant disparity in the K values between the second-tier subsets compared to the first tier, and the K values were lower than those of the same-tier subsets in 2019, approaching those of the third tier. Overall, in 2020, cooperation among local governments along the Corridor showed significant disparities and uneven distribution, with the cooperation between Sichuan and Chongqing serving as the cornerstone for the overall increase in network density (see Fig. 8.8).

In 2021, as the epidemic management entered a phase of normalcy, government collaboration progressively returned. After three years of construction, the maximum and minimum values of Lambda reached new highs of 157 and 44, respectively. This suggests that local governments along the Corridor are now more cooperative and that their connections are even closer. Notably, the rapid development of the southwest region centered around Chongqing Municipality and Sichuan Province resulted in a significant strengthening of cooperation among local governments with the introduction of the "Plan Outline for the Chengdu-Chongqing Economic Circle" in 2021. Southwest provinces and cities gradually entered the top four tiers of subsets, elevating their positions in the

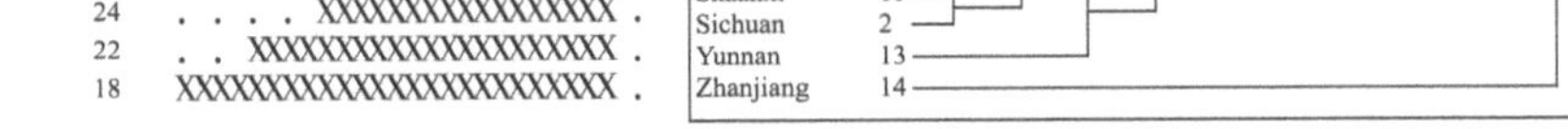

Fig. 8.6 Analysis of lambda set for local governments along the New International Land-Sea Trade Corridor in 2018

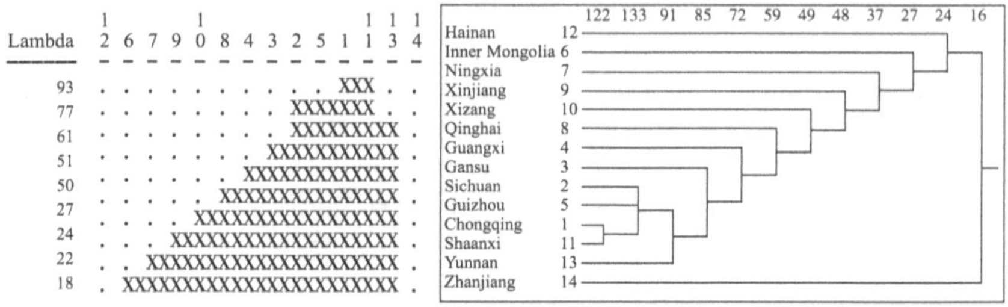

Fig. 8.7 Analysis of lambda set for local governments along the New International Land-Sea Trade Corridor in 2017

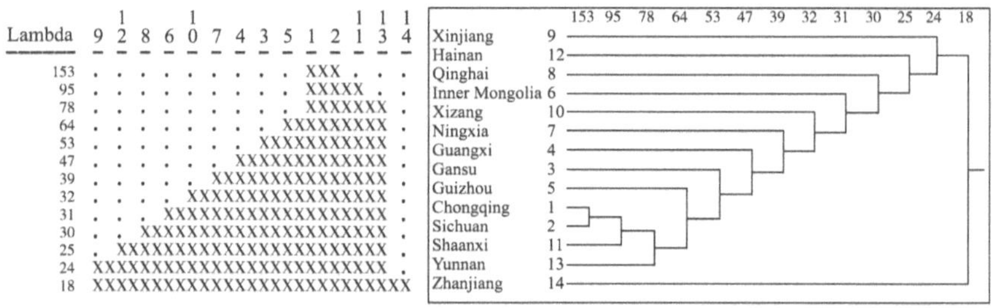

Fig. 8.8 Analysis of lambda set for local governments along the New International Land-Sea Trade Corridor in 2020

network. However, the previously core position held by Shaanxi Province in the cooperation network saw a decline in its status, like that of other provinces in the northwest region (see Fig. 8.9).

Overall, from 2016 to 2021, local government cooperation along the Corridor fluctuated upward. The Master Plan's implementation in 2019 provided more cooperation opportunities and a larger collaboration platform for local governments. As a result, from 2019 to 2021, there was a higher increase in cooperation intensity than there was between 2016 and 2018. Along the entire corridor, cooperation has developed due in large part to the construction of the Chengdu-Chongqing Economic Circle, which has improved cooperation density and intensity, especially in the Sichuan-Chongqing region. Additionally, cooperation within urban agglomerations such as the Guanzhong-Tianshui Urban Cluster, cooperation between Yunnan, Guangxi, and Guizhou, as well as collaboration

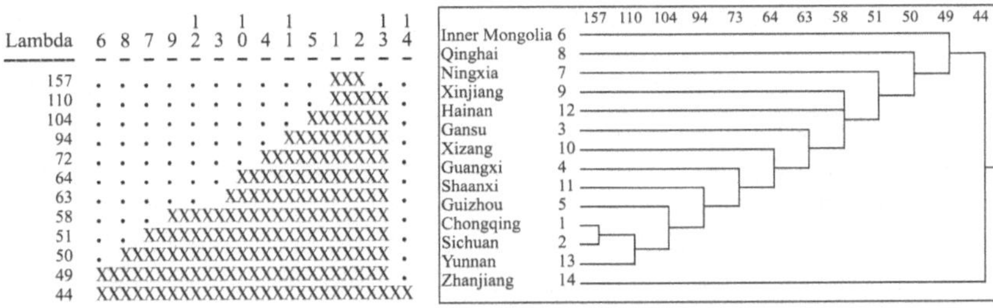

Fig. 8.9 Analysis of lambda set for local government cooperation along the New International Land-Sea Trade Corridor in 2021

involving Guangxi, Zhanjiang, and Hainan based on the Qiongzhou Strait, has all contributed significantly to the overall increase in cooperation density. However, in comparison to the northwest region, the southwest region's provinces and cities cooperated more closely. Nonetheless, due to administrative hierarchy and geographical location, Zhanjiang City has remained on the periphery of the cooperation network.

8.4 Challenges and Future Prospects of the New International Land-Sea Trade Corridor

8.4.1 Challenges for the High-Quality Development of New International Land-Sea Trade Corridor

8.4.1.1 Inadequate Infrastructure Network

The New International Land-Sea Trade Corridor saw a nearly 33-fold increase in the number of international freight trains it carried from 178 in its first year to 6000 in 2021, making it one of the fastest-growing international freight train routes in China in recent years. The rapid growth in freight train demand relies heavily on robust infrastructure support. But even as the New International Land-Sea Trade Corridor moves from its initial phase of strategic planning and infrastructure development to a new stage of removing bottlenecks and rapid development, it still has infrastructure limitations and flaws.

In terms of transportation infrastructure construction, there is an increasing bottleneck problem. Local governments have initiated infrastructure projects aimed at "improving roads in the eastern line, expanding capacity in the central line, and ensuring smooth roads in the western line," as part of the national strategy of simultaneous development along the eastern, central, and western railway lines. Although the eastern line has been electrified, the central line's capacity is limited, and the western line is not fully operational. Efforts are being made to upgrade older railways to meet new technical standards and increase capacity. Furthermore, there are additional infrastructure projects in underdeveloped areas of the western line to establish an integrated railway network in the region.

Overall, due to current railway infrastructure deficiencies and a lack of integration with the Beibu Gulf ports and the Yangtze River waterway, multimodal transportation that connects railways, waterways, and shipping has not yet reached full development (Zheng Hou and Yonghui Huang 2021). As a result, the logistics industry's overall level of development is relatively low, as is its level of standardization (Xian Liu 2019). Looking ahead, as the Corridor takes on more important logistics tasks, challenges may arise in terms of efficiency enhancement, brand building, and environmental development.

For port and waterway construction, insufficient navigational capacity is a significant barrier in current logistics transportation. Some ports, such as the eastern channel of Qinzhou Port in Guangxi, still have one-way channels, limiting the passage of large container vessels. Meanwhile, Yangpu Port also faces development constraints. As of 2021, Yangpu Port had only 38 routes and a container throughput of 1.3183 million TEUs. Achieving the target of five million TEUs by 2025 requires further development, and there is room for improvement in port scale, deepening, and specialization. As of 2021, the number of foreign trade routes at North Bay ports was 65,[3] whereas Guangzhou Port had 141[4] container routes, and Ningbo-Zhoushan Port had 287 routes.[5] Compared to these ports,

[3] State-owned Assets Supervision and Administration Commission of the State Council. Beibu Gulf Port's container throughput exceeded 6 million TEUs in 2021. [2021-01-12]. [EB/OL]. http://www.sasac.gov.cn/n2588025/n2588129/c22689055/content.html.

[4] Guangzhou Municipal People's Government. With Nansha Port Area as the core, the ports along the coastal economic belt of western and eastern Guangdong as two wings, and the Pearl River water system ports as the link, Guangzhou Port is creating a new pattern of "major logistics" in South China. [EB/OL]. [2022-02-18]. http://www.gz.gov.cn/xw/zwlb/gqdt/nsq/content/post_8081677.html.

[5] Ningbo Municipal People's Government. The Great Eastern Port. [EB/OL].http://www.ningbo.gov.cn/col/col1229099791/index.html.

the Beibu Gulf ports have fewer routes and a single route, leading to lower freight volumes. Additionally, the increased costs associated with transshipment and waiting time may reduce the attractiveness of freight transportation, further contributing to insufficient port freight volumes.

In terms of hub construction, there is room for improvement in the development of the integrated transport system. While Beibu Gulf ports are benchmarked against international top-tier ports, a significant gap remains in terms of port throughput and transportation volume compared to other large domestic ports. Furthermore, there is not enough automation in these ports. The ports of the Beibu Gulf, namely Qinzhou Port, Fangchenggang Port, and Beihai Port, do not fully utilize their unique locational advantages and lack collaborative capabilities. Furthermore, while a number of infrastructure projects, including railway container terminals, logistics ports, and logistics parks, have been gradually completed, many key projects in hub cities are progressing slowly. And the rail support lines and secondary and higher-grade highways that connect Beibu Gulf ports and operating areas are severely lacking. There is also a shortage of large-scale container handling facilities, highlighting the shortcomings in the integrated transport system. This leads to congestion in ports, prolonged transportation times, low efficiency in ship loading and unloading, and the inability to fully leverage the comparative advantages of maritime transportation (Pei Yu 2021).

The infrastructure development of the Corridor still encounters notable challenges. The economic impact following its completion heavily hinges on the level of refinement of the corridor itself. Hence, in future development endeavors, the construction of the channel and transportation hubs along the route remains a focal point.

8.4.1.2 Low Operational Efficiency and Scale Benefits

The New International Land-Sea Trade Corridor serves as a bridge and link to promote domestic and international land-sea interaction and mutual benefit between the east and the west. However, in the process of improving efficiency and effectiveness, there are still some issues. Firstly, logistics costs are relatively high. Apart from the costs incurred by the incomplete connectivity of the east-west corridor, freight rates also significantly impact logistics costs. The discounted proportion of sea-rail intermodal train fares is only 7% to 30%, constrained by factors such as stations, routes, and cargo types. Compared with the discount proportion of 45% to 55% for sea-rail intermodal transportation along the Yangtze River, the former's comprehensive logistics costs are significantly higher.[6] Secondly, the incomplete multimodal transportation system adversely impacts operational and service efficiency. The New International Land-Sea Trade Corridor primarily relies on railway transportation and rail-sea intermodal transport. However, the regulatory frameworks governing land-based logistics, primarily railway transport, lack synchronization with those governing maritime transport. Consequently, transit times suffer from inefficiencies, and the regulations governing transshipment trade remain ambiguous.[7] Additionally, the level of informatization, digitization, and intelligence in various links of the supply chain is not high, and there is room for improvement in customs facilitation. Moreover, alternative intermodal transportation modes, such as river-rail-sea intermodal transport and air-rail intermodal transport, require further development. Thirdly, the development of the corridor lacks efficient operational entities. Currently, the operational organization of the corridor primarily revolves around coordinating logistics, with railways serving as the focal point for the westbound corridor. Initiatives pertaining to goods sourcing, transportation, multimodal transport, pricing mechanisms, and financial services are still in their nascent stages and have yet to reach maturity. Operational entities are mostly small, fragmented, and weak, with inadequate collaboration among different corridors.

8.4.1.3 Collaborative Building Mechanism Needs Improvement

The cooperation and coordination between provinces and cities along the Corridor still needs to be improved. In theory, local governments could engage in fierce competition to maximize their regional interests. In reality, provinces and cities compete for resources, have blind rivalries, and duplicate public infrastructure projects. The Corridor, a critical strategic initiative for cross-regional cooperation in the western region, includes numerous provinces and cities. In the context of national attention, the performance-oriented governance system that holds local governments "accountable upwards" guides their competitive behavior, resulting in

[6] *The Central Committee of the Taiwan Democratic Self-Government League (TDSL): Proposal on Further Improving the Level of Joint Construction of the New International Land-Sea Trade Corridor* – Special Report – CPC News Website (people.com.cn) [EB/OL]. [2022-03-01]. http://cpc.people.com.cn/n1/2022/0301/c442049-32362623.html.

[7] *Continuously Expanding the "International Circle of Friends" of Western Provinces* – CPPCC Website (rmzxb.com.cn) [EB/OL]. [2022-03-15]. https://www.rmzxb.com.cn/c/2022-03-15/3074270.shtml.

ineffective cooperation mechanisms and unstable relationships among local governments. Although the national level has planned the regions along the New International Land-Sea Trade Corridor as a whole, the "'14th Five-Year Plan' Implementation Plan for the High-quality Construction of the New International Land-Sea Trade Corridor" proposed a plan to promote overall coordination and coordination work in 2021. Overall coordination work is still in its infancy, and it is too soon to tell how well mechanisms like joint meetings at the provincial level will function once they are put into place. Interdepartmental cooperation mechanisms are not supported by policies or by more specific behavioral arrangements. Local governments have begun to negotiate in some capacity due to pressure from higher-level governments. Since the Corridor's proposal, local governments along the route signed a series of cooperative framework agreements in 2019. These framework agreements are primarily directional and intentional documents, with little binding force and frequently lacking detailed content. These framework agreements have long served as the foundation for intergovernmental cooperation, eroding local governments' enthusiasm to participate. However, the construction involves a number of parties, including governments, businesses, and industries, and covers a wide range of topics such as industrial layout, transportation planning, and enterprise operations. However, there is a lack of effective and reliable incentive and benefit-sharing mechanisms, making it difficult for businesses to form substantive alliances.

In terms of infrastructure development and integrated administration, the Hainan Yangpu Port and its nearby Beibu Gulf Port in Guangxi (Qinzhou Port) are critical ports along the Corridor. However, there is overlap in terms of freight scope and maritime routes between these ports, showing a lack of coordination in planning. It is critical to immediately streamline the relationships between national ministries, western provinces (cities, districts), and leading departments in each province (city, district), in order to establish a joint cooperation mechanism with clear rights and responsibilities and a well-defined division of labor. In the construction, there is significant potential for cooperation among provinces (cities, districts) in customs clearance, logistics informatization, and interaction between industrial parks (Chen and Long 2020). Due to the absence of unified planning and technical standards, coordination in goods import and export operations is lacking, and the systems of railways, customs, ports, and shipping remain relatively independent. This leads to "information silos" and presents challenges to information exchange for multimodal transportation. The objective of "single declaration, single inspection, single release" has not been fully realized, and the level of interconnectivity between provinces is inadequate.

Additionally, the cooperation mechanism between provinces (cities) along the Corridor and ASEAN countries is not sufficiently developed. Theoretically, there is good trade complementarity between China's imports and ASEAN's exports (Yu et al. 2022). However, due to the limited economic connections between the Corridor and Southeast Asia, the balanced interaction of commodity demand has not been stimulated, making it challenging to establish a "two-way" cooperation mechanism. Furthermore, international cooperation encounters more obstacles due to differences in economics, culture, and institutions among different countries. Currently, communication between countries along the Corridor mainly relies on irregular meetings of leaders, with a single and unstable format. Regarding international project cooperation, it is primarily led by countries like Singapore and Vietnam, with limited participation from other countries.

8.4.1.4 Lack of Rational Planning and Layout in Industrial Development

The asynchronous states in the economic growth of different locations along the New International Land-Sea Trade Corridor can be attributed to historical reasons and resource endowment. Taking the Corridor as a whole into consideration, each region should make the most of its geographic advantages to create the strongest possible industrial plan. Chongqing and Sichuan, two of the corridor's most rapidly developing regions, are leaders in sectors like electronics, rail transportation, and machinery production. On the other hand, despite their slower rates of development, provinces and autonomous regions such as Yunnan, Guangxi, and Guizhou have comparatively developed sectors related to agriculture, forestry, animal husbandry, petrochemical refining, port and marine, and liquor manufacturing. Many regions along the Corridor tend to prioritize becoming regional hubs over considering the Corridor's overall development. They often focus on short-term gains when planning industrial layouts and growth strategies (Lu and Wang 2021). Instead of basing their industrial designs on regional characteristics, they often blindly follow trends to attract high-profile businesses. Local governments along the corridor establish numerous industrial parks and make significant investments in technology, talent acquisition, and key industries to attract investment. However, these efforts often fail to consider the holistic development of the Corridor. They are primarily driven by the industrial structure of individual provinces, leading to the growth of conventional, low-value industries and the duplication of industries between provinces. This approach hinders the creation of a modern industrial system and undermines the corridor's economic competitiveness. As a result, the economic development of the corridor's regions lacks long-term sustainability and does not contribute to high-quality growth. Furthermore, the interconnection of favorable industries in provinces and cities along the Corridor is low. Particularly, cooperation between the Southwest and Northwest regions is still in its early phases, making it difficult to establish maximum synergies to drive the corridor's economic development. To accomplish regional economic integration and increase the quality of economic development, it is critical to strengthen cooperation and joint construction procedures throughout the corridor, as well as industry collaboration.

8.4.2 *Prospects of the New International Land-Sea Trade Corridor*

8.4.2.1 *Strengthening Infrastructure Construction to Accelerate Connectivity Along the Route*

In the realm of transportation infrastructure, it is crucial to advance the construction of primary railway lines and address the bottlenecks that hinder multimodal transportation integration between rivers, seas, and railways. Efforts should focus on developing large-scale, specialized, and intelligent port and maritime infrastructure. This includes establishing smart storage logistics and ensuring adequate land use, funding, and regulatory support for the construction of terminals, ports, and related public infrastructure. Moreover, there is a need to enhance the development of global aviation hubs in Kunming and Chengdu, while positioning Nanning as a key hub for international air cargo operations with ASEAN. Emphasis should be placed on highway construction, further expanding and strengthening the highway transportation industry, leveraging highways' vital role in short-distance transportation and multimodal transportation, and promoting seamless connectivity and coordination among various transportation modes and freight hubs to unleash the comprehensive efficiency of multimodal transportation.[8]

In terms of hub construction, efforts should be accelerated to build national logistics hubs with port, land-port, and airport characteristics in cities such as Chongqing, Chengdu, Kunming, Guiyang, and Nanning. Continued monitoring of key projects such as the Pinglu Canal and other transportation hub projects, ensuring smooth transport channels between ports and stations, accelerating the construction of important railway lines for port transportation, and strengthening seamless connectivity between hubs are essential. At the same time, attention should be paid to the construction of transportation links to ports and the connectivity of transportation infrastructure between China and ASEAN countries. This aims to create a modern logistics operation system based on "corridors + hubs + networks."[9]

8.4.2.2 Promoting Mutual Recognition and Sharing to Enhance Corridor Operational Efficiency

The development time of the Corridor is relatively short, and its shipping routes are relatively limited. However, with its gradual improvement and development, issues such as the planning of shipping routes, route planning, and infrastructure improvement can be addressed over time. Yet, more importantly, it is crucial to promote the genuine implementation of multimodal transportation and facilitate the connectivity of various transportation modes among provinces and cities by formulating feasible plans for multimodal transportation. To achieve this, consideration can be given to advocating for the formulation of a "single document" policy for multimodal transportation, promoting the use of a single document for conversion between different provinces, cities, and transportation modes, with legal safeguards in place.

[8] CPPCC National Committee Member, Deputy Director of the Tianjin Committee of the Taiwan Democratic Self-Government League, Sun Changlong, *Leveraging the "Connecting Points and Lines" Function of Highways to Deeply Release the Comprehensive Efficacy of Multimodal Transport*—People's Political Consultative Conference Website (rmzxb.com.cn). [EB/OL]. [2021-06-18]. https://www.rmzxb.com.cn/c/2021-06-18/2884947.shtml.

[9] Zheng Hou, Yonghui Huang. Research on Strategies for Promoting High-Quality Development of the New International Land-Sea Trade Corridor under the New Development Pattern[J]. *Journal of Nanning Normal University (Philosophy and Social Sciences Edition)*, 2021, v. 42; No. 184(06):29–47.

Creating both online and physical service platforms is crucial for enhancing coordination and collaboration between departments, cities, and provinces. These platforms will improve big data services, make it easier to manage entire digitization of freight trains, and provide services like traceability, information sharing, and warehouse and distribution management. Through this effort, multimodal transportation will be efficiently connected to increase cost-effectiveness and improve transport efficiency. The offline service system will be positioned strategically along the corridor, with an emphasis on logistics hubs. It will encourage collaborative development and sharing between the relevant departments and provinces and cities, including transportation, customs, finance, and other relevant departments. To improve customs clearance facilitation, it will offer full services such as supply chain financing, tax declaration, customs clearance, and application for foreign trade subsidies.

Standardized logistics service functions will be implemented, with assistance and active promotion of innovation in railway waybills, supporting legislation, and international overland trade standards. The use of multimodal transport documents in the market will be investigated and promoted, with businesses encouraged to produce multimodal transport bills of lading and a solid mechanism built for mutual confidence, recognition, and connectivity with maritime joint carriage. Furthermore, corridor rule standards will be actively developed, with operating regulations and safety procedures improved across provinces, cities, and industries.[10]

8.4.2.3 Enhancing Top-Level Design and Establishing Coordinated Mechanisms

Building the New International Land-Sea Corridor and advancing trade and logistics will require the establishment of a long-term coordination and communication system on a national and international level. On a domestic level, more needs to be done in terms of cross-regional coordination and collaboration, strengthening the system of joint construction between provinces and central ministries, and improving inter-provincial coordination mechanisms. It is imperative that channel construction and

[10] CPPCC member and member of the Chongqing Municipal Committee of China Democratic National Construction Association, Wang Jiguang: *High-Quality Construction of the New International Land-Sea Trade Corridor International Logistics and Operations Organization Center* – Chongqing Municipal Committee of the China Democratic National Construction Association (cqmj.org.cn). [EB/OL]. [2022-03-10]. https://www.cqmj.org.cn/?Political/15116.html.

operation in provinces and autonomous regions like Chongqing, Guizhou, and Guangxi improve in terms of quality. Furthermore, it is critical to improve the state-led government joint meeting system, concentrate on long-term development and overall coordination, remove regional obstacles, and set up a functional framework for both local regional linkage and central overall coordination. Unfortunately, the system of provincial-level joint meetings that is now in place to encourage cooperation across western regions at the national level has only been used twice, has not received enough attention, and is not well known to the public. Therefore, efforts should be made to promote them and raise public awareness in addition to holding joint meetings at the provincial level. It should also be stressed how to use the joint meeting method to promote cooperation and investment amongst businesses. The public and social organizations play important roles in addition to those of businesses and governments. It is critical to encourage industry associations and social organizations in various regions to cooperate ahead of time, to experiment with inter-provincial cooperation models at a low cost, to improve information communication between provinces and cities, and to reach an agreement on the Corridor's construction. To encourage collaboration between provinces and cities, regional cooperation should be incorporated as an assessment indicator for local governments, and national efforts may be made to form regional economic development communities.

Cities and provinces should work together more closely, shifting from coordinating resources within their borders to doing so along the corridor. They should coordinate connections, unify branding, and gather advantages in niche items based on the demands at both ends of the corridor. For instance, the Sichuan New International Land-Sea Trade Corridor Development Company was founded by the Sichuan Port and Shipping Investment Group Co., LTD. (SPSI) in association with the China Railway Chengdu Group and the Guangxi Beibu Gulf International Port Group Company Ltd. By working together with cities and prefectures, they run under the single name "Sichuan New International Land-Sea Trade Corridor Train" and travel southward,[11] connecting with ASEAN nations by land- or sea-rail multimodal transit, so increasing the Corridor's influence. The construction of a new development pattern

[11] *Heading Southward, Creating a Three-dimensional Open New Brand* – Sichuan Daily Electronic Edition (scdaily.cn). [EB/OL]. [2022-04-10]. https://epaper.scdaily.cn/shtml/scrb/20220410/272256.shtml.

along the corridor will be aided by improving the top-level planning of international collaboration. The RCEP, which includes ten ASEAN nations and economies including China, Japan, South Korea, and Australia, went into force on January 1, 2022. Utilizing various policy and project benefits, developing cooperation mechanisms with the Lancang-Mekong Cooperation Framework, and aligning with the Master Plan on ASEAN Connectivity 2025 are all important to take advantage of the opportunity presented by the implementation of the RCEP. By extending its radiation range, the Corridor will become an integral part of the BRI, acting as the primary route for goods from the western region to reach borders and the sea, and providing a quick and easy means of communication between China and the ASEAN nations.[12]

8.4.2.4 Optimizing Regional Layout to Accelerate the Integration of Industries Along the Route

Localities along the route should make the most of their geographical and resource advantages and aggressively support the integration of freight trains with industrial development. It is critical not only to effectively organize the sources of goods to promote industrial restructuring, but also to leverage the role of open platforms such as international land ports, international airports, and customs special supervision areas to facilitate deep collaboration between large-scale logistics enterprises and supply chain management companies. It is imperative to advance regional economic integration, foster a strong corridor economy, and reinforce the coordinated development of industries along the route. In particular, efforts ought to be directed toward the development of the border, coastal, and aviation industries; toward improving the efficiency of industrial park development; and toward stepping up the establishment of cooperative parks, like the China-Malaysia "Twin Parks," the China-Singapore Nanning International Logistics Park, and the Guizhou-Guangxi Cooperation Zone. Every province should be encouraged to develop and build "corridor enclaves," drawing and combining industries, capital, resources, and technologies along the corridor; planning should be done in concert; brands should be shared; industrial chains should be built; and advantages should be shared. Utilizing the corridor as a link,

[12] *Sea-Rail Intermodal Transport Facilitates Land and Sea Trade Along the Silk Road*, China Transport News Website. (zgjtb.com). [EB/OL]. [2022-03-10]. https://www.zgjtb.com/2022-03/10/content_308331.html.

efforts should be made to guide the two-way linkage of varieties, scale, and structure of import and export goods, achieve two-way integration of logistics resources, and efficiently match industries, thereby forming a new pattern of "industrial support for the corridor and corridor-driven industries."[13] Furthermore, it is critical to strengthen talent exchange, talent cultivation, and recruitment mechanisms between provinces and cities along the Corridor, as well as to increase the introduction of diverse investment entities and innovative investment and financing models to provide strong support for the Corridor's high-quality development in terms of talent, funds, and other elements.

References

Liangdong Chen, Jiayong Gong. Strategies for Promoting Qinnorth's Integration under the Background of the New International Land-Sea Trade Corridor [J]. *Transportation Enterprise Management*, 2021, 36(4): 5–7.

Xiaohui Chen, Jianliang Long. Research on the Development and Countermeasures of Sea-Rail Combined Transport in the New International Land-Sea Trade Corridor[J]. *Railway Freight Transport*, 2020, 38(06): 32–36.

Qiushuang Cui, Qin Dong. Research on the Impact of the "Chongqing-Xinjiang-Europe" International Railway on the Development of Chongqing's Manufacturing Industry[J]. *Economic Review of the Bohai Rim*, 2018, (1): 68–70.

Hongxia Gao. The Necessity and Path to Enhance the Benefits of Transportation and Transportation Economy[J]. *China Small and Medium Enterprises*, 2021, (10): 204–205.

Zheng Hou, Yonghui Huang. Research on Promoting the High-quality Development of the New International Land-Sea Trade Corridor under the New Development Pattern[J]. *Journal of Nanning Normal University* (Philosophy and Social Sciences Edition), 2021(11): 29–47.

Shimin Jiang. Revitalizing the Economy Along the Golden Waterway[J]. *Creation*, 2016, (9): 40–43.

Jiheng Li. On "Road and Bridge Economy"[J]. *Academic Forum*, 1999, (6): 56–60.

[13] *Expanding and Enhancing the Comprehensive Efficacy of the New International Land-Sea Trade Corridor* – Dynamic News, China-ASEAN Information Harbor Website – zgdmxxg.gxzf.gov.cn. [EB/OL]/[2021-04-13]. http://dmxxg.gxzf.gov.cn/xxfb/dtyw/t8544112.shtml.

Xian Liu. Construction of the New International Land-Sea Trade Corridor: Status, Problems and Countermeasures of Guangxi Zhuang Autonomous Region of China[J]. *Southeast Asia Horizons*, 2019(06): 67–76.

Yongmin Long. Research on the Development of the Corridor Economy and Its Characteristics and Basic Laws—Also on the Implementation of the Corridor Economic Development Strategy in Donglan County, Bama Yao Autonomous County, and Fengshan County[J]. *Guanghai Tribune*, 2005, 21(2): 67–69.

Gengfeng Lu, Bailin Wang. Research on the Construction and Development Countermeasures of the New International Land-Sea Trade Corridor[J]. *Contemporary Economy*, 2021, (3): 43–47.

Shan Qin, Yangkun Wang. Theoretical Explanation of "New Infrastructure" in Transportation from the Perspective of Network Economy[J]. *Comprehensive Transportation*, 2021, 43(5): 30–33.

Meichao Shi. Discussion on the Development Strategy of Guangxi Zhuang Autonomous Region Toward ASEAN Based on the Theory of Corridor Economy[J]. *Logistics Engineering and Management*, 2011, 33(2): 105–107.

Zhengfang Shi. Research on the Connotation and Countermeasure Orientation of the Comprehensive Cross-Strait Passage Construction in Haixi—Based on the Perspective of Passage Economic Evolution Theory[J]. *Taiwan Research Journal*, 2012, (6): 47–55.

Yihong Tang. Research on the Synergetic Development of Port Logistics and Regional Economy—Taking Beibu Gulf Economic Zone as an Example[J]. *Statistics and Applications*, 2021, 10(3): 488–495.

Peng Yang (Ed.). *Channel Economy: A New Model for Regional Economic Development*[M], 2012. Beijing: Economic Press China.

Chuanjiang Yu, Qinlin Gong, Zhongzhong Li, Ying Tan, Lina Zhang. Research on the Development Path of the "New International Land-Sea Trade Corridor" from the Perspective of the Development Model of Open Corridor Economy—Based on the Analysis of Domestic Provincial Analysis and International Competitive Complementary Relations[J]. *Journal of Chongqing University (Social Sciences Edition)*, 2022 28(01): 65–80.

Liyan Yu, Jie Li. Research on the Development Strategy and Policy of China-ASEAN Agricultural Product Logistics Hub—Taking Beibu Gulf Port as an Example[J]. *Direction of China Market & Marketing Research*, 2021, (4): 7–8.

Pei Yu. Research on the Development Countermeasures of Beibu Gulf Port Multimodal Transport under the Background of the New International Land-Sea Trade Corridor[J]. *Popular Science and Technology*, 2021, 23(12): 146–148.

Hui Yue. Research on the Layout of the "Diamond Economic Circle" Comprehensive Transportation Corridor[J]. *Railway Transportation and Economy*, 2020, 42(7): 7–11.

Qixian Zhu. Transportation Corridors: Analysis of the Basic Carrier of Corridor Economy—Research on Corridor Economic Theory III [J]. *Journal of Guangxi University for Nationalities*, 2010, 27(3): 70–73.
Qixian Zhu. The Evolutionary Process of Corridor Economy: Research on Corridor Economic Issues II [J]. *Journal of Hezhou University*, 2009, 25(4):123–126.

CHAPTER 9

Conclusion: Comparative Analysis of China-Europe Railway Express

Bai Gao

The comparative analysis of the five cases in this book reveals both common characteristics and regional variations in the development of the China-Europe Railway Express (CRE).

Local governments, acting as the primary driving forces, provide fiscal subsidies through industrial policies to promote the development of the CRE. The motivations behind these subsidies exhibit striking similarities across regions. These shared factors demonstrate that the enthusiasm of local governments in advancing CRE transcends mere political considerations linked to central directives and individual career advancements. Local authorities also consider various local interests, including the comprehensive economic advancement of the region and abstract goals such as winning the status of a "National Central City." These considerations far surpass the concerns for financial viability and profit-making typically emphasized by businesses.

One goal behind the local government supports for the development of the CRE is market building. In the initial stages, local governments

B. Gao (✉)
Department of Sociology, Duke University, Durham, NC, USA
e-mail: bai.gao@duke.edu

B. Gao, Z. Zhen (eds.), *The China-Europe Railway Express*, China and Globalization 2.0,
https://doi.org/10.1007/978-981-19-2882-6_9

provided substantial subsidies to deliberately lower the freight prices, attracting a diverse range of market participants to contribute to the growth of the logistics market. These local governments hoped that with the support of subsidies, market players would be able to identify and capitalize on new market opportunities and pave the way for indispensable operational mechanisms, supply chains, and lateral market connections needed for a mature market. As these government-subsidized activities attain a certain scale, they would generate the economies of scale, thereby reducing the costs for companies' independent operations in the market and diminishing their reliance on government subsidies over time.

Differences in the operation of the CRE across these five cities primarily stem from two factors: the openness of the logistics platform supporting the rail services and the ownership structure of the operating companies, whether state-owned or private. These variations can be attributed to the impact of the state as a structural factor. Local governments with centralized power often create closed platforms dominated by state-owned enterprise monopolies. In these regions, leaders, aiming for quick policy effects, frequently choose relying on state-owned enterprises to carry out their policies. Conversely, regions with decentralized power structures are more inclined to establish open platforms. In these regions, it is easier to use an open framework to reconcile the conflicts of interest and checks-balances among different authorities. Additionally, the state-business relationship significantly affects the operational mode. In regions where private and foreign companies hold sway, they tend to exert more influence on the operation of this logistics platform.

9.1 The Political Implications of Industrial Policies

The CRE's development in these five cities demonstrates that industrial policies adopted by developmental states are closely related to politics. This is particularly underscored by the fact that since the central government officially announced the "Belt and Road" Initiative, all local governments in these five cities have strengthened the already initiated CRE services. It is undeniable that local governments, while vigorously promoting the CRE, may have a component of performance-driven motivations. In many cases, the weight of this component might be considerable. Existing research highlights that China's economic growth is propelled by intense competition among local governments centered around GDP figures. Officials at the provincial, autonomous region, and municipality levels in China are appointed by the central government and are periodically evaluated, with local economic performance being a key criterion for these assessments. Local officials must engage in intense competition in economic development to secure promotions.[1] This mechanism precisely constitutes a crucial condition for the rapid development of the train services. In response to the BRI (Belt and Road Initiative), various local governments heavily subsidized the CRE. This local competitive dynamic has played a crucial role in the rapid development of the rail services.

9.2 National Policy and the Direction of Local Development

This book underscores another strong institutional aspect in the dynamic interactions between central and local governments: the decisions of the central government often push local governments to explore new avenues and redefine their spatial positioning for their economic development. The BRI has profoundly impacted how local governments perceive the significance of the CRE in their regional development strategies. Following the initiation of the BRI, these five cities underwent significant revisions to their economic development plans, reevaluating emerging opportunities from a new perspective. While this phenomenon was already apparent in the pioneering city of Chongqing, it became especially pronounced in subsequent cities such as Yiwu, Chengdu, Wuhan, and Zhengzhou.

Chongqing stands as an early example of Chinese local governments exploring the potential opportunity of the BRI. The initiation of the "Yuxin'ou" route in Chongqing stemmed from the necessity of attracting investments, particularly from major international laptop manufacturers. The municipal government faced a major challenge related to inconvenient inland logistics due to Chongqing's distance from coastal ports and associated transportation costs. It was during this period that Chongqing recognized the potential value in establishing the "Yuxin'ou" route.

After the central government officially adopted the BRI in 2013, it brought about substantial changes to the spatial planning of other cities. Yiwu had initiated the exploration of the "Yixin'ou" route back to 2008,

[1] Lian Zhou, "A Study on the Promotion Tournament Model of Chinese Local Officials," *Economic Research*, No. 7, 2007.

driven by a decline in traditional exports following the global financial crisis. Seeking access to new markets, Yiwu initially aimed to transport small commodities to Central Asian countries. The central government's adoption of the BRI served as a catalyst, providing Yiwu with a renewed sense of clarity and opportunity, akin to the sudden opening of a large window, revealing an entirely new world waiting beyond. Wuhan, inspired by the "Yuxin'ou" route, had previously experimented with the "Wuhan--Europe" or "Hanou" route, albeit with limited success. However, after the BRI was officially announced, Wuhan started to perceive westward expansion from a new perspective. The city leveraged its geographical advantage, integrating it into a comprehensive spatial strategy focused on westward expansion. In contrast, Zhengzhou had already been pursuing a local development strategy centered around air and road transportation, aiming to establish a logistics corridor connecting inland areas with coastal regions before the BRI. However, the central government's vision made the Zhengzhou government realize the value of railways and provided a new direction for their development.

9.3 Local Government and Market Building

The literature on industrial policies highlights the development of strategic industries with high added value. While the individual CRE may not currently demonstrate substantial high added value, their strategic significance lies in their potential to propel the economic integration of the entire Eurasian landmass. Local government officials do want to boost their political achievements. Nevertheless, they also have to cope with financial constraints. The question here is, beyond political considerations, do local governments harbor economic motives when supporting the CRE, even if these motives have not been explicitly articulated in economic terms? Are there any economic considerations underpinning the substantial subsidies to the CRE provided by local governments? We argue that local governments' substantial fiscal expenditures, restructuring of local administrative institutions, and active involvement of state-owned enterprises in the development of logistics platforms are all geared toward harnessing the vast logistics market across the Eurasia, as well as the opportunities for trade and investments facilitated by the CRE. From a purely economic perspective, it seems that the CRE heavily depend on subsidies from local governments. In contrast, industrial policies adopted by developmental states emphasize broader industrialization goals rather than simplistic input-output balances. Economic sociology, which analyzes economic phenomena by examining their connections with other factors, can shed light on the reasons behind these subsidies: if we treat the process of developing CRE as a market-building process, then the subsidies provided by the local governments would become the public goods or externalities that are crucial for market development but the market itself cannot furnish.

9.4 Industrial Policy and Economies of Scale

The five case studies illustrate that the formation of a new market and its independent development can only be achieved after it reaches a certain degree of economies of scale.

Currently, the cost of transporting a standard 40-foot container from China to Europe through the CRE is as high as $6000 to $7000, whereas it is only around $1800 by sea. Such market development would likely never be completed by relying solely on a natural process. In the initial stages, logistics companies lack the capacity to absorb the expensive market transportation costs due to high initial investments and low volumes. If the freight rates for rail transport cannot be reduced to a level considered reasonable for businesses, logistics companies would have to struggle to find shippers, rendering this market existing only in theory. In other words, without government subsidies, the logistics market spanning Eurasia represented by the CRE probably cannot develop solely based on the efforts of enterprises. The role of government subsidies in the initial stage of the railway transport logistics market is to artificially lower freight prices to a level acceptable to businesses through strong and sustained intervention. This intervention helps attract enough market participants, enlarge market capacity, achieve economies of scale, lower unit transportation costs, and ultimately enable the market to operate independently in the future.

9.5 Industrial Policy and Market Participants

Government subsidies have a positive externality on market building by attracting new participants to engage in the development of the market, thereby creating conditions for the economies of scale. When companies decide to enter a new market, they typically assess the anticipated market returns. In the absence of government intervention, establishing a new international logistics market represented by the CRE would be a formidable challenge. Companies actively entering a new market in China often occur after a clear call-to-action from the central government, with the expectation of active involvement and various supports from local governments. Zhengzhou's logistics companies have demonstrated their determination under these circumstances. A clear indicator is their establishment of offices in many cities across the country and abroad. One of the main functions of these offices is to gather cargo from various regions. The role of government subsidies in this case extends beyond increasing the willingness of logistics companies in Zhengzhou to participate in the CRE.

HATRANS, a company based in Łódź, Poland, is another example. Originally a small family business, HATRANS seized the opportunity when Chengdu chose Łódź as the gateway city for the CRE (Chengdu) in Europe and provided subsidies for the service. Within a few years, HATRANS transformed from a small family business into a prominent company, accounting for a quarter of the total logistics market of the "Rong'ou" freight trains, competing on par with European logistics giant DHL (Dalsey, Hillblom and Lynn) from Germany.[2]

Companies from various regions in China are also planning to establish overseas branches for storage, bonded zones, and cargo consolidation. This significantly expands the scale of market building for the development of the CRE.

9.6 Industrial Policy and Market Development

Industrial policy plays a crucial role in facilitating the development of rules, mechanisms, and related businesses in a new market. In the early stage, the establishment of an international market involving cross-border activities often encounters challenges: while companies and governments from one country actively promote market development, differing governance rules in other countries can pose significant obstacles. Some companies might hesitate to participate due to limited knowledge about the market's potential or constraints imposed by local divisions of labor in the industry. Without collaboration with foreign governments and companies, such new markets may face management and operational gaps. In this context, continuous subsidies provided by Chinese local governments play an active role in nurturing this new international market. These

[2] Based on the interview with HATRAMS in Łódź, Poland, on May 5, 2017.

subsidies not only incentivize foreign governments and businesses to see the potential of the CRE market but also inspire their collaborations. Concurrently, these subsidies motivate Chinese counterparts to fill the gaps in foreign markets, spanning various sectors from logistics to trade and from trade to investment.

Government subsidies have significantly aided entrepreneurs in the development of the CRE market. The Chinese Business Center in Hamburg, Germany, was initially established to provide services such as accommodation, office space, consulting, and legal support to Chinese companies utilizing the CRE services ending in Hamburg. As the rail services expanded, it became evident that the CRE market was not just a logistics platform but also a vital hub for trade and investments. Despite services being available in the German market, local businesses were often unaware of the immense opportunities in the CRE market due to information gaps. Consequently, the Chinese Business Center swiftly expanded its operations. Not only did they establish a database of various business opportunities in Germany and actively seek Chinese partners for these opportunities, but they also organized various promotional events for Chinese companies interested in investing in Germany, addressing the gaps that Chinese counterparts faced in the German market.[3]

The CRE serves as a vital link, connecting previously isolated local markets within China and facilitating trade growth across the Eurasia. Beyond enhancing logistics and increasing trade, this interconnected transportation network also acts as a robust platform for direct investments and the development of diverse market mechanisms and institutions. The CRE's operation has encouraged entrepreneurs from different countries to bridge gaps in segmented supply chains, fostering cooperation among varied economic entities. Entrepreneurs are adapting their businesses to seize CRE-driven market opportunities, entering previously unexplored sectors. By uniting fragmented railway networks across countries, the CRE has become a crucial transportation artery spanning Eurasia. Supported by this platform, an integrated logistics system, incorporating railways, highways, maritime, and air transport, alongside various institutions facilitating trade, investment, and economic exchanges, is flourishing and solidifying.

[3] Based on an interview with the Chinese Business Centre on May 10, 2017 in Hamburg, Germany.

9.7 National Development and Grand Market Building on Eurasian Landmass

A new supranational governance mechanism has emerged, encouraged by the prospects of a grand market on the Eurasian landmass, as Chinese local governments continuously subsidize the development of transnational railway transport networks. On April 20, 2017, railway authorities from seven countries—China, Belarus, Germany, Kazakhstan, Mongolia, Poland, and Russia—formally signed the "Agreement on Deepening Cooperation on the CRE." With the goals of increasing the market share of railway freight transportation between Asia and Europe, promoting economic development in the countries along the route, and facilitating economic and trade cooperation, this agreement aimed to jointly build an international logistics brand for the CRE, and provide institutional guarantees for the deepening development of the CRE. The main content of this agreement includes: first, align these countries' development plans for railway infrastructures, build a railway transportation corridor between China and Europe, and collaboratively organizing the railway transportation between China and Europe that is safe, smooth, fast, convenient, and competitive; second, enhance the organization of the entire transportation process by accelerating the speed of container handling, leveraging information technology, and increasing the travel speed of trains within each country; third, promote unified service standards and information platforms by encompassing comprehensive information tracking, establishing collaborative mechanisms for reporting and handling emergencies, and ensuring the safety of goods transportation; fourth, strengthen the marketing and promotion of the CRE by expanding the regions of services, developing new transportation and logistics products, advancing the growth in volumes for cross-border e-commerce, international parcels, and cold chain transportation; fifth, coordinate customs and inspection agencies in countries along the route, simplifying customs clearance procedures for train cargo, optimizing operations at railway ports and stations, and ultimately reducing clearance times; sixth, establish joint working groups and expert teams dedicated to the CRE services, ensuring timely negotiation and resolution of any issues that may arise during the transportation process.[4] This agreement, as a supranational governance

[4] "Seven Countries' Railway Departments Sign Agreement to Deepen China-Europe Railway Express Cooperation," *The Paper.* http://www.sohu.com/a/135866635_260616,

mechanism, aims at providing strong guarantees for the CRE to develop the transportation and logistics markets spanning the Eurasian landmass.

Since the transcontinental railway logistics system, spanning across Eurasia, stands as an international market, it also affects the trade balances among nations. Facilitating economic integration across the vast expanse of Eurasia and establishing an intercontinental market covering the entire continent require unwavering support from participating countries. If the creation of such a market is perceived as a threat to national interests, it will not generate strong political support. A crucial variable, directly related to the potential protectionist reactions, is whether the interests of nation-states are compromised during the process of regional economic integration. The development of the CRE offers some unexpected insights into addressing this challenge.

An important aspect of reducing freight costs for the CRE is the volume of cargos for the return trip. When the containers are empty on the return trip, it is difficult to lower transportation costs. However, attracting enough return cargos presents a significant challenge for these Chinese cities. China serves as the world's factory, and Europe is a major destination for Chinese exports. To attract adequate return cargos, Chinese cities must explore various goods that Europe can export to China. Consequently, red wine and various agricultural products have become popular imports for these Chinese cities. From this perspective, a significant positive externality generated by local government subsidies is the promotion of a more balanced trade relationship between China and European countries. A more balanced international trade will be a crucial prerequisite for the economic integration of Eurasia. Regional economic cooperation based on a healthy international trade foundation forms the fundamental basis for developing the market that the CRE service aims to serve.

In the course of developing the railway logistics market exemplified by the CRE, Chinese local governments have proactively sought to fill the cargos on the return trip from Europe, aiming to cultivate a more balanced trade relationship between China and Europe. Although their primary goal was to lower freight costs, the methods they employed to achieve this objective have yielded unforeseen positive outcomes. The impact of state building in the market building in the international arena is an aspect often overlooked in the existing literature. However, Chinese

April 24, 2017.

local governments have played a pivotal role in the market building for the intercontinental logistics industry sustained by the CRE.

9.8 Returns Beyond a Singular Market

In recent years, affected by the efficiency principle in resource allocation advocated by the mainstream economic theories, projects such as high-speed railways and the CRE are often criticized for lack of enough returns for the investments. Critics often question whether the outputs justify the amount of investments. While evaluating return on investment is undoubtedly important, these critiques frequently overlook a significant factor: the criteria used by Chinese governments, either central or local, to measure their investment returns differ significantly from those used by private enterprises. It's not that the governments do not seek returns; rather, it's about the type of returns they are pursuing.

Among the five cities studied, four have been designated as "National Central Cities." This designation is closely related to their efforts in developing the CRE, as the CRE is directly linked to many key projects pursued by the central government. National Central Cities play a pivotal role in executing major national projects. When China tries to advance the BRI, these cities must serve as core nodes in the initiative. In addition, National Central Cities are required to play important roles in industrial upgrading, transitioning the development model from "Made in China" to "Invented in China," participating in the international division of labor of global production system, and establishing open platforms such as free trade zones. They are instrumental in elevating the levels of China's internationalization and global competitiveness, serving as international comprehensive transportation hubs, and enhancing the status of China's international gateways. The evaluation of these cities encompasses a comprehensive assessment of economic strength, innovation capabilities, degree of internationalization, and comprehensive transportation capabilities, with specific indicators such as transportation hubs and openness being pivotal. The presence of platforms such as free trade zones and national technology districts, coupled with capacities in aviation, shipping, and rail transit, is indispensable. These measurements aim to attract inflows of Fortune

500 companies, international innovation bases, and foreign consulates and offices of international organizations.[5]

Attaining the title of "National Central City" signifies that the city's development potential, advantages, and prospects have received recognition at the highest level of the country. This recognition undoubtedly bestows a highly valuable brand upon the city, representing a successful marketing of the city's image. Moreover, once designated as a National Central City, these cities receive priority consideration in the new measures of national reform and opening-up policies. These cities are strategically important and serve as forerunners in piloting new initiatives. Furthermore, these cities hold a relatively advantageous position when it comes to the location selection of major projects at the national level. They are more likely to win the competition for projects such as free trade zones and pilot zones for airport economy.[6]

9.9 The Organizational Structure of Local Government and the Operational Model of the CRE Logistics Center

Economic sociology emphasizes the impact of institutional arrangement on economic activities. In the five case studies included in this book, it highlights the importance of how administrative responsibilities are allocated within each local government. In a country like China, where the government employs various intervention methods in the economy, the variations in the governance structures of the logistics industry and the operational models of logistics platforms among these five cities can be attributed to their different models of internal division of labor and power distribution.

[5] Hao Xu, Hongru Wang, Xin Yin. "The Number of National Central Cities is 12: What are the Selection Criteria?" *China Economic Weekly*, No. 7, 2017. See also. http://news.xinhuanet.com/city/2017-02/21/c___129487224.htm.

[6] Hao Xu, Hongru Wang, Xin Yin. "The Number of National Central Cities is 12: What are the Selection Criteria?" China Economic Weekly, No. 7, 2017. See also. http://news.xinhuanet.com/city/2017-02/21/c___129487224.htm.

The characteristics of Wuhan's logistics platform highlight the impact of organizational structure of local government on the operation of the CRE. A notable distinction of Wuhan from other cities lies in the division of authorities: the power to allocate subsidies and the power to develop and supervise logistics platform are distributed to different bureaucracies. The Business Commission oversees subsidy distribution, while the Logistics Office directly manages the logistics platform. These bureaucracies have different interests and policy goals. The Business Commission aims to attract as many companies as possible to use Wuhan's logistics platform, thereby boosting the volume of international trade year by year. In contrast, the Logistics Office strives for a monopoly position by the logistics platform under its supervision to maximize profits and returns on the initial investment. When conflicts arise, the Business Commission insists on providing subsidies only if the logistics platform operates openly. Under the subsidy constraint, Wuhan's logistics platform has to emphasize increasing the freight value of individual containers.

Zhengzhou serves as another compelling example. The Zhengzhou municipal government has consistently pursued a development strategy centered around logistics. As a result, not only is its internal management relatively centralized, but the logistics platform serving the CRE also shows a tendency of vertical integration. This approach has enabled Zhengzhou's logistics platform to establish branches not only in cities across the country but also in various foreign countries, creating a unified logistics network. In addition, Zhengzhou has eliminated the traditional boundaries among air, railway, and road transportations, forming a highly integrated logistics system that incorporates diverse modes of transportation. This government structure strongly supports Zhengzhou's regional economic development strategy, which perceives the city's comparative advantage in serving as a major commercial and logistics hub.

9.10 State-Business Relationship and the Operational Model of the China-Europe Railway Express

The existing state-business relationships in different regions significantly affect their responses to new challenges in a novel environment. The inherited state-business relationship usually shapes the initial trajectory of market building. However, as crises often occur in the early stage of market building, these inherited relationships also face frequent disruptions. This will lead to the rebalance and restructure of state-business relationships. This rebalancing-restructuring process always involves political maneuvering among different actors, including various government agencies and powerful companies. These actors seek to establish institutional arrangements aligned with their interests, and such efforts directly influence the direction and mechanisms of market building.

Tianmeng Company, the operator of "Yixin'ou" route, is a private company, and its success is benefited from the special pattern of state-business relationships fostered by its geographical location. Zhejiang, historically situated on the frontline facing the East China Sea, has maintained a state of military readiness. Consequently, state-owned enterprises have never thrived here, leaving room for private companies to flourish in Zhejiang's market. Yiwu, representing the province's private economy, has consistently received support from the local government. Tianmeng Company, proactive in exploring the Central Asian market from its early stage, showcased remarkable flexibility and entrepreneurial spirit when the decision was made to launch freight services to Spain. These qualities, inherent to a private company, proved to be a major advantage in market competition.

Chongqing's approach to developing the "Yuxin'ou" route differs significantly from Yiwu's. The city's initiative aimed at attracting foreign investment, considering it a pivotal market player right from the inception of the rail service. To incentivize foreign investment, Chongqing actively promoted the establishment of a joint venture logistics company, aligning the interests of various countries along the "Yuxin'ou" route. This distinctive approach provided the city with a unique advantage, setting it apart from others. Notably, the "Yuxin'ou" achieved uninterrupted travel to Europe after clearing customs in Chongqing, avoiding additional inspections by foreign countries en route.

The development of Chengdu's "Rong'ou" route underwent a complex transformation involving a shift in the logistics platform. In the local economy, state-owned enterprises have always held significant influence. When Chengdu initially launched the "Rong'ou" route, it followed Chongqing's model and established a joint venture company, Chengdu Eurasian Railway Logistics Co., Ltd., funded jointly by Poland's HATRANS Logistics Co., Ltd., Jiangsu's Feilika International Logistics Co., Ltd., and Shenzhen's YH Global Logistics Co., Ltd. However, by 2016, when Chengdu wanted to significantly increase the number of freight train services, it found that relying solely on an operator composed of non-local and foreign companies could not meet its needs. Consequently, the Chengdu municipal government instructed the Transportation Commission to invest in a state-owned enterprise responsible for operating Chengdu's logistics platform.

9.11 Challenges Facing the China-Europe Railway Express

The challenges confronting the CRE stem primarily from disparities between the Chinese system of formulating and implementing industrial policies and classical developmentalism. As previously discussed, China's industrial policies involve distinct roles for local governments and state--owned enterprises, diverging significantly from the contexts in Japan and South Korea.

In the organization of the CRE operations, a notable internal tension exists between China Railway and regional interests. From the perspective of macro-level management of the logistics industry, centralizing cargo collection and train assembly at Alashankou in Xinjiang might enhance efficiency. This approach could ensure fixed itineraries, making negotiations on transportation tariffs with foreign railway partners more favorable for China Railway. However, the operations of the CRE heavily rely on subsidies from local governments. If centralized operations at Alashankou do not clearly demonstrate local contributions, local enthusiasm is likely to wane. Without substantial subsidies, shipping companies might prefer maritime transport. Despite unifying the name of CRE under a single brand, China Railway had to establish multiple large cargo collection centers nationwide. Whether this tension in the logistics industry can be resolved through nationwide dynamic train assembly using big data or by developing a new method, reflecting each region's contribution to CRE's development and meeting the performance evaluation needs of local governments remains to be seen.

Cities operating the CRE strongly criticize China Railway for its failure to set constraints on new entries to the CRE market. Conflicts often arise between early-bird cities and latecomer cities. The early-bird cities face reduced government subsidies as the market expansion has begun to attract customers willing to pay significantly higher freight prices. However, when new cities enter the CRE market, local governments offer exceptionally high-level subsidies. This disrupts the established equilibrium of freight prices due to the lack of coordination in industrial policy. Unlike the Japanese industrial policy that emphasized controlling excessive competition and encouraging oligopolistic competition, China's central government faces a significant gap in policy coordination concerning market access. In order to enhance economies of scale in the logistics industry and improve the international competitiveness of related companies, the National Railway Administration should encourage oligopolistic competition in the CRE market. This may help the industry avoid repeating the mistakes of excessive competition observed in the automobile, photovoltaic, and iron ore industries.

Various local logistics platforms face a significant challenge regarding the dominance of state-owned enterprises, often established by local governments, in building the logistics platform for the CRE. The challenge lies in whether these cities can avoid the monopoly of state-owned enterprises over the entire logistics industry. Creating an open and highly competitive logistics platform is essential for the CRE to attract more market participants, especially foreign and private companies. Such a platform would increase economies of scale, potentially reducing or eliminating government subsidies, and enabling the independent operation of the Eurasian logistics market. For local governments, the correct way of generating returns for the huge amount of investments in the initial stage of the CRE development, is to increase taxation, instead of allowing their state-owned enterprises to operate the logistics platform to make monopoly profits. This would prevent the exclusion of potential market participants, especially foreign and private enterprises, from the CRE logistics market. This is essentially an issue of state building alongside the progress of market building.

To achieve the long-term goal of promoting economic integration across the Eurasian landmass, the increase of China's imports would serve not only as a basic prerequisite for lowering the freight costs of the CRE but also as a critical measure aiming at rectifying the imbalance in the China-Europe trade. In this sense, the CRE could serve as a lever for transforming China's economic development model, shifting away from its previous role as the world's factory. Actively seeking importing goods from countries along the routes of the CRE will fundamentally change China's relationship with the world economy, transforming it from an exporting powerhouse into an importing giant that offers development opportunities to many countries. Such a transformation of China's development model will also help to prevent the reversal of globalization.

Appendix: Chronology of China-Europe Railway Express

Man Tang and Ying Yang

Assistant Research Fellow at the China High-Speed Rail Development Strategy Research Center, Southwest Jiaotong University, Chengdu, China

10.1 Key Events of China-Europe Railway Express

On March 19, 2011, the first China-Europe Railway Express (Chongqing-Duisburg) was inaugurated.

On August 14, 2014, the inaugural domestic coordination meeting of the China-Europe Railway Express (CRE) took place in Chongqing. Attended by representatives from local governments and platform companies of China-Europe Railway Express in cities like Chongqing, Chengdu, Zhengzhou, Wuhan, Suzhou, and Yiwu, significant developments were made during this meeting. During the session, key initiatives were introduced, including the issuance of the "Interim Measures for the Organization and Management of China-Europe Railway Express" and the signing of the "Memorandum on Establishing the Domestic Transport Coordination Council of China-Europe Railway Express." These measures encompassed unified branding, streamlined transportation organization, standardized pricing, consistent service standards, cohesive operational teams, and unified coordination platforms across various

B. Gao, Z. Zhen (eds.), *The China-Europe Railway Express*, China and Globalization 2.0,
https://doi.org/10.1007/978-981-19-2882-6

routes. These steps aimed to bolster mechanisms and enhance equipment support, fostering a more cohesive and efficient CRE network.

On December 16, 2014, the second domestic coordination meeting of CRE was held in Zhengzhou, organized by China Railway Container Transport Corporation (CRCT). Representatives from six cities including Chongqing, Zhengzhou, Chengdu, Wuhan, Suzhou, and Yiwu engaged in in-depth discussions on the CRE's operation, pricing bundled with volume, and transit assembly issues.

On April 15, 2016, the China-Europe International Freight Train Alliance Conference convened in Urumqi, leading to the formation of the China-Europe International Freight Train Alliance under the "Belt and Road" Initiative. Comprising 11 members from provinces, cities and municipality such as Chongqing, Zhengzhou, Chengdu, Xiamen, and Xinjiang, this market-oriented alliance actively engaged in collaborative discussions for the advancement of the China-Europe International Freight Train. Their goal was to achieve cooperative and mutually beneficial outcomes. This significant development solidified the establishment of operating enterprises for China's westbound CRE in Xinjiang. It also laid the groundwork for regulations that facilitated the sharing and joint development of achievements within the alliance.

On June 8, 2016, under the coordination of the National Development and Reform Commission and the China Railway, a unified branding strategy for China-Europe Express was officially adopted. This marked a significant milestone in its evolution. All 39 routes originating from 16 major Chinese cities, including Chongqing, Chengdu, Zhengzhou, Wuhan, Changsha, Suzhou, Dongguan, and Yiwu, and destined for Europe, were uniformly rebranded as China Railway Express.

On October 17, 2016, the National Development and Reform Commission unveiled the "China Railway Express Construction and Development Plan (2016-2020)," a pivotal blueprint outlining the CRE's strategic development. This plan defined CRE as "international railway intermodal trains operating on fixed train numbers, routes, schedules, and full journey times, traveling between China and Europe and countries along the Belt and Road." It concurrently outlined three key spatial layouts for China-Europe railway transport channels, hub nodes, and transport routes. Specifically, the plan proposed three primary routes: the western route through China's western regions, exiting at Alashankou (Khorgos); the central route crossing China's northern regions, exiting at Erenhot; and the eastern route along China's southeastern coastal areas, exiting at Manzhouli (Suifenhe). Additionally, the plan established 43 CRE hub nodes, categorized into major inland cargo source nodes, major railway hub nodes, major coastal port nodes, and borderland land ports. It also detailed 23 existing direct routes, 20 planned direct routes, and 5 mail transport routes.

On April 22, 2017, railway authorities from China, Belarus, Germany, Kazakhstan, Mongolia, Poland, and Russia inked the "Agreement on Deepening Cooperation of China-Europe Express." This marked the first instance of China's railway department signing a cooperation agreement on CRE operations with railway departments of Belt and Road Initiative (BRI) countries. The agreement chiefly aimed to align railway infrastructure development plans, streamline whole-process transportation organization, promote unified service standards and information platforms, and bolster the marketing and promotion of CRE.

10.2 Major Events for Each China-Europe Railway Express Route

10.2.1 China-Europe Railway Express (Chongqing)

On January 2, 2011, the "Yuxin'ou" international railway intermodal test train departed from Chongqing, reaching Moscow after an 11-day journey covering 8129 kilometers. This test train laid a solid foundation for the full-scale trial operation of the "Yuxin'ou" International Railway Corridor.

On March 19, 2011, the Yuxin'ou (Chongqing to Duisburg) international railway intermodal train completed its maiden full journey, marking the inaugural run of the first CRE. Laden with electronic products manufactured in Chongqing by HP, the train commenced its journey from Chongqing Tuanjie Village Station, passing through cities such as Dazhou, Ankang, Xi'an, Lanzhou, and Urumqi. It exited through Alashankou, transited through Kazakhstan, Russia, Belarus, and Poland before successfully arriving at Duisburg, Germany. The entire journey covered a total distance of 11,179 kilometers, taking 16 days to complete.

In September 2011, Chongqing hosted the "'Yuxin'ou' Five Countries and Six-Party Joint Meeting," during which a memorandum of cooperation was signed to facilitate the regular operation of the "Yuxin'ou" international railway. The meeting proposed the establishment of the

"Yuxin'ou" platform company, aiming to promote shared interests, enhance operational efficiency, reduce transportation costs, and ensure the smooth flow of return shipments. These initiatives were strategically significant for enhancing the competitiveness of the "Yuxin'ou" International Railway Corridor.

In March 2012, the "Yuxin'ou" achieved a breakthrough in low-temperature operations, successfully transporting electronic products manufactured in Chongqing to Europe at −40 °C.

On April 12, 2012, Yuxin'ou (Chongqing) Logistics Co., Ltd. was officially established, marking a new milestone in the construction of the "Yuxin'ou" International Railway Corridor and signifying an important step in transforming Chongqing into a western logistics hub.

On August 1, 2012, the "Yuxin'ou" Customs Facilitation Seminar was successfully held. Eight countries including China, Russia, and Germany reached consensus on further simplifying customs clearance procedures and implementing mutual supervision principles.

On November 16, 2012, the "Yuxin'ou" Acer-ASUS combined train successfully arrived at Duisburg, Germany, marking three significant milestones for the "Yuxin'ou" international intermodal transportation network that established the "Five-fixed Train": the first successful use of the international unified waybill, the first successful combination of multiple types of cargo for transport, and the first successful unloading of the "Yuxin'ou" along the route.

In February 2013, the first return test train of the "Yuxin'ou" departed from Duisburg and arrived in Chongqing on March 18. This marked the first return freight train on the "Yuxin'ou" international railway intermodal transportation network two years after its establishment, breaking the dilemma of one-way transportation and establishing a two-way connection for goods transport on the route.

In July 2013, the "Yuxin'ou" officially launched the trial operation of the China-Europe Safe and Smart Trade Route, significantly improving customs clearance efficiency.

On September 2, 2013, the "2013 Shenzhen-Chongqing and 'Yuxin'ou' International Logistics Corridor Promotion Conference" was held in Shenzhen, laying the foundation for opening a new international trade route between South China and Central Asia and Europe through the "Yuxin'ou International Railway Corridor.

On September 18, 2013, the memorandum of understanding for the tripartite "Yuxin'ou," namely "Chongqing-Xinjiang-Russia" ("Yuxine") meeting, was signed in Chongqing. The meeting aimed to further deepen China-Russian international cooperation, optimize the route's regular operation, and enhance its influence in serving China-Europe trade.

Starting from October 2013, the "Yuxin'ou" achieved a regular weekly service, operating three times a week during peak seasons, laying a robust foundation for the regular operation of public trains on the route.

On April 8, 2014, the "Yuxin'ou" public trains were officially launched, becoming accessible to the entire market. This initiative enabled a wider range of products to benefit from the efficient, secure, and cost-effective advantages offered by the "Yuxin'ou" International Railway Corridor. Additionally, it streamlined the transportation of goods from Chongqing and its surrounding areas, while also attracting European products to swiftly enter the Chinese inland market.

On August 14, 2014, the first batch of imported carriages from Duisburg, Germany, marked a solid foundation for the regular transportation of imported cars by the "Yuxin'ou." It also provided source support for the regular operation of the "Yuxin'ou" public return trains.

On August 14, 2014, the first domestic coordination meeting of China-Europe Railway Express was held in Chongqing. The meeting aimed to promptly resolve issues related to the operation of the trains, improve its quality, establish, and improve service standards.

On September 1, 2014, the "Yuxin'ou" international railway postal trial containers were successfully transported to Almaty, Kazakhstan, achieving the first-phase goal of international postal exports. This achievement laid the groundwork for realizing the strategic goal set by the Chongqing municipal government and China Post to transport international mail from Chongqing to Europe via the "Yuxin'ou" route.

On September 3, 2014, the "Yuxin'ou" trains to Russia were officially opened, marking the first time that China's inland container trains were shipped to Russia.

On November 22, 2014, the 16th mayor's Joint Meeting of Central Cities Conference of Yangtze River Economic Coordination was convened in Hefei, Anhui Province. The strategic decision to "rely on the golden waterway to promote the development of the Yangtze River Economic Belt" breathed new life into Chongqing's economic landscape through the Yuxin'ou" International Railway Corridor.

On December 29, 2014, a momentous event unfolded with the departure ceremony of the 100th "Yuxin'ou" train. This marked the year when "Yuxin'ou" ascended to a national strategic status. The railway became a gateway for Chongqing's external engagement, propelling the city's economy to unprecedented heights.

On June 26, 2015, the first batch of cross-border e-commerce return freight of "Yuxin'ou" trains arrived in Chongqing. This event marked a significant milestone in the history of cross-border e-commerce, as it was the first instance of goods being returned from abroad through railway transportation, disrupting the previous practice of relying solely on sea and air transport.

On July 16, 2015, the inaugural "Yuxin'ou" Hogood Coffee international special train was launched, diversifying the cargo transported via the route. This initiative integrated the Maritime Silk Road, Yangtze River Golden Waterway, and the Silk Road, establishing Chongqing as a key hub for Chinese coffee distribution and advancing the BRI.

On April 16, 2016, to promote the strategic upgrade from "Yuxin'ou" to "Yaxin'ou," the Chongqing municipal government specifically organized an "The China-Singapore (Chongqing) Demonstration Initiative on Strategic Connectivity."

On July 5, 2016, the General Administration of Customs approved Chongqing as the pilot city for the "Yuxin'ou" train postal service, and Chongqing took the lead in conducting "Yuxin'ou" postal tests to Russia and Germany.

On July 22, 2016, new routes for the "Yuxin'ou," passing through Manzhouli and Khorgos ports, were added, further enhancing its radiation capability to Central and Eastern Europe.

10.2.2 China-Europe Railway Express (Yiwu)

On September 26, 2014, during a meeting with Spanish prime minister Mariano Rajoy in Beijing, Chinese president Xi Jinping expressed that the development momentum of the CRE was strong. The China-Europe Railway Express (Yiwu to Madrid) was planned to depart from Yiwu in Zhejiang Province and reach its destination in Madrid.

On November 18, 2014, the inaugural "Yixin'ou" departed from Yiwu, China. It exited through the Alashankou Port in Xinjiang, passing through Kazakhstan, Russia, Belarus, Poland, Germany, and France, and arrived in Madrid, Spain, on December 9 after a 21-day journey. This railway line, spanning over 13,000 kilometers, is currently the longest among all CRE routes.

From 2014 to 2015, the market operator of the "Yixin'ou," Yiwu Tianmeng Industrial Investment Co., Ltd., established branches and constructed overseas warehouses in Madrid. They also planned to build overseas sorting centers and Yiwu product display centers in key cities along the route, such as Warsaw, Berlin, and Paris. These centers provide services including receiving goods, transportation, customs clearance, and delivery, offering effective logistics solutions for China-Europe trade and cross-border e-commerce.

On January 30, 2015, the first return trip of the "Yixin'ou" train (Madrid to Yiwu) departed from Madrid. It traveled through Spain, France, Germany, Poland, Belarus, Russia, and Kazakhstan, arriving in Yiwu, China, on February 22. The journey covered over 13,000 kilometers and took 22 days.

Starting from 2014, Yiwu has opened international freight train routes to eight destinations, including Central Asia, Madrid (Spain), Tehran (Iran), Mazar-i-Sharif (Afghanistan), Chelyabinsk (Russia), Riga (Latvia), Minsk (Belarus), and London (UK). Yiwu has become the city with the most extensive international railway container transport routes.

On June 28, 2015, the "Yixin'ou" added Duisburg as a midway station for unloading, establishing a weekly regular service.

On October 9, 2015, the market operator of "Yixin'ou," Tianmeng Company, signed a memorandum of cooperation with a subsidiary of DHL in Germany, establishing a long-term strategic partnership to promote railway logistics services for the China-Europe Railway Express (Yiwu).

On January 28, 2016, the first freight train from Yiwu to Tehran officially departed and arrived on February 15.

On March 14, 2016, Yiwu and the Aragon Autonomous Region in Spain signed a strategic cooperation agreement to promote regular operations of the "Yixin'ou," marking the first cooperation agreement between the city and a foreign local government regarding the route.

On May 31, 2016, the first batch of German-produced infant formula transported via the "Yixin'ou" arrived in Hangzhou Cross-Border E-Commerce Industrial Park after secondary customs clearance. This successful collaboration between the "Yixin'ou" and cross-border import e-commerce marked the perfect integration of "Yixin'ou + Cross-border E-commerce."

On June 8, 2016, Yiwu, alongside Chongqing, Chengdu, Zhengzhou, and eight other cities, hosted the inaugural ceremony introducing the unified brand of the China Railway Express. This collaborative effort established the China Railway Express (CRE) as a globally competitive and esteemed logistics brand, significantly boosting market competitiveness.

In July 2016, "Yixin'ou" established a logistics distribution point in Hamburg, Germany.

On August 13, 2016, the first Yiwu-Russia freight train departed from Yiwu West Freight Station and arrived in Chelyabinsk approximately eight days later, covering a total distance of 7200 kilometers.

On the afternoon of January 18, 2017, the first CRE from China to the UK successfully arrived at a railway station in London. The train, which departed from Yiwu West Station on January 1, exited through Alashankou, and traveled through Kazakhstan, Russia, Belarus, Poland, Germany, Belgium, France, and the Channel Tunnel, covering a total distance of 12,451 kilometers. The journey took 18 days, opening a new logistics route for China-UK trade.

As of the end of March 2017, the China-Europe Railway Express (Yiwu) has completed 162 round trips, transporting 12,612 standard containers. This includes 136 outbound trips with 11,746 standard containers and 26 return trips with 866 standard containers. Currently, the Yiwu-Madrid route has achieved two outbound trips per week and one return trip per week, reducing the journey time from the initial 21 days to as fast as 16 days and decreasing operational costs by nearly 30%.

On April 10, 2017 (local time in London), the first train carrying British goods departed from the UK to Yiwu. Covering a total distance of 12,451 kilometers, the train arrived in Yiwu approximately 18 days later.

10.2.3 China-Europe Railway Express (Chengdu)

On April 26, 2013, the China-Europe Railway Express (Chengdu-Lodz) was inaugurated. Originating from Chengdu Qingbaijiang Railway Port, it passed through Baoji, Lanzhou, Urumqi, and exited at Alashankou. Crossing Kazakhstan, Russia, Belarus; it finally reached Lodz, Poland, covering a total distance of 9826 kilometers in just 11 days. This route was among the earliest "Five-fixed" public trains. Upon arrival, the goods were promptly sorted and distributed across Europe within one to three days.

On October 25, 2014, the Chengdu hosted the "Rong'ou Express" promotion conference, marking a significant event for regional collaboration. Chengdu forged strategic partnerships with Kunming and Guiyang within the ambit of the "Rong'ou Express" initiative. The purpose of this collaboration was to extend the network of "Rong'ou Express" to Kunming and Guiyang, capitalizing on the unique strengths of these cities. The overarching goal was to enhance economic and trade interactions between the western regions of China and various European nations. Moreover, the Chengdu Logistics Office inked a pivotal "Chengdu-Shenzhen Train Cooperation Framework Agreement" with China Logistics Group. This agreement aimed to streamline and enhance goods transportation between the Pearl River Delta region and Europe through the efficient conduit of the "Rong'ou Express."

In February 2015, Chengdu was approved to establish a port for the import of complete vehicles, breaking the historical practice of transporting imported vehicles from Tianjin or Shanghai for several decades.

On June 26, 2015, Sichuan, Xiamen, and Xinjiang entry-exit inspection and quarantine bureaus signed a joint work plan for the integration of inspection and quarantine clearance for the "Xiamen-Chengdu-Xinjiang-Europe"("Xiarongxin'ou") route.

In October 2015, the "Rong'ou Express" was extended to Nuremberg, Germany, rapidly expanding its international market reach to major hub cities in Europe.

On August 16, 2015, intercity trains connecting Chengdu with hub cities in China, such as Xiamen, Shenzhen, Ningbo, Kunming, Nanning, Shanghai, Wuhan, and Guangzhou, were launched. This significantly expanded the domestic market coverage for the China-Europe Railway Express (Chengdu-Lodz).

On August 18, 2015, the first return train of the "Rong'ou Express" departed from Lodz, Poland, marking the beginning of its two-way operations.

In March 2016, the "Rong'ou Express" extended its reach to Tilburg, Netherlands, further expanding its international market coverage to European hub cities.

Starting from April 1, 2016, Chengdu International Railway Service Co., Ltd. took over the comprehensive operation and management of the "Rong'ou Express," changing the previous situation where private enterprises were in charge.

In May 2016, global logistics giant DHL signed a "Cooperation Memorandum on China-Europe Logistics Channel Construction" with Chengdu for enhancing cooperation on the "Rong'ou Express." They reached consensus on jointly developing the city's freight hub and other matters. This marked the deepening collaboration between the route and international logistics enterprises.

In July 2016, the "Rong-Euro Express" marked a historic milestone by transporting the inaugural shipment of 20 imported BMW cars from

Europe. This event marked a paradigm shift in the history of complete car imports, breaking away from the reliance on maritime ports. It established a new avenue for international collaboration in the automotive industry, enabling "Made in Chengdu" cars to be exported from Chengdu and "Made in Europe" cars to enter Chengdu, creating a dual-directional international cooperation channel in the automotive sector.

In September 2016, the "Rong'ou Express" officially launched the southbound international test train from Chengdu to Istanbul, marking the first southbound China-Europe train. This signified the expansion of the "Rong'ou+" strategic overseas coverage to Central Asia and Southern Europe, further promoting economic and trade exchanges between Chengdu and countries along the BRI.

In December 2016, the first batch of over 20 tons of imported meat products arrived in Chengdu from Nuremberg, Germany, via the "Rong'ou Express." This opened a new mode of importing European meat products through rail transportation, enabling the distribution of imported meat products from inland cities to various regions across the country.

On December 20, 2016, China Europe Railway Express (Chengdu) operated its inaugural dedicated train from Wenjiang, transporting flowers and plants to Tilburg, Netherlands. The journey took 13 days and marked the first time Chinese floral and nursery products were exported to Europe via rail transportation.

In March 2017, the China-Europe Railway Express (Chengdu-Moscow) started operating in both directions, facilitating the exchange of goods between "Made in Chengdu" and "Made in Russia."

On March 1, 2017, the first customized train of the China-Europe Railway Express (Chengdu-Belarus) departed from Chengdu International Railway Port and arrived in Minsk, the capital of Belarus, after 12 days. This marked the official opening of the northern route from Chengdu to Europe. With this, Chengdu's connections to Europe via the northern, central, and southern routes were initially established. These three routes form the core part of the "Rong'ou+" strategy. The central route extends from Chengdu to Lodz, serving as a primary freight transportation corridor directly penetrating the heart of Europe, while the northern route extends to Russia, including Moscow, Tomsk, Belarus, Minsk, and Lithuania, covering the Commonwealth of Independent States and Eastern European countries. The southern route leads from Chengdu to Almaty, passing through Istanbul and reaching Southern Europe.

10.2.4 China-Europe Railway Express (Wuhan)

On October 24, 2012, the China-Europe Railway Express (Wuhan-Pardubice), or "Hanxin'ou," was officially launched. The train started from Wuhan, passed through Ankang, Xi'an, Lanzhou, Urumqi, exited through Alashankou, traversed Kazakhstan, Russia, Belarus, and Poland, and reached Pardubice in the Czech Republic. The total distance covered was 10,863 kilometers, and the journey took 23 days.

From October 2012 to April 2014, a combination of factors including supply chain issues, transportation costs, operational infrastructure, and subsidy policies resulted in the inability to meet the prerequisites for the consistent operation of "Hanxin'ou." Consequently, the service was suspended shortly after its initial launch.

In October 2013, the Wuhan railway port achieved successful completion and commencement of operations. Embracing a market-oriented strategy, the Wuhan Asia-Europe Logistics Co., Ltd. was subsequently founded. This company assumed the crucial role of orchestrating the procurement of goods, formulating transportation plans, and overseeing logistical matters along the route for international container freight transport via the "Hanou" railway.

In April 2014, the Wuhan municipal government conducted a work meeting focusing on the standardization of international railway freight transportation for "Hanxin'ou." During this session, the set objective was to establish regular operational procedures for the service.

On April 23, 2014, the inaugural "Hanxin'ou" (Wuhan-Lodz) train for regular international railway freight transportation embarked on its journey. Departing from Wuhan Railway Container Centre Station, the train traversed through Alashankou in Xinjiang, making its way through Kazakhstan, Russia, and Belarus, and ultimately reaching Lodz, Poland. The extensive route covered over 10,000 kilometers, completing the journey in a remarkable 15 days.

On July 2, 2014, a signing ceremony for the China-Kazakhstan cooperation project of the "Hanxin'ou" was held in Astana, the capital of Kazakhstan.

On April 3, 2015, the first China-Europe Railway Express train from Wuhan to Hamburg was launched. The train passed through Xiangyang, Lanzhou, Urumqi, and exited through Alashankou in Xinjiang. It traversed Kazakhstan, Russia, and Belarus before reaching Hamburg, Germany, covering a total distance of approximately 11,000 kilometers and taking about 15 days.

On July 1, 2015, an international freight train originating from Wuhan arrived at Duisburg, Germany. This marked the extension of the terminal station of the China-Europe Railway Express (Wuhan) from Hamburg to the northwest port city of Duisburg in Germany.

On October 24, 2015, the first China-Europe international container train from Wuhan to Moscow departed from Wujiashan Railway Central Station. The train exited through Manzhouli and arrived at Kuntsevo Railway Station in Moscow, covering a total distance of 9779 kilometers in about 12 days.

On April 6, 2016, the inaugural international freight train service directly connecting Wuhan to Lyon, France, named the "Hanxin'ou" international container train, commenced its operations. The train departed from Wujiashan Railway Central Station in Wuhan, exited through Alashankou in Xinjiang, and traveled westward through Kazakhstan, Russia, Belarus, Poland, Germany, and seven other Eurasian countries. It extended several hundred kilometers southwest from the original terminal station Duisburg in Germany and arrived in Lyon, France, on April 21. The total distance covered was 11,300 kilometers, and the journey took 15 days.

On November 2, 2016, the Alashankou Comprehensive Bonded Zone signed a strategic cooperation agreement with Wuhan Asia-Europe Logistics Co., Ltd. (Wae-Logistics), establishing a cooperation mechanism among Wae-Logistics and related enterprises in Alashankou.

On December 8, 2016, the trans-Eurasian new channel "Wuhan-Manzhouli-Europe" ("Hanmanou") international train was dispatched for the first time. Departing from Wujiashan Railway Central Station in Wuhan, the train exited through Manzhouli, traversed Russia, Belarus, Poland, and Germany before reaching its destination. Covering approximately 12,000 kilometers, the route established a new station in Vorsino, Russia, and efficiently distributed goods across Europe through terminal stations in Hamburg and Duisburg, Germany, and Lyon, France.

Currently, the "Hanou" trains have successfully operated 12 new routes, including Wuhan to Hamburg/Duisburg, Wuhan to Lyon, Wuhan to Poland, Wuhan to the Czech Republic, and Wuhan to five Central Asian countries. Among the rail routes opened in 40 cities across the country, the "Hanou" proudly holds the top position in terms of operational routes.

10.2.5 China-Europe Railway Express (Changsha)

On October 30, 2014, the first direct Europe-bound international railway freight service, the China-Europe Railway Express (Changsha-Duisburg) or "Xiangou Express," was officially launched. The service operated on a main line and two branch lines. On its inaugural day, two trains were dispatched: one on the main line and another on a branch line. The main line exited through Manzhouli in Inner Mongolia, passing through Russia, Belarus, and Poland, before reaching Duisburg, Germany. This route covered a total distance of 11,905 kilometers with a travel time of 16 to 18 days. Simultaneously, the branch line started from Changsha, exited through Alashankou in Xinjiang, passed through Kazakhstan, and arrived in Tashkent, Uzbekistan. This branch covered a total distance of 6476 kilometers with a travel time of 11 days.

On November 22, 2014, another branch line of the "Xiangou Express" to Moscow, Russia, was launched. The train started from Changsha's Xianing Railway Port, exited through Erlianhaote (or Manzhouli), and reached Moscow, Russia, covering 8047 kilometers (or 10,090 kilometers) with a travel time of 13 days (or 15 days).

Starting from October 2015, the China-Europe Railway Express (Changsha to Duisburg) operated by China Railway Guangzhou Group Co., Ltd. began regular weekly services, providing strong transportation support for Hunan Province's cross-border e-commerce industry.

At the end of October 2014, the China-Europe Railway Express (Changsha to Duisburg) was launched, marking the first direct international railway freight service from Hunan to Europe. The train exited through Erenhot and passed through Mongolia, Russia, Belarus, and Poland before reaching its destination in Hamburg, Germany, covering a total distance of 11,305 kilometers with a travel time of approximately 16 days.

On January 18, 2017, the 8462nd China-Europe Railway Express from Changsha (Hunan) to Minsk (Belarus) started from Changsha Freight Center's Xianing Logistics Workshop Yard. It exited through Erenhot in Inner Mongolia, crossed the China-Mongolian-Russian railway corridor, and arrived in Minsk, Belarus, after about 12 days of travel. This route marked the fifth new line of CRE launched by China Railway Guangzhou Group Co. Ltd. from Changsha Freight Center, following Hamburg, Warsaw, Moscow, and Tashkent.

10.2.6 China-Europe Railway Express (Zhengzhou)

In March 2013, the Zhengzhou Economic and Technological Development Zone Administration and Zhongyu Port Group jointly established Zhengzhou International Hub Development and Construction Co., Ltd.as the main operator of the China-Europe Railway Express (Zhengzhou). This unique operating model was characterized by "government guidance and enterprise-led operation."

On July 18, 2013, the Zhengzhou-Europe International Block train to Hamburg from Zhengzhou was successfully launched, achieving regular operations twice a week. Departing from Zhengzhou's Putian Station, it exited through Alashankou Port, traversed Kazakhstan, Russia, Belarus, and Poland, and finally arrived in Hamburg, Germany, covering 10,245 kilometers in approximately 15 days. The train established four core consolidation and distribution centers and six secondary consolidation and distribution centers in major European cities including Hamburg, Warsaw, Prague, Milan, Malaszewicze, Paris, Minsk, Moscow, Tashkent, and Astana.

On December 5, 2013, the first China-Europe Railway Express (Zhengzhou-Erlianhaote-Europe), or "Zhenglianou," was launched. The train started from Zhengzhou, exited through Erenhot, passed through Mongolia, Russia, Belarus, and Poland, and finally arrived at Hamburg, Germany, covering a total distance of 10,484 kilometers with a travel time of approximately 12 days.

On January 14, 2014, the return freight train from Hamburg to Zhengzhou was launched.

On March 20, 2014, Zhengzhou International Hub Development and Construction Co., Ltd. established a branch in Germany called ZZH International Multimodal Transport GmbH. This branch played a key role in station layout and consolidation and distribution network establishment for the "Zheng'ou" in Europe. Centered in Hamburg, the company's road consolidation and distribution network swiftly expanded to encompass 112 cities in 22 countries across Europe and Asia, facilitating cross-border e-commerce and international trade development.

On September 1, 2014, the departure ceremony for the return journey of the China-Europe Railway Express (Zhengzhou) was held at the Billwerder-Moorfleet Station in Hamburg, Germany. This event signified the regular operation of the return journey, offering a fresh route for China-European logistics and bolstering the development of the central plains' region.

Starting from September 2015, the China-Europe Railway Express (Zhengzhou) became the first to achieve three outbound trips and two inbound trips per week.

Starting from July 2016, the China-Europe Railway Express (Zhengzhou) successfully maintained a balanced and stable operation with three outbound and three inbound trips per week. It stood out as the sole train in the CRE system to achieve such high-density round-trip schedule and holds the distinction of being the nationwide leader in fully loaded return trips.

On November 23, 2016, the company signed a cooperation agreement with Finland's Kouvola Reform and Development Group in Zhengzhou. Both parties collaborated to create the China-Europe Railway Express route from Zhengzhou to Northern Europe, engaging in cooperation in route development, cargo organization, logistics, and trade.

Since March 2017, the China-Europe Railway Express (Zhengzhou) has further increased its operating frequency, achieving a regular and balanced schedule with "four outbound trips and four inbound trips, totaling eight trips per week." This enhancement solidifies its leading position in the China-Europe Railway Express network.

By mid-March 2017, the China-Europe Railway Express (Zhengzhou) had operated 556 trains (351 outbound trips and 205 inbound trips) with a total cargo value of $2.819 billion and a total weight of 270,600 tons.

10.2.7 China-Europe Railway Express (Xiamen)

On August 16, 2015, Xiamen launched the China-Europe Railway Express "XiaRong'ou" (Xiamen-Chengdu-Europe) and the Central Asia Railway Express, marking the inaugural China-Europe and Central Asia freight train services initiated from a national pilot free trade zone. The CRE route starts from Xiamen, passes through cities including Chengdu and Alashankou, and reaches Lodz, Poland, covering a total distance of 12,733 kilometers and completing the journey in 15 days. Initially, one train operated weekly, but starting from March 2016, the frequency increased to two trains per week. By April 2017, the service further intensified to two or three trains weekly, totaling 127 trains, carrying 6828 containers and goods valued at 1.927 billion yuan ($0.26 billion).

In early 2016, the China-Europe Railway Express (Xiamen) introduced "customized" services. The "TPV Technology Special Train" operates directly from Xiamen to factories in Poland.

In April 2016, the China-Europe Railway Express expanded its reach to the Taiwan region, employing a combination of sea and rail transport. This extension aimed to integrate logistics with ASEAN countries, bridging the Maritime Silk Road with the Silk Road on land.

In October 2016, Xiamen was incorporated into the "China-Europe Railway Express Construction and Development Plan (2016-2020)" with backing from the General Administration of Customs. The visionary plan outlined the establishment of a multimodal transport supervision center and the introduction of new destinations in Nuremberg, Germany, and Tilburg, the Netherlands.

In December 2016, Xiamen was included in the "The EU – China Smart and Secure Trade Lanes" pilot project, becoming the first railway pilot of the initiative.

On April 21, 2017, the China-Europe Railway Express (Xiamen to Moscow) direct freight train departed from Xiamen en route to Moscow. This marked another significant milestone for Xiamen, following the initiation of train services to destinations such as Lodz in Poland and Almaty in Kazakhstan. It represented yet another international freight train bound for countries along the BRI, solidifying its status as the first direct China-Europe freight train departing from Xiamen. Starting from the Haicang Free Trade Zone in Xiamen, the train passed through key cities such as Nanchang, Nanjing, Jinan, Jinzhou, and Manzhouli, culminating its journey in Kuntsevo, Moscow. Covering a total distance of 10,920 kilometers, the train completed the route in approximately 14 days. Initially operating with 35 cars per trip, the service ran three times a month during the first, second, and third ten days. Plans were in place to transition to a weekly service in the latter half of 2017, aiming for regular, normalized operations.

In September 2017, the Ninth BRICS Summit was scheduled to be held in Xiamen. Concurrently, the launch of the China-Europe Railway Express (Xiamen-Moscow) aimed to further enhance Xiamen's role as a hub city on the Maritime Silk Road and the Silk Road on land. This initiative aimed to create an international brand for the route, thereby advancing Xiamen's development as an international hub center for maritime, air, and multimodal transport.

10.2.8 China-Europe Railway Express (Nanjing)

On June 29, 2016, the China-Europe Railway Express (Nanjing to Moscow) departed from Nanjing. This train, originating in Nanjing and terminating in Moscow, covered a total distance of approximately 10,000 kilometers. The route passed through cities including Manzhouli, Irkutsk, and Novosibirsk, completing the journey in 15 days. The inauguration of this service marked the maiden establishment of a train route from Nanjing to Moscow within the Nanjing international train services. This development played a pivotal role in broadening China-Russian trade ties and advancing the BRI.

10.2.9 China-Europe Railway Express (Suzhou)

On November 22, 2012, the "Suzhou-Manzhouli-Europe" or "Sumanou" container train officially commenced operations. The train departed from Suzhou West Railway Station, passed through Manzhouli Port, crossed Siberia, and traveled through cities including Irkutsk, Novosibirsk, Moscow in Russia, Brest in Belarus, and arrived in Central and Eastern European countries such as Poland, covering a total distance of 11,800 kilometers. Covering a total distance of 11,800 kilometers, the journey takes 18 days, reducing the transit time by 15 days compared to sea shipping, which typically takes 35 to 45 days.

On September 29, 2013, the first "Five-fixed Train" of "Suzhou-Inner Mongolia-Europe," or "Sumanou," from Shanghai Railway Bureau started its journey from Suzhou West Station to Warsaw, Poland. Laden with high-tech products such as laptops and tablets manufactured and distributed locally and in the surrounding areas of Suzhou, the train traverses Manzhouli Port in Inner Mongolia, and travels directly to Eastern European countries including Russia, Austria, Hungary, the Czech Republic, and Poland. Covering approximately 11,200 kilometers, the transportation takes about 15 days, saving nearly two-thirds of the time compared to traditional sea shipping methods.

On March 11, 2014, the "Sumanou" achieved regular operations, with a stable departure frequency of three trains per month. The shortest travel time for the journey was reduced to 12 days, making it the only CRE in the country to be scheduled in hours.

On July 1, 2014, "Sumanou" was officially designated as the eastern route of the national CRE network and was included in the national railway schedule.

From August 2014, the departure frequency of the train was increased and stabilized to four trains per month.

On December 10, 2014, the "Sumanou" was upgraded to a rapid cargo train for baggage.

On December 14, 2014, the first return train of "Sumanou," which collected goods from all over Europe and was assembled in Małaszewicze, arrived in Suzhou, taking only 15 days for the entire journey.

On April 18, 2015, the second return train of "Sumanou" departed from Duisburg, Germany, and arrived in Suzhou on May 3, covering the entire journey in 15 days.

Since July 2015, the import train of "Sumanou" has been operating on a regular basis.

On August 16, 2015, the first international freight train of "Sumanou" successfully commenced, completing the entire journey in 12 days. Departing from Manzhouli Port, the train reached Moscow, with flexible stops at stations like Irkutsk, Novosibirsk, Yekaterinburg, and Bryansk based on demand.

10.2.10 China-Europe Railway Express (Dongguan)

On November 22, 2013, the first "Guangdong-Xinjiang-Russia" (also known as "Yuexin'ou") international freight express train departed from Shilong Town of Dongguan. Exiting China via Alashankou, it traveled directly to Central Asia and Europe, covering a total distance of 20,000 kilometers. This maiden voyage significantly reduced the transportation time from the Pearl River Delta to Moscow, slashing it from approximately 35 days to just 15 days. This launch marked the establishment of a rapid logistics route connecting the Pearl River Delta to Central Asia and Europe.

Starting from 2015, the "Yuexin'ou" international railway intermodal service operated two trains per week.

On April 14, 2016, the China-Europe Railway Express set off from Shilong Town in Dongguan, crossed Manzhouli Port, traversed the vast Siberian region, and passed through countries including Russia and Poland before reaching Duisburg, Germany. The journey covered a total distance of over 13,488 kilometers and was completed in 19 days. This service, operating on a fixed schedule every Thursday, established regular operations with fixed departure and arrival times.

On April 5, 2017, the inaugural CRE train departed from Vorsino, Russia, laden with Russian grain and food products destined for Shilong. After 17 days, on April 22, it successfully arrived in Dongguan.

On April 11, 2017, the "China-Europe (Shilong-Vorsino) Bidirectional Train" was officially launched. Originating from Shilong, it passed through Beijing and Shenyang before reaching Moscow via Manzhouli, covering a total distance of about 12,000 kilometers in approximately 15 days. This marked the successful commencement of bidirectional operations for the China-Europe Railway Express (Shilong-Vorsino). Starting from May, this bidirectional train operated on a weekly basis, establishing a regular service.

On December 25, 2015, the first China-Europe Railway Express (Guangdong-Manzhouli-Europe), known as "Yuemanou,"departed from Shilong in Dongguan. Passing through Manzhouli in Inner Mongolia Autonomous Region, the train reached Moscow, Russia, covering a total distance of over 11,000 kilometers within 15 days.

10.2.11 China-Europe Railway Express (Guangzhou)

On August 28, 2016, the China-Europe Railway Express (Guangzhou) was officially launched. Departing from Guangzhou Dalang Freight Station, the train traveled through Manzhouli and Moscow, reaching its destination in Vorsino, Kaluga region, Russia, covering 11,500 kilometers in 14 days. The cargo transported included clothing, fabrics, furniture, lighting fixtures, appliances, and electronic products. This route represented a new international logistics land corridor established by Guangzhou along the Silk Road. The train operated weekly and was jointly managed by CRCT, Guangdong Guangwu Logistics Co., Ltd. Baiyun Branch, and Guangzhou Dashunfa International Logistics Co., Ltd.

On March 27, 2017, CRCT and Guangzhou Dashunfa International Logistics Co., Ltd. discussed cooperation on the operation of the China-Europe Western Route and the China-Vietnam Central Asia express trains.

10.2.12 China-Europe Railway Express (Hefei)

The China-Europe Railway Express (Hefei) was launched on June 26, 2014. Departing from Hefei North Station, the train traversed the heartland of Eurasia, and headed straight to Hamburg, Germany, covering a distance of 11,000 kilometers in about 15 days.

On December 12, 2016, the China-Europe Railway Express completed its inaugural return trip from Hamburg to Hefei, arriving at the logistics base of Hefei North Railway Station. This successful return journey marked the train's transition into regular operations, operating weekly for outbound trips and monthly for return trips.

On February 25, 2017, the China-Europe Railway Express (Hefei-Hamburg) successfully achieved regular weekly operations.

10.2.13 China-Europe Railway Express (Harbin)

On February 28, 2015, the first Harbin-Russia international railway freight express train was officially launched. The train departed from Harbin, traveled 1004 kilometers on the Harbin-Manzhouli Railway to reach Manzhouli for customs clearance, then traveled 5574 kilometers on the Trans-Siberian Railway Network through Siberia, reaching Biklyan, Russia, after ten days, covering a total distance of 6578 kilometers.

On June 13, 2015, the "Haou" train (Harbin-Hamburg) commenced operations. The train departed from Harbin, passed through Russia, Poland, and other countries, and finally arrived in Hamburg, Germany, covering a total distance of 9820 kilometers in 15 days.

On July 14, 2015, the first "Haou" return trip arrived at Harbin Xiangfang Railway Station from Dues Freight Yard in Hamburg, Germany, marking the successful bidirectional connection of the crucial Haou channel in the "Longjiang Silk Road Economic Belt."

On January 5, 2017, the "Haou" train was officially included in the China-Europe Railway Express operating schedule, becoming a well-known brand of China-Europe Railway Express in the country.

On February 27, 2016, the first Harbin-Russia international freight train, which traveled directly from Harbin to Yekaterinburg, was officially launched. Departing from Harbin Xiangfang Railway Station and entering Russia through the Manzhouli Port, the train reached Yekaterinburg, covering a total distance of 5889 kilometers in just ten days.

In June 2016, the Harbin-Russia international freight train (Harbin-Yekaterinburg) officially entered regular operation and densification development.

10.2.14 China-Europe Railway Express (Shenyang)

On October 30, 2015, the first China-Europe Railway Express (Shenyang-Hamburg) named "Shenmanou" was launched. Originating from Shenyang East Station and passing through Manzhouli, Russia, Belarus, and Poland, the train reached its destination in Hamburg, Germany, covering a total distance of 11,000 kilometers within 12 to 14 days. The service operated on a weekly basis. On November 3, 2015, the Manzhouli Inspection and Quarantine Bureau and Shanghai Entry-Exit Inspection and Quarantine Bureau collaborated across regions to establish an integrated inspection and quarantine mechanism for international trains. They introduced an innovative "direct release" approach for "Shenmanou," which involved pre-verifying cargo information and releasing goods directly if they matched the provided details. This streamlined customs clearance, ensuring "zero waiting" and "zero contact" for the international train.

In 2016, the China-Europe Railway Express from Shenyang to Hamburg was included in the "China-Europe Railway Express Construction and Development Plan (2016-2020)" by the NDRC. Shenyang East Station Land Port was included in the "13th Five-Year Plan for Port Development" by the General Administration of Customs of China.

On September 30, 2016, the first Shenyang to Yekaterinburg train and the return train from Novosibirsk were launched.

On April 21, 2017, the first China-Europe freight train from Shenyang to Warsaw officially commenced its operation. This train, carrying 28 containers of domestically produced HP printers, departed from Shenyang East Station en route to Warsaw, Poland. This marked a new chapter in the deep cooperation between CRCT, Shenyang Railway Bureau, and Fortune Global 500.

10.2.15 China-Europe Railway Express (Chifeng)

On May 17, 2016, the first China-Europe Railway Express from Chifeng to Moscow started from the Chifeng Bonded Logistics Center of Shenyang Railway Bureau. This train passed through Manzhouli Port and made stops at three stations: Novosibirsk, Sarepta, and Labinsk, before reaching its destination in Moscow. Covering a total distance of nearly 9000 kilometers, the one-way travel time was 12 days. Following the inaugural run, the Shenyang Railway Bureau planned to operate one train per week and expand the train's destinations to countries such as Poland, Germany, and the Netherlands.

10.2.16 China-Europe Railway Express (Kunming)

On July 1, 2015, Yunnan inaugurated its first China-Europe international freight train, the "Yunnan-Xinjiang-Europe," also known as the "Dianxin'ou" train, establishing a direct rail link between Kunming and Rotterdam. Departing from Kunming, the train journeyed through domestic cities such as Chengdu, Baoji, Lanzhou, and Alashankou. In the international segment, it traversed Kazakhstan, Russia, Belarus, Poland, and Germany before reaching its destination in Rotterdam, Netherlands. Covering a total distance of 14,000 kilometers, the travel time was 15 days. This inaugural run of the "Dianxin'ou" train marked the official commencement of railway transportation from Yunnan to Europe. It also represented the first instance of Yunnan exporting processed coffee products to Europe via rail, thereby opening a new route for Chinese coffee to access the European market. The China-Europe Railway Express (Kunming) operated twice a month starting from July 2015.

10.2.17 China-Europe Railway Express (Lanzhou)

On August 21, 2015, the first China-Europe international freight train from Lanzhou to Hamburg was launched. Starting from Lanzhou New Area and exiting through the Alashankou Port, the train passed through four countries, including Russia, and arrived in Hamburg, Germany, in 13 days, covering a total distance of 8900 kilometers.

On September 21, 2015, China-Europe international freight train from Lanzhou to Hamburg returned fully loaded from Hamburg, becoming the first domestic freight train to achieve a fully loaded return journey from Hamburg.

On September 12, 2016, the "Belt and Road" China (Lanzhou) International Cross-border E-commerce Logistics Convention was held in Lanzhou. Representatives from Lanzhou, Xi'an, Guangzhou, Hangzhou, Chengdu, and other 13 cities signed the "Strategic Cooperation Framework Agreement for China-Europe Railway Express Freight Distribution." The signing was a crucial step for Lanzhou in implementing the BRI and broadening its western opening. It played a pivotal role in advancing the regular operation of the China-Europe Railway Express in Lanzhou.

On January 18, 2017, the inaugural return journey of the "Lanzhou Train" China-Europe international freight service was successfully initiated. Departing from Herne, Germany, the train traversed Poland, Belarus, Russia, and Kazakhstan before entering China through the Alashankou Port in Xinjiang, finally reaching Lanzhou Zhongchuan North Station. Covering a total distance of over 8000 kilometers in 16 days, this marked a significant milestone in the history of China-Europe Railway Express. Notably, it marked the inaugural voyage of a refrigerated container train along this route, signaling a firm stride toward the gradual establishment of regular, bidirectional operations for the "Lanzhou Train" China-Europe international freight service.

10.2.18 China-Europe Railway Express (Changchun)
In August 2015, the "Changchun-Manzhouli-Europe," also known as "Changmanou," route commenced its operations, originating from Changchun. Exiting through the Manzhouli Port, it traversed Russia and reached Schwarzheide, Germany, covering a total distance of around 9800 kilometers. This route connected 18 railway stations of six countries, with a one-way travel time of approximately 14 days.

10.2.19 China-Europe Railway Express (Xining)
On September 8, 2016, the inaugural China-Europe Railway Express journey from the Qinghai-Tibet Plateau commenced its operations. Originating in Xining, Qinghai, the train passed through Gansu Province, exited via the Alashankou, and traversed Kazakhstan, Russia, and Poland before reaching its destination in Antwerp, Belgium, covering 9838 kilometers. The 12-day journey featured 44 containers carrying products from Qinghai's key industries, such as Tibetan carpets and Chinese wolfberries. This route highlighted the secure, convenient, environmentally friendly, and efficient transportation advantages of the Eurasian railway corridor.

10.2.20 China-Europe Railway Express (Xi'an)
On August 18, 2016, the China-Europe Railway Express (Xi'an-Warsaw) was officially launched. The train started from Xi'an International Port District, exited through the Alashankou Port in Xinjiang, passed through Kazakhstan, Russia, Belarus, and finally arrived in Warsaw, Poland, covering a total distance of 9848 kilometers. The journey took 12 days.

On September 2, 2016, the first China-Europe freight train from Xi'an to Hamburg was launched. The train departed from Xi'an Railway Bureau's Xinzhu Station, exited through the Alashankou Port in Xinjiang, passed through Kazakhstan, Russia, Belarus, and Poland, and finally arrived in Hamburg, Germany, in 13 days. The goods included machinery and equipment, home furnishings, clothing, and electronic devices.

On November 18, 2016, the inaugural return journey of the China-Europe Railway Express from Hamburg to Xi'an was launched. After 18 days of travel, the train reached Xi'an Xinzhu Station on the night of December 5, establishing the first "two-way" international trade route between Shaanxi and Europe via railway.

On December 6, 2016, the China-Europe Railway Express from Xi'an to Moscow was officially launched. The train started from Xi'an, exited through the Alashankou Port in Xinjiang, passed through Kazakhstan, and finally arrived in Moscow, covering a total distance of approximately 7423 kilometers. The journey took around 11 days.

On November 28, 2013, the inaugural China-Europe Railway Express journey from Xi'an to Rotterdam commenced. Departing from Xi'an Xinzhu Station and passing through the Alashankou Port, the train traveled through Kazakhstan, Russia, Belarus, Poland, and Germany before reaching its destination in Rotterdam, Netherlands. This route spanned seven countries, encompassing a total distance of 9850 kilometers, and achieving the remarkable feat in a mere 18 days.

On April 21, 2017, the inaugural China-Europe Railway Express from Xi'an to Budapest, Hungary, successfully completed its journey. Starting its expedition on April 1, the train exited through the Alashankou Port in Xinjiang, traversed Kazakhstan, Russia, Belarus, Poland, and Slovakia, and finally reached its destination in Hungary, covering a total distance of 9300 kilometers. The train was carrying 41 containers primarily filled with small commodities from Yiwu, Zhejiang.

10.2.21 China-Europe Railway Express (Lianyungang)

On November 29, 2015, the China-Europe Railway Express from Lianyungang to Istanbul embarked on its official journey. Exiting through Khorgos, the train traversed countries including Kazakhstan, Azerbaijan, and Georgia, making stops in destinations such as Aktau in Kazakhstan, Baku in Azerbaijan, and Poti in Georgia. Covering approximately 9000 kilometers, the entire journey was completed in 14 days, concluding in Istanbul, Turkey.

On December 13, 2015, the inaugural "Lianyungang-Kazakhstan-Europe" freight train, known as "Lianxin'ou," embarked on its journey. This train route spanned Kazakhstan to Europe, passing through six countries and covering a total distance of 11,000 kilometers in just 12 days. The launch of this train marked Lianyungang as the eastern endpoint city of the national-level New Eurasia Land Bridge Economic Corridor. This development signified an enhanced integration of Lianyungang with the BRI, fostering deeper international economic and trade cooperation.

10.2.22 China-Europe Railway Express (Xinjiang)

On May 28, 2016, the inaugural westbound international freight round-trip between China's Xinjiang and Germany, known as the China-Europe Railway Express (Urumqi-Duisburg), was launched. The one-way journey covers approximately ten days, spanning a total distance of 8000 kilometers. Starting from Urumqi, the train departs from the Alashankou Port, a bridgehead on the Eurasia Land Bridge. It travels through Kazakhstan, Russia, and Poland, and finally reaches Duisburg, Germany.

On May 22, 2015, the international container freight train service from Shihezi, Xinjiang, to Chelyabinsk Oblast, Russia, was successfully initiated. Departing from the Tianye specialized railway station in Shihezi and exiting through Alashankou, the train traveled through Kazakhstan and Russia before reaching Chelyabinsk Oblast. The journey covered a total distance of 2500 kilometers and was completed in five days. This marked the official operation of the Xinjiang-Kazakhstan-Russia Chelyabinsk Oblast international logistics corridor project.

On May 7, 2016, the international freight train service from Sangezhuang (Lianyu Company Special Line) in Xinjiang to Moscow was launched, taking approximately eight days.

On February 27, 2017, the China-Europe Railway Express from Xinjiang (Kuitun) to Moscow (Russia) had its inaugural run.

On January 29, 2015, the international freight train service from Xinjiang to Georgia was officially launched. Departing from Kuitun, the train exited through Alashankou, passing through Kazakhstan, Russia, and Azerbaijan before reaching the capital city, Tbilisi, in Georgia. The entire journey covered 5470 kilometers in 25 days.

In August 2014, the international freight train service from Korla, Xinjiang, to Mersin, Turkey, underwent testing. The journey commenced at Korla Station, exited through Alashankou, traversed Kazakhstan and Russia to reach Novorossiysk on the Black Sea. From there, the goods were transported by sea to Istanbul and finally arrived at Mersin, Turkey.

On July 29, 2015, the train service from Korla to Duisburg was launched, marking a direct freight train route from southern Xinjiang to international destinations. This train passes through the Alashankou Port using the Eurasia Land Bridge, traveling through Kazakhstan, Russia, Belarus, Lithuania, and Poland before reaching Duisburg, Germany, covering a total distance of 9100 kilometers.

On October 29, 2015, the first westbound train from Yili to Kupavna, Russia, was launched. The "Yili Express" international freight train departs from Bulie Station in Yining County, exits through the Alashankou Port, travels through Kazakhstan and other countries, and finally reaches Kupavna, Russia, in eight days. The train primarily carries exports such as

PVC building materials, caustic soda, tiles, decorative materials, clothing, industrial silicon, as well as fruits and vegetables.

10.2.23 Linyi-Manzhouli-Europe (Linyi)

On October 20, 2015, the first international direct railway freight service from Linyi, Shandong Province, to Hamburg, Germany, was launched. The train started from Linyi, passed through Harbin, transited at Manzhouli, crossed the border into Russia, and arrived in Hamburg, Germany, on November 9. The total distance covered was over 11,000 kilometers, and the journey took 20 days.

10.2.24 China-Europe Railway Express (Tongliao)

On March 25, 2016, the first "Tongliao-Manzhouli-Europe" or "Tongmanou" international container train, designated as 79007, embarked on its inaugural journey from Tongliao Mulitu Industrial Park. After exiting at Manzhouli, the train passed through three stations in Russia, including Pridacha, and arrived in Saint Petersburg, Russia, on April 8, according to Beijing time. Covering a total distance of 9000 kilometers, the journey took 15 days, significantly reducing transportation time compared to sea freight, saving nearly 30 days in transit.

10.2.25 China-Europe Railway Express (Nanchang)

Launched on November 24, 2015, the inaugural China-Europe international railway freight service (Nanchang-Rotterdam) departed. The train started from Nanchang Henggang Station, exited at Manzhouli Port, passed through Russia, Belarus, Poland, and Germany, and reached its destination, Rotterdam, Netherlands. The total distance covered was over 12,000 kilometers, and the journey took approximately 17 days.

10.2.26 China-Europe Railway Express (Tianjin)

On November 21, 2016, the inaugural journey of the China-Europe Railway Express from Tianjin to Minsk, Belarus, was launched. Departing from Tianjin and exiting at Erenhot, the train reached its destination, the China-Belarus Industrial Park in Minsk, in just 13 days. This service represented a significant initiative by the Beijing Railway Bureau to support the BRI and promote coordinated development in the Beijing-Tianjin-Hebei region. Importantly, it marked the initiation of the first China-Europe Railway Express route directly connecting Tianjin to Belarus.

On November 30, 2016, the inaugural westbound container train of the Tianjin-Moscow bidirectional international route embarked on its journey from Tianjin Port. This marked the first bidirectional international rail service between Tianjin and Europe. The route, spanning approximately 7600 kilometers, operates in both directions between Tianjin and Moscow, passing through locations such as Erenhot and Mongolia. The estimated travel time is approximately 12 days. Prior to this, on November 23, 2016, the first eastbound train from Moscow to Tianjin commenced, marking the first return train from Europe to Tianjin and filling the gap in "bidirectional heavy container transportation" for the "Tianjin-Europe" train service.

10.2.27 China-Europe Railway Express (Yingkou)

On October 18, 2014, the inaugural international train departed from Yingkou Port to Moscow, signifying the commencement of the first domestic international container train directly traversing Manzhouli Port en route to Moscow. This weekly service completed the entire journey in just 12 days.

On June 12, 2015, the inaugural "Yingkou Port-Warsaw" China-Europe international direct train departed from Yingkou Port in Liaoning Province. The cargo mainly consisted of electronic products such as LCD modules and light guide panels, with a value of €25 million. The train completed the journey in approximately 14 days, covering a total distance of 10,500 kilometers. The service operated twice a week.

On June 25, 2015, the first freight train from Yingkou Port to Tsentrolit, Belarus, was launched. The train traveled 8834 kilometers in 10 days, passing through Manzhouli, Zaybaykalsky, Chita, Ulan-Ude, Novosibirsk, Yekaterinburg, Moscow, and Osinovo, finally reaching Tsentrolit, Belarus. The service operated weekly.

On October 23, 2015, the "Yingkou Port-Kaluga, Russia" China-Europe direct train officially commenced operations. The train departed from Yingkou Port, passed through Manzhouli Port, and traveled through Zaybaykalsky, Chita, Irkutsk, Novosibirsk, Yekaterinburg, Moscow, and directly to Kaluga, Russia, a city known for its automobile industry. The total distance covered was 8400 kilometers, and the journey took 13 days.

On August 6, 2015, the "Yingkou Port- Dobrá, Slovakia" China-Europe international direct train officially commenced operations. The total distance covered was 11,000 kilometers, with a transit time of 15 days. The service operated weekly.

On April 9, 2016, the Yingkou Port TREST Premium Train (Yingkou Port to Khovrino, Moscow) was launched. The train runs once a week, undergoes whole train transshipment at Zaybaykalsky, and is transported without disassembly throughout the journey, with a total transportation time of 10 days. It is the fastest-running train in the history of China-Russian railway transportation.

On April 9, 2016, the first return train of the "Yingkou-Manzhouli-Europe," known as "Yingmanou," sea-rail intermodal route arrived at Yingkou Port. This return train, which departed from Krasnoyarsk, Russia, on March 30 and entered China through the Manzhouli Port, significantly increased the freight volume of the "Yingmanou," enhancing the overall operational capacity and market competitiveness of the entire logistics route.

10.2.28 China-Europe Railway Express (Dalian)

In January 2016, the "Samsung" train, starting from Dalian, Liaoning Province, and passing through the Manzhouli Port, was inaugurated, providing a direct route to Kaluga, Russia. This marked the world's first train named after a company, signifying the formal commencement of the China-South Korea-Russia international logistics corridor. Currently, the "Samsung" train operates regularly with three services every month.

On May 18, 2016, the international train service from Dalian Port Railway Center Station to Minsk, Belarus, was officially launched. The train departs from Dalian Port, exits through the Manzhouli Port, and ultimately arrives at the China-Belarus Industrial Park, a Chinese investment project in Belarus.

On July 20, 2016, the Dalian-Moscow train service commenced its operations from Dalian Port Railway Center Station. Following the "Samsung" and Minsk trains, this marked the official opening of the "Liaoning-Manzhouli-Europe" or "Liaomanou" commercial vehicle transit train route from Dalian Port. The train traveled from Manzhouli to Moscow, covering a total distance of 8600 kilometers with a transit time of approximately 12 days. On this occasion, 120 premium Great Wall Haval vehicles were transported from Hebei Province to Dalian Port, and, after loading in Dalian, they were directly shipped to Moscow via the "Liaomanou."

10.2.29 China-Europe Railway Express (Ganzhou)
On April 23, 2017, the first China-Europe Railway Express from Bazaikha, Russia, arrived in Ganzhou, Jiangxi. The train originated from Bazaikha, passed through the Manzhouli Port, and traversed several provinces and autonomous regions including Inner Mongolia, Heilongjiang, and Liaoning, before reaching Ganzhou Port, covering a total distance of over 7000 kilometers. This marks the official launch of the return journey of the China-Europe Railway Express from Jiangxi Province, adding another international logistics channel to enhance economic and trade interactions between China and Russia.

10.2.30 China-Europe Railway Express (Manzhouli)
On March 25, 2016, the first train departed from Manzhouli Port in Inner Mongolia, carrying 43 containers. The train, named "Manzhouli-Russia-Europe" or "Maneou," embarked on an approximately eight-day journey, reaching its destination in Yaroslavl, Russia.

10.2.31 China-Europe Railway Express (Guiyang)
On July 1, 2015, the inaugural departure of the "Guizhou-Shenzhen-Europe," known as "Qianshenou" international sea-rail intermodal train China-Europe Railway Express (Guiyang-Duisburg) commenced officially. Initially, two trains regularly operated each week. Starting from Guiyang Gaimao Railway Station, the route followed the Chongqing-Guiyang Railway to Chongqing, where it merged with the "Chongqing-Xinjiang-Duisburg," or "Yuxin'ou" international rail freight service. The journey continued through Chongqing, Xi'an, Lanzhou, Urumqi, and proceeded westward through Kazakhstan, Russia, Belarus, and Poland before reaching Duisburg, Germany. The total length of the route was approximately 11,200 kilometers, with a transit time of around 16 days.

10.2.32 China-Europe Railway Express (Taiyuan)
On February 15, 2017, the inaugural China-Europe Railway Express (Taiyuan-Lesosibirsk) commenced its journey. Originating from Zhongding Logistics Park in Taiyuan Railway Bureau, the train journeyed through the Manzhouli-Zabaykalsky border station and eventually arrived at Lesosibirsk station in Krasnoyarsk Kray, Russia. Covering a total distance of 6000 kilometers, with 2491 kilometers within China and 3509 kilometers outside China, the train reached Manzhouli on February 20 and arrived in Lesosibirsk in early March.

10.2.33 China-Europe Railway Express (Hefei)

In June 2014, the first China-Europe Railway Express from Hefei to Hamburg was launched, providing a rapid and efficient railway channel for exporting solar photovoltaic products, LCD panels, laptops, textiles, and other products from the East China region to Europe. Currently, the service has achieved regular weekly operations.

On July 25, 2015, the inaugural China-Europe Railway Express from Hefei to Spain departed from Hefei North Station Logistics Base. This route passed through the Alashankou Port, traveled through Central Asia, and reached its destination in Spain, covering a total distance of approximately 12,724 kilometers.

On December 12, 2016, the first China-Europe Railway Express from Hamburg to Hefei arrived at Hefei North Station Logistics Base. The train departed from Hamburg on November 20, traversed Poland, Belarus, and Russia, and entered China through Manzhouli Port on December 8, covering a total distance of 10,600 kilometers, and taking 23 days to complete the journey. Comprising 41 containers, the train transported biomedical products, machine spare parts, special construction materials, and other goods from Europe. The operation was coordinated by Anhui New Eurasian International Logistics Co., Ltd., with Sinotrans Limited overseeing the cargo source.

On February 25, 2017, the China-Europe Railway Express (Hefei to Hamburg) departed from Hefei North Logistics Base with 49 standard containers on board, marking the successful achievement of regular weekly operations after more than two years of market development. It is expected that the return journey of the train will also achieve regular operations in 2017.

Kolibri 360 GmbH
Ferdinand-Jühlke-Straße 7
99095 Erfurt, Deutschland
produktsicherheit@kolibri360.de